First Published in 2022 by Echo Books

Echo Books is an imprint of Superscript Publishing Pty Ltd, ABN 76 644 812 395

Registered Office: Suite 401, 140 Bourke St, Melbourne, VIC, 3000

www.echobooks.com.au

Creator: Barbara Slotemaker de Bruïne

The Golden Age: The extraordinary story of how Australia became the most successful nation in world women's squash from 1962–2010.

ISBN: 978-1-922603-35-7 (hardcover)

NATIONAL LIBRARY OF AUSTRALIA

A catalogue record for this book is available from the National Library of Australia

Book layout and design by Peter Gamble, Canberra.
Set in Garamond Premier Pro Display, 12/17 and Bon Vivant Serif.

www.echobooks.com.au

THE GOLDEN AGE

OF

AUSTRALIAN WOMEN'S SQUASH

The extraordinary story of how Australia became the most successful nation in world women's squash from 1962-2010.

Squash has now been included into the Olympics in Los Angeles in 2028 and a new journey begins!

Barbara Slotemaker de Bruïne
(née Baxter) AM

echo))
BOOKS

This book is dedicated to the early pioneers of the women's game in the 1950s, Betty Meagher and Judith FitzGerald (née Tissot) and to Heather McKay (née Blundell). Her outstanding achievements led to the amazing success of subsequent teams through the development of an enduring competitive culture, where the Aussies refused to let the side down and did everything in their power to win!

From 1962 to 2010, many Australian women continued to fly the flag and we were the most successful squash nation during this time. Congratulations to everyone for their dedication and long-term pursuit of excellence.

Heather's opponent, team member, friend and early roommate, Barb

Heather Blundell and the author after the final of the NSW Championships
(Photo: Courtesy of Barbara Slotemaker de Bruïne (née Baxter)

Contents

Introduction		xi
Foreword		xv
Abbreviations		xvii
1	Brief History and Development of the Game	1
2	The 1930s and 1940s—The Beginnings	5
3	The 1950s—The World Awaits	7
4	The 1960s—The Golden Age Begins	13
5	The 1970s—Australia's Dominance	29
6	The 1980s—Time to Regroup	43
7	The 1990s—The Golden Age Continues	51
8	The 2000s—Change was in the Wind	55
9	Inspirational Women	59
	Betty Meagher (1919–1986)	59
	Judith (Louise) FitzGerald (née Tissot) (1930–2020)	62
	Yvonne West (deceased–dates unknown) 1960s	64
	Aline Smith (deceased–dates unknown) 1960s	64
	Jan Tilly (née Shearer)	64
	Heather (Pamela) McKay (née Blundell) AO MBE 1960s–1980s	66

Jenny Irving 78
Pat McClenaughan (Trish Faulkner) 80
Barbara Slotemaker De Bruïne (née Baxter) AM 82
Helen Muir (née Plaisted) 93
Marion Jackman (née Hawcroft) 96
Marlene Tierney 99
Robyn Howard (née Kennedy) 100
Bev Johnson 102
Margaret Zachariah 105
Chris Van Nierop 110
Lyle Hubinger 110
Anne Smith 112
Sue King (née Newman) OAM 114
Barbara Wall 118
Vicki Cardwell (née Hoffmann) BEM 123
Rhonda Thorne (née Shapland) 130
Barbara Oldfield 135
Dianne Davis 138
Jan Miller 143
Carin (Alexia) Clonda 145
Robyn Lambourne (née Friday) 153
Liz Irving 159
Michelle (Susan) Martin OAM 164
Danielle Harte (née Drady) 170
Sarah Fitz-Gerald (AM) 173
Carol Owens 181
Rachael Grinham 188
10 Unsung Heroes 199
Beverley Gould (1936–2019) 199
Dawn Moggach (OAM) 202
Chris Sinclair 204
Rita Paulos 207
Robyn Prentice 211

Margaret Campbell   215

Marie Donnelly   216

Heather Rhead   218

Jan Honeycombe   219

Patricia (Jean) Walker OAM (1930—2016)   221

Carol Murray (née Hunter)   227

11 Australian Squash Families   233

The Meagher Family   234

The FitzGerald Family   236

The Hunt Family   237

The Irving Family   241

The Martin Family   244

The Grinham Family   245

12 Professionalism and Prize Money   249

13 The Olympics   255

14 Future Directions   259

Timeline   267

Appendix–Results   297

Quiz   313

Acknowledgements   317

About the Author   323

Endnotes   329

Quiz Answers   338

Introduction

This book has been written to record the amazing performances of Australian women squash players over several decades. Many of these performances had not been previously recorded and it has been my aim to obtain this information from the players to 'set the record straight'. It is also to commemorate the 70th Anniversary of the formation of the Australian Women's Squash Rackets Association (AWSRA) in Melbourne Australia in 1952. The Association was founded by Betty Meagher (Australian Champion in 1946, 1949 and 50). On her return from her overseas squash tour in 1950, she decided that if Women's Squash in Australia was to develop, it needed to get organised. The English women had already formed their Association in 1934, and were playing international matches against the USA (the American game*). In 1954, the AWSRA invited, the top two English players, Janet Morgan and Sheila Speight, to tour Australia to promote the game. They were of a much higher standard than the Australian players and all of our top players were thoroughly defeated. Still the bar had been raised! In 1954/55, Judith Tissot (Australian Champion 1952) travelled by sea to the UK, where she managed to reach the fourth round of the British Open and win a couple of County tournaments. However, we still had a long way to go!

In 1962, Heather Blundell flew across, and whilst she lost her first match 3–2 to Fran Marshall, the British No 1, in the Scottish Championships, she would never lose again, to anyone! Heather dominated the British Open, the unofficial World Championship of Squash, winning for 16 consecutive years from 1962–1977. She also won the first two official World Open Championships in 1976 and 1979, before she retired. In 1963, after the Australian Women's Championships, Heather stated to the top women players, 'that it was time to go and knock the Poms off'. This five-person team had to do their own fund raising and travel as individuals—two by a 28-day sea voyage and the other three by air. They played one official match. Heather thought they were ready and they were—her instincts were right! The Australians defeated the British women—for the first time by any country playing the British game, 3–2. As a result of this match, the international series began with the English team visiting Australia in 1965, seeking revenge. This time the best of three matches were played with three players per team. Australia won this series 3–0. A total of nine series were played between 1964 and 1980 and Australia won all of them. The Golden Age had begun. Eventually, in 1979, a World Championship Teams event was organised as a Biennial event. England won this event and the challenge had been issued. We subsequently won the event nine times and were runners-up five times between 1979 and 2010.

In 1976, the World Individual Championships had commenced and Australia's record was equally impressive. Fifteen times our women held the trophy aloft between 1976 and 2010 and thirteen times they were runners-up. The stories of these incredible champions are told here, based on the information gained in interviews with the players. They reflect the self-sacrifice, determination and 'will to win' attitude required to succeed at the international level. Hopefully, future generations will be inspired by their stories. Match results are also recorded here, otherwise they would have been lost forever.

At the time of writing, Australia does not have any female player in the top 50 in the world! What has led to this demise? Now that Squash has been included into the Olympics in Los Angeles in 2028, can we recover in time? These are some of the issues I wish to address. I hope that you enjoy the journey.

* The ball, size of the racket, court dimensions and method of scoring are different.

> Barbara Slotemaker de Bruïne (née Baxter) AM
> Australian Representative 1962, 1964 and 1967
> ACT Coaching Director 1984–1988
> National Coaching Director 1988–91
> Australian Coach of the Year 1993
> NCAS Level 3 Coach 2006–14
> Coach of Nationally ranked Junior players 1976–21

Foreword

Thanks to the research of the author, Australian Women's Squash now has a greater understanding of how our pioneers led the way. An inspiring journey that allowed Australia's female players to shine on the international squash stage. After playing overseas and seeing first-hand how organised the English women squash players were, Betty Meagher formed the Australian Women's Squash Rackets Association (AWSRA) in Melbourne, Australia, in 1952. Within a few years, contributions from other leading Australian female players including Judith Tissot, my mother, inspired the beginning of international competition. However, it didn't really get 'off the ground' until the success of Heather McKay. Her outstanding performances eventually led to the commencement of International Teams' events, World Individual Championships and the World Teams' Championships.

The dominance of Australian Women over several decades was due to several other factors as well, including the support of families, the surge in court construction in the 60s and 70s, the availability of excellent coaches and the infrastructure established through the outstanding administration of the sport during this time. These stories and more are told with information obtained from interviews with the champions including Judith FitzGerald, Heather McKay, Jenny Irving, Marion Jackman, Margaret Zachariah, Sue King, Barbara Wall, Vicki Cardwell, Rhonda Thorne, Liz Irving, Michelle Martin, Sarah Fitz-Gerald, Carol Owens and Rachael Grinham. Their stories will hopefully inspire the next generation to shine on the world stage.

Australian female squash players will forever be grateful to our pioneers and everyone else involved that enabled this success to occur. Now, it is by examining our history that we may gain insights for our future directions in the sport.

> Sarah Fitz-Gerald, AM
> President of Squash and Racquetball Victoria
> Vice-President of the World Squash Federation

Front cover:

Centre; Heather McKay, clockwise from top right; Sue Newman, Barbara Wall, Rhonda Thorne, Vicki Cardwell, Michelle Martin, Sarah Fitz-Gerald, Carol Owens, Rachael Grinham.

British Open titles: Heather McKay(16), Sue Newman(1), Barbara Wall(1), Vicki Cardwell(4), Michelle Martin(6), Sarah Fitz-Gerald(2), Rachael Grinham(4)

World Open titles: Heather McKay(2), Rhonda Thorne(1), Vicki Cardwell(1), Michelle Martin(3), Sarah Fitz-Gerald(5), Carol Owens(1), Rachael Grinham(1).

Back cover image

Steve Line–SquashPics.com

Abbreviations

The major source of much of the information contained in the earlier part of this book was Australian Squash—The Belsham Years 1976–1992. Because so many references have been used, an abbreviated form has been employed to cite them e.g., Belsham and the relevant page. In addition, in some instances, newspaper articles have been obtained from players' scrapbooks with no dates or newspaper name. These have been included; however, I can't obtain the exact dates or name due to the length of time since they were published. Emails have also been a great source of information and these dates have been provided. There are also references to various Associations, Administrative positions and scoring systems. These are explained below:

ACC	Australian Coaching Council
AIS	Australian Institute of Sport
ASRA	Australian Squash Rackets Association
ASSA	Australian Society of Sports Administrators
AWSRA	Australian Women's Squash Rackets Association
IOC	International Olympic Committee
NCAS	National Coaching Accreditation Scheme

NCD	National Coaching Director
NSWWSRA	NSW Women's Squash Rackets Association
PARS	Point a Rally scoring
PSA	Professional Squash Association
PSCAA	Professional Squash Coaches Association of Australia
SA	Squash Australia
S&RV	Squash and Racquetball Victoria
SWOT	Squash Without Tears
VSF	Victorian Squash Federation
WISRF	Women's International Squash Rackets Federation
WISPA	Women's International Squash Professionals Association
WSPA	Women's Professional Squash Association
WSF	World Squash Federation

1 Brief History and Development of the Game

It is thought that the game of squash rackets developed from the game of rackets, in 1830, by the pupils of Harrow school in the United Kingdom.[1] Its beginnings resulted from a desire of rackets players to develop their skills in a more restricted area. Squash courts were cheaper to build than rackets courts, and due to the British weather, squash became more popular. It started off as an old boys sport as it was primarily played at the few schools that had rackets courts, or at the homes of those who went to those schools. The early courts were not standardised in shape, size or construction and it was not until the 1920s, that efforts were made to rectify this situation.

Scoring was also adapted from rackets and was the first to 15 and length shots formed the basis of the game with lobs, drops and angles rarely used. The Squash Rackets Association (SRA) was formed in 1928 in the UK and a greater degree of organisation came into the game. However, North America (1904) and Canada (1915) did not adhere to these guidelines and therefore their court dimensions, type of ball used (a hard ball) and racket dimensions differed to those recommended by the SRA. They have only more recently (1990s) adopted the softer ball game to attract international players.

The early days of squash. Boys at Harrow School waiting to play rackets with a softer ball in a courtyard
(Guinness Book of Squash by Michael Palmer, 1984, p7)

In Australia, the first Rackets Club was built in 1876 at the Melbourne Club in Collins Street.[2] The first squash rackets courts were built in July 1913, just before World War 1, at the Melbourne Club which was a conversion of the original Rackets court. The courts were not thought to be of the standard dimensions, as they were nine inches too short and started at the fifteen-foot line. However, they were in regular use after 1921 and after a brief decline from 1927–29, the courts were altered again in 1932 and there was regular play until 1942 when play ceased due to World War II. The first commercial court was built in Australia in 1926 in the Bjelke-Petersen Centre at 360 Collins Street Melbourne which was owned by the uncle of future QLD Premier Joh Bjelke-Petersen.[3] Three courts were built at St Kilda in Canterbury Rd around 1930.

Courts were also built at Sandringham in Melbourne in 1935.[4] Private courts were built in Sydney, on private properties (Dame Edith Walker's at Yaralla and Dangar's Property 'Gostwyck' near Yaralla) and 'Barford' the home of W.O. Fairfax. Royal Sydney Golf Club (1929), Langridge's (1935), Sydney University (1937) and Killara Golf Club (1939) also had courts, but it was very much a 'boys' club' with little evidence of women being invited to play.[5].

The game continued to be played predominantly in men's clubs with one or two courts until the late 1950s, however organisational structures were being formed much earlier.[6] The women of NSW were one of the first to form an association in Australia. They formed the NSWSRA (NSW Squash Rackets Association) on 21/12/1933.[7] The NSW Men formed their Association on 11th July 1938. They called themselves the Squash Rackets Association of NSW.[8] To make it even more confusing the NSWWSRA (NSW Women's Association disassociated themselves from the men) but was not formed until 1957.[9] In 1934, the Australian Squash Rackets Association was formed and was based in Victoria.[10] The Squash Rackets Association of Victoria was formed in 1937 and inter-club pennant competitions for men commenced with teams from six clubs. The women's equivalent started in 1946 and consisted of 4 teams. It was during 1952 that the Australian Women's Squash Rackets Association (AWSRA) was formed and the Victorian Squash Rackets Association (VWSRA), under the initiative of Betty Meagher. The game was very much in its infancy.

2 The 1930s and 1940s—The Beginnings

As early as 1932, a small band of female enthusiasts not only held their first squash rackets tournament in Melbourne, but persuaded the Royal Melbourne Tennis Club, which had for 51 years been a strictly male sanctuary, to set aside a court for their use and to admit them as squash players.[11] Whilst there were many more men playing the game, there were some women who did play. The first Australian Women's Championship was won in 1932 by Mrs Ross Grey Smith of Victoria defeating B. Jackson of Victoria 9–1, 5–9, 9–6, 9–1. Her brother owned a private court, one of only two private courts in Melbourne, which gave her the opportunity to play. The other private court was owned by the late E.C. Dyson, whose sister, Lady Scott, was an even earlier squash player.[12] Mrs Ross Grey Smith made additional sporting history in the 1930s by being the only woman member of the squash rackets club at Bjelke Petersen's and after insisting, was allowed to play against the male members in the club's annual tournament.[13] Meanwhile in Sydney, Mr Justice Reginald Long Innes became the patron for the NSW Association and in 1926 went to England to gather information on court construction at Rugby School, whose courts he thought were the best model.

He suggested 5 courts be built at Royal Sydney Golf Club however, due to financial difficulties at the time, only two were built.[14] These courts were the first ones to be open to women players in general.[15]

By now the Langridge Club had been formed and this was a very fine court indeed. Already, Joan Long Innes was requesting that more courts be built in the city so that squash was available to everyone.[16] She also expressed the desire to go abroad.[17] Another Australian, Lewis Shaw, who was living in England at the time and was a member of the Queen's Club, stated 'I do feel that the Australia standard is not very far behind the English'[18] Was this really the case?

The Victorian Women's Championship was first held in 1935 and was won by that year's National champion Robyn Traill of NSW who defeated Mrs Ross Grey Smith 9–2, 9–4, 9–6.[19] In fact, from 1935 to 1941 there were five separate winners of the Victorian Women's Championship. These included the first overseas winner in 1938, Londoner Mary Armitage who also won the National Championship that year. Isobel Collingwood won the title in 1939 and 1941 and there were no women's events held in 1940 and 1942 through until 1945.[20] 1946 saw the emergence of Betty Meagher, who won her first Australian Championship. She won the title in 1949 and again in 1950 when she was 3 months pregnant with twins. In a rather nice touch, there were two pairs of booties inside the trophy! She then became a driving force for the development of the women's game. Another player dominant at this time was Val Watts who was Australian Champion in 1947, 1948 and 1951. These two players dominated the Australian Women's Championship from 1946 to 1951.

3 The 1950s—The World Awaits

Joan Watson was the Australian Champion, in 1953.[21] During the '50s the Australian Championships were held at the Royal Sydney Golf Course and there was no Interstate Teams event. However, Victoria did play NSW and the Victorian girls were far stronger, winning easily 4–0. Western Australia, while having women players, were precluded from playing because of the time and expense involved. [22] Even in Victoria, squash was predominantly played in Men's Clubs by men.[23] According to Betty Meagher, 'there were very few public courts and, in our first Championships after the War, we were greeted with a sign in our dressing room, converted from the butler's pantry, which read 'A Penny a Peep at the Popsies!' Of course, it was all in good fun. There were only a handful of competitors and the girls had a good giggle about it.'[24] It was coming from this background, that Betty travelled to London in 1950, accompanied by her husband Alan and Gordon Watson, Joan Watson's brother-in-law. She was the first Australian female squash player to compete in the British Championships, however, she was defeated in the second round losing to Betty Hilton 9–7, 9–6, 9–0[25] She had been more successful at the Hampshire Open, where she had been runner-up to V.N. Ord. On her return, the opportunity arose for her to purchase the Flinders Lane Squash Courts from Gordon Watson of Gordon Watson's Squash Academy, which she did for 1,000 pounds. It was her intention to make it the centre of women's squash activities and she decided to combine her career of accountancy with that of squash court management along with her husband Alan, and this venture succeeded.[26]

Betty Meagher's remarkable drive and vision then enabled her to form both the Victorian and Australian Women's Associations in 1952.[27] The Victorian Women's Association very quickly had about 70 members and Betty had pioneered the beginning of organised Women's Squash Competition in Australia. It was soon after this that Judith Tissot won the 1952 Australian Women's Championship and sailed off to England and Europe—more of this later. In August 1953 a tour to New Zealand was arranged.[28] The team comprised Florence Williams, Maria Maher, who became Australian Champion in 1955, Beverley Malcolm and Rae Maddern who was Honorary Secretary of the newly formed Victorian Squash Association and team captain. Yvonne Swan, the NSW Champion who became wife of well-known coach Fred Barlow, was invited to join the team but was unable to travel. Betty Meagher, President of the Australian WSRA and Victorian WSRA and three times Australian Champion, would join the team prior to the New Zealand Championships.[29] At this stage, women's squash had grown enormously. There were now interstate teams' events and

Betty Meagher—the founder of the AWSRA and VWSRA as usual at full stretch
(Photo: Courtesy of Bev Garfield)

Alan and Betty Meagher and Gordon Watson, in London in 1950.
(Photo: Courtesy of Bev Garfield)

there were about 1000 women players throughout Australia. Betty Meagher stated that it was the Australian WSRA's intention to send the Australian Women's Squash Champion in alternate years to compete in the British Open Squash Championships. This didn't eventuate for some time, but the seed had been sown.

Overseas Visitors

In 1954, an invitation was issued to the British Women's Association to send two players to tour Australia and New Zealand. These players were Janet Morgan and Sheila Speight. 'The purpose of the tour was to play in two state championships and the Australian Championship and to play exhibition matches throughout both countries. It was hoped that the tour would stimulate the growth and interest in women's squash.'[30] Sheila Speight sailed to Australia on 19th June 1954, while Janet Morgan flew out on 28th July. In those days, the ship was packed with immigrants while Janet's flight was delayed for 24 hours in Basra, Iraq with engine trouble. A bit different to the comforts of today's international travellers.

Donald Bradman, Janet Morgan and
Sheila Speight—Adelaide 1953
(Photo: Sheila Macintosh—Speight)

Sheila Speight
(Photo: Sheila Macintosh—Speight)

They started the tour in Perth, playing in the Western Australian Championships. Janet defeated Sheila in the final 9–7, 9–1, 9–6.[31] They then flew through the night to Adelaide, where they gave two exhibitions on the day of arrival. From there it was on to Melbourne for three weeks, where there were more exhibition matches and the Victorian and Australian Championships. Janet defeated Sheila in the final of the Victorian Championship 9–3, 9–2, 9–1 and defeated Betty Meagher, the former Australian Champion, 9–0, 9–1, 9–0 in the semi-final of the Australian Women's Championships. Such was the difference in the playing standard at this point in time. It would take only 10 years to rectify this situation. Janet also defeated Sheila in the final of the Australian Championships, but with greater difficulty. Janet won 9–3, 6–9, 9–2, 9–3. It must be remembered that Janet, as Heather McKay would be in future years, was the dominant player of her time she went on to win 10 British Opens.

Judy Tissot getting ready to play in England, 1955
(Photo: Courtesy of Sarah Fitz-Gerald)

The tour was a resounding success. They visited schools, gave radio interviews and were honoured with the presence of Sir Donald Bradman sitting in the gallery whilst they played an exhibition in Adelaide. After the Australian Championships they went on to New Zealand. The enthusiasm of the Kiwis, like the Australians, was tremendous. In 38 days, which included time spent in travelling, they played 41 matches: 11 championship matches, 6 exhibitions against each other and 18 against men. They also played 6 doubles matches and spent four afternoons playing the women players. If you thought that was exhausting, Hashim Khan apparently played 8–10 people per day when he toured.

Janet observed at the end of this tour that 'the women's game is handicapped in both countries by a lack of facilities. Much of the women's game is played on public courts in Australia and in both countries few squash clubs have mixed membership. However, I feel that the interest and enthusiasm is such, that with encouragement, the popularity of the game will improve rapidly'.[32]

Meanwhile, another champion had emerged in this period. Judith FitzGerald (née Tissot) won her first Australian Women's Championship in 1952. She had first played squash in 1947 and was a State Grade tennis player. It was a natural transition to squash for her and she was the next to tour in 1953–4, mainly to play tennis and to catch up with a nice Italian boyfriend! She gained valuable experience, reaching the 4th Round of the British Women's Championship and was runner-up in the Plate, being defeated by R. Pendered in 5 hard fought games. During her time in the UK in 1954 and 1955 Judy won the East of England

Judy FitzGerald (Tissot) in her prime
(Photo: Courtesy of Sarah Fitz-Gerald)

Championship and the West of England Championship and twice won the Isle of Wight Championship. In those days squash was completely amateur and Judy had to support herself working in a range of jobs including as a lift operator at Simpson's in Piccadilly, a cook for children at the Bournemouth Hotel, and a supervisor at the Quality Inn hotel in Regent Street.[33]

On her return, Judy played squash more seriously and won the Australian Championship again in 1956, 1957 and 1958. After her marriage six children quickly followed and Judy's playing career came to an end. She did however start coaching, which she continued for 40 years! Her star pupil was of course her daughter Sarah, who became a legend in her own right in the late 1990s and early 2000s. Her career will be more fully outlined later. Judy also coached Carol Owens, who became a World Champion. Judy received a Distinguished Service Award in 2007 from Squash Australia for her services to Squash. When asked what it took to become a champion, her reply was 'love of the game, perseverance, hard work, desire to learn, independence of thought and the ability to analyse and apply tactics'. That advice still applies today.[34]

4 The 1960s—The Golden Age Begins

After Judy FitzGerald's win in the Australian Championships in 1958, women's squash just trundled along, but change was in the wind and Janet Morgan's prediction that the game would improve rapidly, was about to occur! Pat Parmenter won the Australian Championships in 1959, and in 1960 a decision was made to send an Australian Women's Team to the UK along with the men.

The administrators had decided BEFORE the Australian Championships that the State Champions from NSW, Victoria and South Australia would comprise the team. So, NSW Champion Yvonne West, Victorian Champion Aline Smith and South Australian Champion Jan Shearer were selected. This meant that the winner and runner-up of the 1960 Australian Championship, NSW junior player Heather Blundell and QLD's Dot Linde who were effectively the first and second ranked players in Australia, were not selected in the Australian team. Dot Linde was also the Queensland Champion. Heather had earlier won the NSW Junior Championship and had had to play qualifying to get into the main draw at the Australian Championship. Needless to say, she had swept through the Championship claiming her first Australian title.

Australian Women's team 1960-61 Left To Right: Yvonne West (NSW) Aline Smith (Vic) Jan Shearer (SA) (Captain) (Photo: Courtesy of Jan Shearer)

She upset the apple cart by defeating the players who had already been selected to represent Australia in the UK! Obviously, this possibility had not been foreseen.

The team (without Heather) sailed on a 28-day voyage to the UK and upon arrival in the UK were met by Fran Marshall, the no. 1 British player. Now Fran was a Kenyan and, as we would say in Australia, 'as fit as a Mallee bull'! She decided that the Aussie team needed some fitness work and, as her husband Jimmy was a Major in the Army at Catterick near Sheffield, she had access to the Commando course! So, the Aussies were put through their paces, with some difficulty I might add—it was the middle of Winter! They later came down with the 'flu and were soundly beaten 3–0 by the British team of Fran Marshall, Sheila Macintosh (née Speight) and Di Corbett in an unofficial match.[35] Fran did get into trouble over her actions and Jan Shearer did score some brownie points by winning the British Junior Championship. In the British Open she lost in the third round to Pauline White 9–5, 4–9, 8–10, 6–9 which was a very good effort. Aline Smith lost in the third Round to Gowthorpe 1–9, 3–9, 6–9 and Yvonne West lost to Fran Marshall 1–9, 0–9, 2–9.[36] Clearly, we still had a long way to go.

The Emergence of a Champion—Heather Blundell

So now the dominance of Australian squash over the rest of the world began, thanks mainly to the emergence of Heather Blundell. Much has been written about this amazing squash player's achievements, but very little has

On arrival in the UK Left to Right: Jan Shearer (SA–Captain) Fran Marshall (UK) Aline Smith (Vic), Yvonne West (NSW)
(Photo: Courtesy of Jan Shearer)

been recorded as to her background, how she started in the game and the trailblazing role she played in putting Australia at the forefront of international Women's Squash for over 50 years. The baton was taken up by other Australian players after she retired, namely Sue King (née Newman), Barbara Wall, Rhonda Thorne, Vicki Cardwell, Michelle Martin, Sarah Fitz-Gerald, Carol Owens and Rachael Grinham. However, without Heather's pioneering and success on the world stage, much of this may not have happened.

Heather was one of a family of eleven children and was born in Queanbeyan, NSW in July 1941. Her brothers and sisters played sport regularly, some at a high level in hockey, tennis, rugby AFL, squash and golf. Her Dad was a champion country Rugby League player and both parents played tennis. More of this story will be outlined in the chapter on Inspirational Women. It was in 1959, as squash was starting to emerge in Australia that Heather, whose main sport was tennis at the time, started to dabble in squash. She played squash at the Squash Bowl courts in Canberra to get fit for hockey. 'It was pretty much hit and giggle stuff'. There was no coaching, just a good cardio workout. One of her squash partners, Alan Netting, suggested in 1960 that she

A young Heather!
(Photo Courtesy of Heather McKay)

should enter in the NSW Country Women's Championships. As a point of interest, Heather's eventual mentor Vin Napier had become President of the NSW Association in 1955 and it was his suggestion that a Country Championship be held to encourage country players.[37] This motion was passed by John Cheadle and Vin Toohey, both prominent players and coaches, and the first Country Championships were held in Wollongong, in 1960. Without these top players becoming involved at the administrative level, Heather may not have been discovered! With her parents' approval and with no formal coaching, she entered in the Junior and Women's titles, winning both. This is how the local newspaper described the matches. 'It was her great retrieving shots and low driving shots to the corners that were factors in her wins. After only playing the game socially for about 12 months she could easily have a great future in squash.'[38] How right they were!

Heather was fortunate that Vin Napier was present at these Championships and she caught his eye. He suggested that she should attend the NSW Championships in Sydney.

It was at the NSW Championships that I first met Heather. I was actually ranked no. 1 for the NSW Junior Tournament. Heather was ranked no. 3 behind Pat McClenaughan, who also later became an Australian representative. Somebody suggested that I should go and watch this kid from the country play. I travelled to Ashfield and distinctly remember her being up near the front wall, when her opponent drilled a cross court drive straight at her. Anyone else, would have made an error! Not Heather! She took one step to the side and hit the ball down the side wall for a winner! I thought, oh sh*t!

It was this capability that was evident throughout her career—the ability to turn defence into attack. As it turned out it was an indication of her potential, as she had only been playing the game competitively for such a short time and was totally untutored. In the quarter finals of the NSW Open, she extended the no.1 seed, Yvonne West, after leading 2–0, to eventually lose in five games. It was the first of her two losses in her whole career! On the same night, I was on a nearby court defeating the no. 2 seed Thea Moore in 4 games. Change was afoot! Unfortunately, I had made the mistake of entering 3 events and was completing exams at Teacher's College, during the day. My court owner John Luscombe had arranged for free coaching with Vin Toohey, a former NSW Champion, and I hadn't realised how much I'd improved. So, I had entered the A Reserve, the Juniors and the Open, the latter for experience. I was now into the semis in all three events and doing exams during the day, whilst Heather was resting at home. A fatal mistake. It was my only chance of possibly defeating Heather, as she defeated me in the final of the NSW Juniors in five hard fought sets, 10–8 in the fifth. A lesson for all youngsters out there. Don't go in too many events.

On these performances, Heather was selected as no. 4 in the NSW team and travelled to Brisbane for the Australian Championships. My court owner generously shouted me the trip and, being the new kids on the block, we shared a room together. At this stage, Heather hadn't won any National title, was a country kid and very shy. Here she was unseeded and had to play in a qualifying round before she scrambled through the draw. She didn't know what a let or stroke was, and she lost the odd game. She managed to defeat the No1 seed, June McCraw ('Speedie') in five games in the semi-finals and emerged as Australian Champion, defeating Dot Linde from Queensland in four games in the final. Jean Walker, Captain of the NSW Women's team, cleaned up that night, as she ran a book on the match and the Queenslanders lost heavily! Little did they know what was to come! The next week, now no. 1 in the NSW team, she defeated the same players she had previously struggled against, 3–0. This was evidence of her ability to learn quickly and adapt and change her game so that she could defeat players more easily. This was a trait she demonstrated throughout her career.

Heather did not go on the Australian tour that year (1961), which in many ways was a blessing in disguise, as it enabled her to move to Sydney and consolidate her game under the tutelage of John Cheadle and Vin Napier.[39] The Australian women were still a long way behind the British at this stage. The team that was sent was Yvonne West from NSW, Aline Smith from Victoria and Jan Shearer from South Australia. They were easily defeated 3–0 in the unofficial test match; however, the time was approaching when this would no longer be the case.[40] In 1961, Heather defeated Jan Shearer, the British Junior Champion, in the Australian Open final in 4 games. In 1962 Heather set off to the UK on her own, after having won the 1961 Australian title, attempting to win the British Open which was the unofficial World Championship at the time. This had been made possible because the locals of Queanbeyan had held several fund-raising events to help her on her way.

Two fine champions Heather and Janet
(Photo: Courtesy of Heather McKay)

In addition, the Australian Women's Squash Rackets Association (AWSRA) and the NSW Women's Squash Rackets Association (NSWWSRA) assisted with funding, as they did throughout her career.

On her arrival in the UK, Heather was met by Janet Bisley (née Morgan) a former great and a very shrewd tactician in her own right. She had won the British Open for 10 consecutive years from 1950–59, only losing 3 games on the way and she graciously took Heather under her wing, whenever she was in the UK. Heather's first tournament was the Scottish Open, where she reached the final and had to play the vastly more experienced British no. 1 Fran Marshall. She was defeated 3–2 and commented afterwards, 'She'll never beat me again'—and she never did! Heather had suffered her second loss and this would be the final loss of her career. She then travelled to London, after winning the North and South of England tournaments, to play in the British Open Championship. It was here that Janet introduced Heather to her former coach, Robert (Bob) Johnson, from the Surbiton Lawn Tennis Club in Sutton. She was beginning to suffer from tennis-elbow and she needed to correct her backhand stroke. He then proceeded to demonstrate the stroke. Heather said, 'You mean like this?' So just like that she changed her backhand three weeks before the British Open! A quick learner, if ever there was one! She defeated Fran Marshall, 9–6, 9–5, 9–4 and this was the first of her sixteen consecutive British Open titles.

As mentioned previously, the first team, to travel overseas to play against the UK was in 1960–61 and it would be three years before another team would visit the UK. It was only as Heather started to make inroads into the British dominance that it became a possibility. With the 1962 British Championship under her belt, Heather was ready to spread her wings even further. She was the one who was instrumental in encouraging the Australian women to get a team together, when at a party after the 1963 Australian Open which she had won, she said, 'I think it's time we went and knocked the Poms off!' At that time the top women after Heather were Dot Linde from Queensland, Jenny Irving from Victoria, Barbara Slotemaker de Bruïne (née Baxter) from NSW, and Pat McClenaughan from NSW. Pat had been the NSW and Australian Junior Champion in 1961–63. Unfortunately, Dot couldn't make it as she was moving to New Zealand and getting married, so Helen Plaisted from Western Australia was invited. This was a completely spontaneous decision by the players. Jenny was going to the UK with her husband, Brian, by sea on a holiday, Barbara stated that she was free to go, as she had completed her bond for teaching and was no longer obligated. She would join Jenny and Brian and travel on the 'Canberra' to the UK, a 28-day trip! Pat was going for a year, sponsored by her father, to see how far she could go in her tennis and squash career and Helen was going to play tennis. So, it was game on.

In 1963 permission was sought for an invitational test against the British team, which was granted and, in 1964 the players made their own way across to the UK by air and sea. This was the start of the international series and the Australians won in a marathon 4 and ½ hour match. The results are recorded in the order they played below:

5. Helen Plaisted (Australia) d Pauline White (UK)
   10–8, 4–9, 4–9, 9–5, 9–5
4. Mary Muncaster (UK) d Barbara Baxter (Australia)
   9–5, 6–9, 2–9, 9–2, 9–6
3. Pat McClenaughan (Australia) d Anna Craven-Smith (UK)
   10–9, 7–9, 5–9, 10–8, 10–8
2. Sheila Macintosh d Jenny Irving (Australia)
   9–2, 7–9, 9–3, 2–9, 9–2

As you can see the match was levelled at 2–2 before Heather majestically demolished Fran Marshall 9–1, 9–0, 9–0 in 3 games and 15 minutes and Australia had won the match 3–2. We had indeed 'Knocked the Poms off!' though it had taken 4 and ½ hours to achieve it. Future test matches were restricted to 3 members to avoid the exhaustion of the spectators—not to mention the players! Heather earned the nickname 'Blunders' on this occasion as she didn't make any!

At this time, the stage had also been set on the international scene by the men, as the Australian Men's team of 1962–63 comprising Ken Hiscoe,

Australian and Great Britain's Women's Teams 1964.
Back row (Left to Right): Pauline White, Sheila Macintosh, Janet Bisley, Mary Muncaster,
Fran Marshall, Anna Craven-Smith
Front row (Left to Right): Jenny Irving, Helen Plaisted, Pat McClenaughan, Barbara
Baxter, Heather Blundell
(Photo courtesy of Heather McKay)

Owen Parmenter, Ken Binns, John Cheadle (Captain) and Dick Carter of NSW and Doug Stephenson of South Australia. The team had also been successful. They defeated the UK for the first time and after that South Africa. Ken Hiscoe won the 1962 British Amateur squash crown on this tour.[41]

Their improvement had been rapid, as only a few years earlier in 1959 a British team comprising Michael Oddy, Nigel Broomfield and Roy Wilson had soundly defeated the Australian team.[42] The environment was ripe for Australia to become the leading nation in both men's and women's squash throughout the '60s and beyond. It took some time for a team series to eventuate for the women, however the men defeated the UK in 1966–67, 1969, 1971 and 1973.[43] Meanwhile, Heather went on her merry way, starting to accumulate the rest of her consecutive Australian titles from 1960 to 1973 and British Open titles from 1962–1977.

The Australian Men's Team 1962-63.
Left to Right: Owen Parmenter (NSW) Doug Stephenson (SA), Ken Binns (NSW), John
Cheadle (Manager—NSW), Ken Hiscoe (NSW) and Dick Carter (NSW)
(*Squash the Australian Way* by Vin Napier,1978, p77)

In 1965 the United Kingdom sent out a team for the first time to play a series of Test matches in Australia. The team was Pauline White (Captain), Fran Marshall, Anna Craven-Smith, Sylvia McClure and Ann Price. This tour was made possible through the provision of a British Government grant and the fact that there had been a change in the definition of amateur status.[44] It was a seven-week tour consisting of 3 international matches, 4 state matches and 2 exhibition matches. In addition, they were to compete in New Zealand for 3 representative matches and to compete in the New Zealand Championships. An exhausting tour, by anyone's standards.[45] At this stage, there was already talk of the possibility of a World Squash Championship. Australia's team consisted of Heather Blundell at no. 1, Marion Hawcroft at no. 2 and Jenny Irving at no. 3. The matches were tight and the results are listed below:

First test

1. H. Blundell d F. Marshall, 9–1, 9–0, 9–1

2. M. Hawcroft d S. McClure, 4–9, 9–5,9–2, 9–6.

3. J. Irving lost to P. White, 3–9, 6–9, 9–2, 9–7, 7–9

Australia won 2–1

Second Test

1. H. Blundell d. A. Craven-Smith, 9–0, 9–2, 9–6

2. M. Hawcroft lost to F. Marshall, 2–9, 0–9, 5–9

3. J. Irving d. P. White, 3–9, 10–8, 9–4, 9–4

Australian won 2–1

Third Test

1. H. Blundell d. A. Craven-Smith 9–0, 10–8, 9–7

2. M. Hawcroft lost to F. Marshall 2–9, 9–5, 9–10, 5–9

3. J. Irving d. P. White 4–9, 9–4, 9–3, 10–8.

Australia won 2–1 and the series 3–0

British Women's Team 1965.
Left to Right: Fran Marshall, Sylvia McClure, Pauline White, Anna Craven-Smith, Ann Price
(Photo: Courtesy of Marlene Tierney—The Australian Program,1965)

From these results it is apparent that, without the dominance of Heather, Australia would have been in some difficulty in these matches. Anna Craven-Smith, who was fleet of foot and an excellent games player, who later played off scratch in golf, was emerging as a possible threat to Heather's supremacy. They were later to have several battles in the British Open Championships in 1966 and 1967. Anna lost to Heather in 1966, 9–0, 9–0,10–8 and in 1967, 9–1,10–8, 9–6 keeping Heather on court for 57 minutes! She was one of the few players, who actually pushed Heather. If only she'd trained! Heather stated after this match 'If I'd lost the third, I would have been in trouble. I was exhausted'[46] That was one of Heather's many strengths. She never got complacent and trained harder than anyone else. It was her professional attitude that pulled up the standards of the other Australian and international players.

Not to be underestimated in Heather's achievements was her marriage to Brian McKay in December 1965. He was a State 1 player in NSW, was a valuable practice partner, provided stability at home and kept her motivated. In fact, on her return from winning her sixth successive British Open title in 1967, she felt she was slowing up a bit and might retire in a couple of years![47] Little did she know how long she would keep going! Another thirteen years! Brian played a major role in keeping her on task, but of course she still had to play the matches.

1966–67

An official team was sent to the UK and this time the whole team went by air. Funds of $6,000 were raised by Barbara Baxter, in her role as Secretary of the Australian Women's Association. The team even had official uniforms and a spending allowance of $500.00 to cover incidental expenses. UTA (Air France) provided Heather's ticket and the other players were given discounted air fares. There was much wrangling over the itinerary, as the canny Manager of the UK team, Janet Shardlow (née Morgan) had the test series organised so that the first Test was played in Sheffield in the North of England. This was in the first week, when they had just arrived from

Heather and Brian at Dickson Squash Centre in Canberra
(Photos courtesy of Heather McKay)

Australian and UK Women's Teams 1966–67.
UK Team Back Row: (l to r) Anna Craven Smith, Fran Marshall,
Sheila Macintosh (Speight), Janet Shardlow (Manageress) Ann Price, Sylvia McClure
Australian Team Front Row: (l to r) Robyn Kennedy, Barbara Baxter, Heather McKay,
Marion Hawcroft, Marlene Tierney
(Photo: Courtesy of Barbara Slotemaker de Bruïne)

the summer of Australia. The ball was like a plum pudding, with no bounce at all! The next two tests were played in the sixth and seventh week of the tour. Again, in the North (Birmingham) after the Aussies had been playing down South, where the weather was warmer and the ball bounced more! The final one was played on the hot courts of the Lansdowne Club. This gave the Australian players very little time to acclimatise to the varying conditions. The Australian team comprised: no. 1 Heather McKay of NSW, no. 2 Marion Hawcroft from Queensland and no. 3 Barbara Baxter from NSW. Marlene Tierney from South Australia was the reserve and Robyn Kennedy from Victoria, was the Australian Junior Champion, who joined the tour to gain experience.

Again, Heather was the stalwart of the team, winning all of her matches 3–0. The results were as follows:

First test—Sheffield

    1. Heather McKay d Anna Craven-Smith 9–3, 9–5, 9–0

    2. Fran Marshall d Marion Hawcroft 9–10, 9–5, 9–2, 9–7

    3. Sheila Macintosh d Barbara Baxter 9–7, 7–9, 9–10, 9–7, 9–1

    UK won 2–1

Second test—Birmingham

    1. Heather McKay d Anna Craven Smith 9–1, 9–5, 9–4

    2. Marion Hawcroft d Fran Marshall 9–4, 10–8, 9–6

    3. Barbara Baxter d Sheila Macintosh 9–6, 4–9, 9–2, 9–6

    Australia won 3–0

Third Test—London

    1. Heather McKay d Anna Craven Smith 9–0, 9–2, 9–2

    2. Marion Hawcroft d Fran Marshall 9–5, 9–6, 8–10, 9–0

    3. Barbara Baxter lost to Sheila Macintosh 7–9, 4–9, 4–9

    Australia won 2–1 and the series 2–1

Once again, Heather had delivered the knockout blow for Australia and they had now defeated the UK three times in five years. This also was an indication that Heather relished in her role of playing for her country and she wasn't just an individual player, a factor that was evident in the years ahead. It would be four years before another challenge was mounted by the UK in 1971.

5 The 1970s—Australia's Dominance

Report on Australian Women's Team Tour 1971

(Courtesy of Jean Walker—Team Manager)

The tour of 1971 was far more ambitious. It lasted for 8 weeks with many promotional visits to several countries, including Indonesia, Pakistan, Germany, Denmark, UK, USA and Canada as Australian women endeavoured to take Women's Squash to the world! In addition, they competed in Test matches, the British Open and County tournaments. Costs of the around the world airline tickets were met by the AWSRA and the home State of the players. As the players were billeted in most countries, their only out of pocket expenses were for extra fares, official trophies and souvenirs—a mere $150.00, plus their team uniform. In addition, the individual players were allowed to raise funds from exhibitions prior to the tour, raising approximately $350–$400 each.

The team members this time were: Heather McKay of NSW, Jenny Irving of NSW, Marion Jackman of Qld, Mavis Baker of NSW and Manager Jean Walker of NSW. As one can see from this list, NSW was very much the dominant state at this point in time.

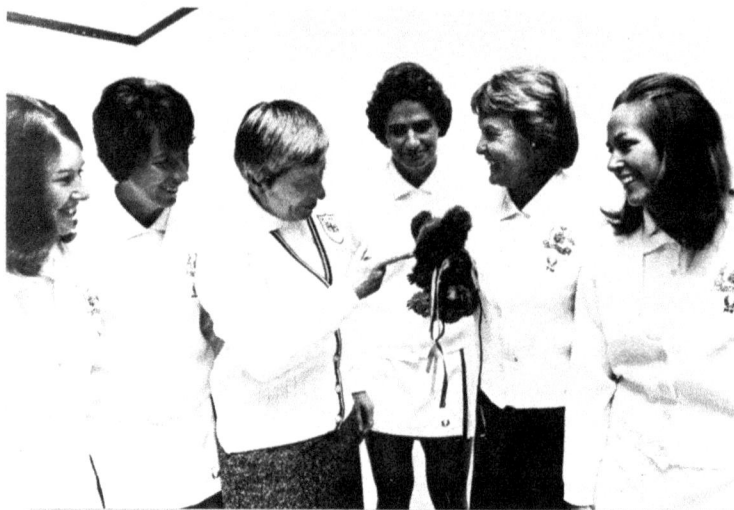

Australian Women's Team 1971.
Left to right: Marion Jackman, Heather McKay, Janet Shardlow (former British Open Champion—British Captain), Jenny Irving (with Lucky II, the Mascot), Jean Walker and Mavis Baker
(Photo: *Squash the Australian Way*, Vin Napier, 1978, p93)

The number of women players in Europe was practically non-existent, however contact was made with Rosanah Rashid, the national champion of Pakistan, who expressed an interest to visit Australia. She had been coached by the famous Khan family. The only other nation with a fair number of women players was Sweden. The standard in the UK was gradually improving however, at this stage, Australian Women were the best players in the world and they remained undefeated throughout the tour.

The tour did achieve its objectives of not only promoting interest among the top players in Australia, but liaising with other countries and encouraging girls from other countries to visit Australia to improve their game. Jean Walker in her report stated that 'we hope, in the near future to have girls visit from Pakistan, Sweden, England, USA and Canada. At first these visits will be individual, but it is certainly a start to a future Teams Competition'.

In the UK, the team played in the North of England and South of England tournaments.

Heather defeated Mavis Baker in the final of the North of England Championship and defeated Marion Jackman in the South of England Championship. Her opponent in the British Open was Jenny Irving, whom she defeated 9–0, 9–3, 9–1, claiming her 10th consecutive British Open crown.

The test results are listed below:

First Test
1. Heather McKay d Fran Marshall 9–2, 9–0, 9–1
2. Jenny Irving d Jean Wilson 9–4, 9–2, 9–0
3. Marion Jackman d Claire Chapman 9–3, 9–2, 9–4
Australia won 3–0.

Second Test
1. Heather McKay d Fran Marshall 9–0, 9–4, 9–1
2. Jenny Irving lost to Jean Wilson 9–3, 8–10, 9–6, 7–9, 3–9
3. Marion Jackman d Claire Chapman 9–2, 9–5, 9–2
Australia won 2–1

Third Test
1. Heather McKay d Fran Marshall 9–3, 9–0, 9–1
2. Marion Jackman d Jean Wilson 3–9, 9–5, 9–3, 9–1
3. Mavis Baker d Claire Chapman 9–5, 9–4, 9–2
Australia won 3–0 and the series 3–0

An outstanding result, with Heather winning all of her matches 3–0

The American tour was also a resounding success and the girls were unbeaten throughout, even though the ball, size of the racket, court dimensions and method of scoring were different. The tour did stir up interest, however, and at least 4 of the girls in Canada and America expressed an interest in visiting Australia. It was during this tour that Team Captain Jean Walker laid considerable groundwork to establish the first Women's World Championship, which was eventually held in Brisbane in 1976.

Report on UK Women's Tour 1972

Australian Women's team 1972
Left to right:, Marion Jackman (Queensland), Heather McKay (NSW), Jean Walker
(NSW Manageress), Jenny Irving (Victoria) and Mavis Baker (NSW).
(Photo: The Australian v Great Britain Programme,1972)
Note: the point 3 position! Mavis had recommended this as the best photographic
position from her earlier training in ballet!

After their resounding defeat in 1971, the British sent out another team in 1972. This was the first team to tour Australia since 1965. Unfortunately, their hopes were not realised and this team was soundly defeated in all of the three tests, without any of the Australian players losing a game.

First Test in Melbourne

1. Heather McKay d Fran Marshall 9–2, 9–0, 9–0
2. Marion Jackman d Jane Barham 9–1, 9–2, 9–0
3. Jenny Irving d Margaret Claughton 9–4, 9–0, 9–1.
Australia won 3–0

Second Test in Sydney

1. Heather McKay d Fran Marshall 9–0, 9–4, 9–1

2. Marion Jackman d Jane Barham 10–8, 9–0, 9–3

3. Jenny Irving d Jean Wilson 9–4, 9–0, 9–1

Australia won 3–0

Third Test in Brisbane

1. Marion Jackman* d Fran Marshall 9–3, 9–1, 9–3

2. Jenny Irving d Jane Barham 9–2, 9–2, 9–3

3. Mavis Baker d Jean Wilson 9–7, 9–6, 9–5

Australia won 3–0 and the series 3–0

Note* Heather McKay was out (injured) for this test with cracked ribs. One of the few times in her career, where she couldn't play!

Great Britain Women's Team 1972
Back Row (L to R): G.E Marshall, M. Claughton, J. Wilson
Front Row (L to Rt: J. Barham, H.G. Macintosh (Capt.) J. Wainwright
(Photo: The Australian v Great Britain Programme,1972)

Report on Australian Women's Team Tour 1975

(Courtesy of Carol Murray—Team Manager)

As Heather McKay had turned professional in 1974, it was now up to the next group of girls to show their mettle! The team of Manageress Carol Murray of NSW, Marion Jackman of Queensland (the 1974 Australian Champion), Sue Newman of NSW, Lyle Hubinger of Queensland, Margaret Zachariah of Victoria and Chris van Nierop of WA was given the task of taking over the reins. They did not disappoint. The tour started with 6 days in Sweden where the team played exhibitions and matches against the top men and women players. The tour had two roles, promotion and competition. Then the team moved on to England for the British Open and the test series. The Aussie women had graduated to the top of women's squash without the legendary Heather, a testimony to the extent that her presence had lifted the women's game in Australia. Such was the dominance of this team that the Australians won every tournament in which they participated and every final was an all-Australian event. In the British Open Australia filled 6 of the top 8 seeds. For the first time, the semi-finals were all-Australian. Players included Heather McKay, who was now professional, but allowed to compete as it was an Open event, Marion Jackman, Sue Newman and Margaret Zachariah. All of these players were either Australian Champions or future Australian Champions: Heather 1960–73, Marion 1974, Sue 1975–76 and Margaret 1977. Heather defeated Marion in the final 9–3, 9–1, 9–5.

In the Test Series, Australia was fortunate to have players of the calibre of Marion Jackman, Sue Newman, and Margaret Zachariah. They all proved to be excellent players under test conditions and they won the test series 3–0, only dropping one rubber out of 9 played. This meant that Australia had won every series since its inception eleven years earlier! Their impeccable behaviour on court and the fact that they were dressed immaculately, thanks to the assistance of Billie Woodgate from Fred Perry's, meant that their whole approach was first class.

Australian Women's Team 1975
Top to bottom: Carol Murray (NSW—Manager), Marion Jackman (Queensland),
Sue Newman (NSW), Lyle Hubinger (Queensland) Margaret Zachariah (Victoria)
and Chris van Nierop (WA)
(Photo: Courtesy of Carol Murray–Team Manager)

First test results:

1. Marion Jackman d Sue Cogswell (UK) 9–6, 9–1, 9–2

2. Sue Newman d Jean Wilson (UK) 10–8, 9–0, 9–4

3. Lyle Hubinger lost to Jane Courtney (UK) 1–9, 2–9, 9–10

4. Reserve—Margaret Zachariah d Teresa Lawes (UK) 9–10, 9–2, 9–1, 9–0

Australia won 2–1

Second test results:

1. Marion Jackman d Sue Cogswell 9–7, 9–7, 7–9, 9–2

2. Sue Newman d Jean Wilson 9–4, 9–2, 9–6

3. Margaret Zachariah d Jane Courtney 9–6, 9–3, 9–3

4. Reserve: Chris van Nierop lost to Teresa Lawes 5–9, 9–10, 8–10,

Australia won 3–0

Third Test results:

1. Marion Jackman d Sue Cogswell 9–4, 9–2, 9–5
2. Sue Newman d Jean Wilson 10–8, 9–4, 9–3
3. Margaret Zachariah d Teresa Lawes 9–3, 9–4, 9–2
4. Reserve: Lyle Hubinger d Jane Courtney 9–5, 9–7, 5–9, 9–3

Australia won 3–0 and the series 3–0

Note: The reserve matches gave the chance for other members of the team to gain experience for the future and Manageress Carol Murray recommended it be continued.

For this tour, the girls had to meet their own internal travelling costs which averaged $9.30 per day! Their overall costs for just living, meals etc. was $425. Accommodation was mainly billeting and, in fact, the girls only paid for accommodation for 4 days out of 6 and ½ weeks. The overall impression of this tour was that in the UK squash was still popular, with new courts continuing to be built. There were capacity galleries at every test, however 'the standard of the English girls was way below ours and they didn't appear to be as dedicated, energetic or as determined as our players' [48]

'In Canada, squash was booming as they have converted to the soft ball game exclusively, and there was also evidence of some English courts being built (different dimensions to the US). Their players were very enthusiastic and keen to learn and there were plans to send at least two girls to Australia in the near future. Sweden was also advancing with many new centres under construction; however, the game was still very much at a social level, with the Swedes more casual in their approach to competitive squash' .[49]

Recommendations from Carol Murray included travelling expenses for all members to be paid before leaving Australia, a daily living allowance, gifts for opponents in test matches as a goodwill gesture, to be paid for by the AWSRA, hotel accommodation should be provided prior to test matches to maximise rest and luggage should be limited to one bag plus one squash bag. It was felt that this would be enough luggage provided the girls have been supplied with team uniforms. Sponsorship should be sought for Australian teams and, finally, tournaments should be held earlier in the evening so that press coverage is maximised.

Inaugural World Individual Championship 1976

This was a turning point for the sport, with players who were deemed to be professional allowed to play. It really was a Championship to prove who was the best player in the World! Could Heather, who was now 35 and not playing in any tournaments as there were very few available for professionals, weave her magic?

The Championship was held in Brisbane and four Australians reached the semi-finals—Margaret Zachariah was defeated by Heather 9–1, 9–4, 9–1 and Sue Newman was defeated by Marion Jackman 9–1, 9–7, 9–3. Heather was not to be denied. She defeated Marion Jackman 9–2, 9–2, 9–0 in the final. The champion had not lost her touch. She dropped 16 points in 5 matches, 4 of those in the final. She was now World Champion (as if we didn't already know this), however it was nice to have it confirmed. As an aside, Heather always wore her lucky charm—a 4 leaf clover necklace. Was that her secret weapon?

International Teams' Championships 1976

International matches had now developed into a teams' event, including New Zealand, Great Britain and Australia. This was a tri-nation event as South Africa, Canada and Ireland only competed as individuals. It was a round robin event, as it was necessary for 6 teams to compete for it to be classified as a world championship event. The Australian team now had to continue to fly the flag without Australia's Nos 1 and 2, Heather and Marion. They could not compete as they were professionals. And fly the flag they did!

The team was—Margaret Zachariah, Victoria, Sue Newman, NSW, Jenny Irving, Queensland (Captain) and Chris van Nierop, Western Australia. Jean Walker, NSW was Manageress.

Great Britain and Australia had both beaten New Zealand in their pool, so in the deciding test match played at Miranda in Sydney in August 1976, the old rivals played off. Sue Newman had a mighty battle against Sue Cogswell. The awesome power of Sue Newman was met and matched by Sue Cogswell

Australian Women's Team 1976.
L to R: Margaret Zachariah (Vic) Sue Newman (NSW), Jenny Irving (Qld—Captain)
Chris van Nierop (WA)
(Photo: Courtesy of Carol Murray)

Participating teams and individuals at the Inaugural World Championships in 1976
(Photo: Courtesy of Margaret Zachariah)

who threw in a mix of volley drops and boasts that confused and finally tired the Aussie. Chris van Nierop was next on court and, after her tour overseas in 1975, her game now had a maturity acquired from this international experience. She was put to the test, however, and after losing the first game 4–9, she settled to win in 4 and it was left to Margaret Zachariah to claim victory for the Aussies. She took only minutes to convince the gallery and she was untroubled to win in three games.[50]

Sue Newman (Aust) l to Sue Cogswell (UK) 10–8, 9–7, 7–9, 3–9, 3–9

Chris van Nierop (Aust) d Angela Smith (UK) 4–9, 10–8, 9–5, 9–2

Margaret Zachariah (Aust) d Teresa Lawes (UK) 9–6, 9–2, 9–2

Australia won this test 2–1 and their dominance continued.

(*South Africa, Canada and Ireland did not compete in the Teams' events).

The UK team comprised: Sue Cogswell, Angela Smith, Karen Gardner, Therese Lawes, Joyce Maycock, with Claire Chapman (Captain)

Australian Women's Test series 1978

This team comprised Margaret Zachariah, 1977 Australian Champion, Vicki Hoffmannn, 1978 Australian Champion, Anne Smith, Australian representative 1974 and 1977–79, and Rhonda Shapland, Australian Junior Champion 1972 and 74–76. The Manager was Jan Honeycombe who was President of the Brisbane Women's Association. This tour was more diversified with teams from Canada, Ireland and New Zealand competing. It was part of a tour by the Australian team to the U.S. and England and the test matches were played in Birmingham in the UK. Australia defeated Great Britain 2–1 in the final. Margaret was injured; however, it was agreed that she should still play in the no. 1 position.[51]

Margaret Zachariah l to Sue Cogswell 4–9, 6–9, 5–9

Vicki Hoffmann d Barbara Diggens 9–5, 9–1, 9–4

Anne Smith d Jayne Ashton 9–1, 8–10, 9–6, 9–1

Reserve—Rhonda Shapland d Lesley Moore 10–8, 9–5, 9–1

Australia won 2–1

World Individual Championship 1979

Could Heather, who was now 38 and still not playing in many tournaments due to other commitments, maintain her record? Could another Australian lift the trophy, as 6 out the 8 Aussies were seeded, or would a Brit finally lift the coveted crown? With 64 entries, including 11 Aussies, let the games begin!

By the quarter finals, there were still 6 Aussies left: Heather McKay, Anne Smith, Barbara Wall, Sue King, Rhonda Thorne and Vicki Hoffmann. The two remaining players were British; Sue Cogswell and Angela Smith. By the semis there were two Aussies and 2 Brits left, fortunately, in opposite halves of the draw. (See full list in references at the back of the book). Heather managed to defeat Angela Smith (UK) 8–10, 9–4, 9–3, 9–1, dropping a game due to lack of match practice. Sue Cogswell (UK) defeated Vicki Hoffmann 9–5, 9–6, 7–9, 9–7. The stage was set for a UK–Australian final. Was Heather sufficiently prepared? Could the Brits pull off a much-desired result? No. The queen prevailed in a close tussle 6–9, 9–3, 9–1,9–4. Heather McKay had successfully defended her title—World Champion and it was time to retire from the World scene as a player.

World Teams Championships 1979

The World Teams' Championships now included teams from Canada, Ireland, Sweden, USA, Great Britain and Australia. Australia was without the inimitable Heather McKay. The team comprised Barbara Wall, Vicki Hoffmann and Sue King. Barbara and Sue were professional at that time, but were allowed to play as it was an Open event. The event came down to Australia v Great Britain in the Final. With two British Open Champions in the Australian side (Sue and Barbara) and an Australian Champion—Vicki! It was a foregone conclusion, or was it?

Results:

1. Sue Cogswell (GB) d Barbara Wall (Aust) 9–6, 9–3, 9–1.
2. Angela Smith (GB) d Vicki Hoffmann (Aust) 9–7, 7–9, 9–3, 9–5
3. Teresa Lawes (GB) d Sue King 5–9, 9–5, 7–9, 9–7, 9–5
Great Britain d Australia 3–0

Australian Women's Team 1979
L to R: Sue King (NSW—Captain), Barbara Wall (WA) Anne Smith (Vic) Vicki Hoffmann
(Vic) and Rhonda Shapland (Qld)
(Photo: Courtesy of Sue King)

Great Britain Women's Team 1979
Top row: Sue Cogswell and Lesley Moore. Middle Row: Jayne Ashton and Barbara Diggens
Front Row: Angela Smith and Teresa Lawes
(Photo: Courtesy of the WSRA History 1934–89, p31)

No! The Brits achieved the impossible and defeated Australia 3–0! This was a well-earned result and one which would have been most exciting to watch! The British thoroughly deserved their win and were now Champions of the World!

Fortunately, several players were emerging on the Australian front who would lead Australia into a role of dominance, into the next decade. Sue King, Barbara Wall, Vicki Cardwell had or would be British Open Champions, whilst Rhonda Thorne and Vicki Cardwell were to become World Champions in 1981 and 1983, respectively. Let's see how this evolved.

6 The 1980s—Time to Regroup

By now many of the top players had turned professional, as with the formation of World International Squash Players Association (WISPA) in February 1978 and the Women's International Squash Federation in March1979, more opportunities would emerge for a full-time playing career. The Australian players that were professional were Bev Meagher (1965) Bev Johnson (1969) Barbara Wall (1973) Heather McKay (1974), Marion Jackman (1976) Lyle Hubinger and Sue King (1977). Now with Open prize money, many more were to follow in their footsteps. Between 1983 and 2011, the WISPA tour involved over 80 tournaments world-wide annually and over 200 players were registered with WISPA. The way was clear for a full-time professional playing career.[52]

Note: Please see the Appendix–Future Directions.

Women's Test Series 1980

This time the Test series was battled out in Australia.[53] The team comprised Vicki Hoffmann, now 1980 British and Australian Open Champion, Sue King, 1978 British Open champion, Rhonda Thorne, former Australian representative, Margaret Zachariah, Australian Open Champion 1977, and Barbara Oldfield. This was a strong side with enormous experience and the Manager of this team was well-known Victorian coach Brian Boys. The British team also had Sue Cogswell, the British Closed Champion, who had been a member of the team that defeated Australia in the World Teams event in 1979. Barbara Diggens and Lesley Moore were not to be underestimated as well!

First Test Perth 31-8-80

>   1. S. Cogswell d R. Thorne* 10–8, 9–10, 9–3, 9–4
>   2. L. Moore d M. Zachariah 9–5, 9–3, 10–9
>   3. B. Diggens l S. King 8–10, 1–9, 9–7, 9–2, 6–9
>   Great Britain d Australia 2–1

*Note:(Vicki Hoffmann could not play due to an injured elbow)

Second Test Sydney 4-9-80

>   1. S. Cogswell d V. Hoffmann 6–9, 9–1, 9–4, 9–3
>   2. L. Moore l R. Thorne 5–9, 0–9, 4–9
>   3. B. Diggens l S. King 7–9, 3–9, 9–5, 6–9
>   Australia d Great Britain 2–1

Australian Women's Team 1980.
L to R: Margaret Zachariah (Captain–Vic), Rhonda Thorne (Qld), Vicki Hoffmann (Vic),
Barbara Oldfield (WA) and Sue King (NSW)
(Photo: Courtesy of Margaret Zachariah)

Third Test Brisbane 12-9-80

    1. S. Cogswell l V Hoffmann 7–9, 8–10, 5–9

    2. L. Moore l R Thorne 0–9, 1–9, 0–9

    3. B Diggens d S. King 10–9, 9–3, 9–4

    Australia d Great Britain 2–1

Australia won the series 2–1 in what had been a most exciting and seesawing test. They had avenged their loss to GB in the World Teams' Event the previous year. From now on, there would only be a World Teams Championship.

World Teams Championship 1981

Now it was time to see if Australia could regain its top spot! This time Heather was the Manager-Coach and in her team, she had Vicki Hoffmann, British Open Champion 1980, Australian Amateur Champion 1978 and Australian Open Champion in 1979 and 1980, Rhonda Thorne, who later became World Champion in 1981, Barbara Oldfield and Rae Anderson. Could they win the coveted crown? They could!

Australian Women's Team 1981.
L to R: Heather McKay (Coach-Manager), Rae Anderson (Vic), Vicki Hoffmann (Vic),
Barbara Oldfield (WA)and Rhonda Thorne (Qld)
(Photo: *The Belsham Years 1976–1992*, p22)

1. Rhonda Thorne d Angela Smith 9–1, 9–6, 9–0
2. Vicki Hoffmann d Lisa Opie 9–5, 9–6, 9–7
3. Barbara Oldfield l Sue Cogswell 8–10, 9–3, 9–4, 7–9, 9–10
Australia 2–1

World Teams Championship 1983

This Tournament was played in Perth, Australia and now the teams entered were from all corners of the globe. Teams from Ireland, the United States, Wales, Sweden, England, Scotland, Canada, New Zealand and Australia participated in two separate pools. Note: Teams from the UK played as independent countries. Australia won through to the final and the inevitable close tussle with England. It would have been exciting to watch.

The results were:

1. Rhonda Thorne d Lisa Opie 2–9, 9–6, 5–9, 10–8, 10–8
2. Carin Clonda d Martine le Moignan 9–4, 9–5, 9–1
3. Jan Miller l Angela Smith 6–9, 4–9, 6–9
Australia d England 2–1

Australia were World Champions again after a very close contest!

Australian Women's Senior and Junior Teams 1983
L to R: Marie Donnelly (Manager), Rhonda Thorne (Qld), Di Davis (WA),
Jan Miller (SA), Carin Clonda (NSW), Judy FitzGerald (Coach-Manager),
Carol Kennewell (Vic), Liz Irving (Qld), Robyn Friday (WA), Helen Paradeiser (Q)
(Photo: *The Belsham Years 1976–1992*, p29)

Robyn Friday wins Inaugural
World Junior Championship—1983
(Photo: *The Belsham Years, 1976–1992,* p28)

Note: Whilst the WISRF had agreed to include a World Junior title in the programme, they would not agree to a World Junior Team's event.[54] As the Championships were being played in Australia, other Junior players were entered in the Individual event for experience.

Robyn Friday won the inaugural World Junior Championship.

1985 World Teams Championship

This year saw the changing of the guard. Vicki had retired from international Competition in 1983 to start a family, Rhonda had retired and Liz Irving was out with a back injury.[55] Australia had lost three of its top players. It was time to regroup. The Australian team selected to play in Ireland were Jan Miller (Captain), Carin Clonda, Dianne Davis and Tracey Smith, who replaced Liz Irving. Jan was the only player who made it through to the Quarter finals in the British Open, where she was defeated by Lucy Soutter 3–0.

In the teams' event, there were now 14 countries competing. They were: Australia, Canada and Zimbabwe in Pool 1, England, the Netherlands, Sweden and Wales in Pool 2, New Zealand, Scotland, Finland and West Germany in Pool 3 and Ireland, the US and Hong Kong in Pool 4.[56] Australia won their pool but then were defeated by England in the semi-finals. In the play off for third, Australia defeated Ireland 2–1. England defeated New Zealand in the final 2–1 with Susan Devoy being the only winner for New Zealand.

On a more positive note, our Junior Women's team were showing signs that they would be a force to be reckoned in the future. This team of

Australian Senior and Junior Women's Teams 1985.
Back Row (L to R) Jan Miller, Tracey Smith, Di Davis, Danielle Drady, Michelle Martin,
Sarah Fitz-Gerald
Front Row (L to R) Sally Ann Robbie, Carin Clonda and Margaret Zachariah (Manager)
(Photo: *The Belsham Years 1976–1992*, p29)

Sarah Fitz-Gerald (Captain), Danielle Drady, Michelle Martin and Sally Ann Robbie won the World Junior Teams' Championship defeating England 2–1

There were developments on the home front, at this stage, with Heather McKay and Geoff Hunt, former Australian and World Champion, being recruited to run the Australian Institute of Sport Program on the Gold Coast. This was to enable Australia to perform to a higher level on the World stage. Players would learn how to be professional athletes, manage themselves and learn how to train, prepare for a major tournament and react mentally.[57] There was a great support staff with a Strength and Conditioning Coach Jeff Wollstein, Nutritionist Holly Frail, Sports Psychologist Ian Lynagh, Physiologist Enid Ginn and Athletics Coach Garry Brown. In addition, housing was provided. The players had to work a minimum of 15 hour per week in addition to their training. Michelle Martin, Sarah Fitz-Gerald, Danielle Drady and many others came through this programme and the results would show, a bit further up the track.

England World Champions 1987.
Left to Right: Lisa Opie, Martine Le Moignan, Alex Cowie, Lucy Soutter,
Alison Cummings and Suzanne Horner.
(Photo: *A History of the Women's Game of Squash Rackets Association, 1934–1989*, p47)

World Teams Championship 1987

This year, the Australian team was Vicki Cardwell (Captain), Sarah Fitz-Gerald, Michelle Martin and Robyn Lambourne (née Friday) This time the World Championships were played in New Zealand and there were again 14 nations competing: England, New Zealand, Australia, Ireland, Canada, Scotland, the United States, the Netherlands, Wales, Sweden, West Germany, Norway, France and Japan in that order. [58] Australia had defeated New Zealand 2–1 in a thrilling match in the rounds Vicki had defeated Susan Devoy, the reigning World Champion, in 5. They played Ireland in the semi and won 3–0, whilst England defeated New Zealand 3–0. In the final against England the results were:

1. Lisa Opie d Vicki Cardwell 9–3, 9–3, 6–9, 9–4.
2. Robyn Friday d Martine Le Moignan 9–5, 5–9, 9–0, 6–9, 9–5
3. Lucy Soutter d Sarah Fitz-Gerald 9–6, 9–3, 9–4.
England 2–1.

We still weren't quite there, however Sarah won the World Junior event defeating Donna Vardy of England 3–0.[59]

World Teams Championship 1989

The World Teams' Championships were played in the Netherlands and the English team were on a roll. Our team, comprising some of the old (Vicki Cardwell and Liz Irving) and the new (Danielle Drady—with Michelle Martin waiting in the wings), were no match for their more seasoned opponents—Martine Le Moignan, Suzanne Horner and Lisa Opie. The results were:

1. Liz Irving l Martine Le Moignan 3–9, 2–9, 10–8, 4–9.
2. Danielle Drady l Suzanne Horner 9–5, 4–9, 9–6, 9–5, 9–5. *

England 2–0

* If Danielle had managed to pull this off maybe we could have won with another eminent tussle between Vicki and Lisa, however, this was not to be and the last match wasn't played due to the result, already having been determined.

England World Champions 1989.
Back row: L—R: Martine le Moignan and Suzanne Horner
Front Row: L–R Lisa Opie, Alex Cowie (Manager) and Barbara Diggens
(Photo: *A History of the Women's Game of Squash Rackets Association, 1934–1989*, p47)

7 The 1990s—The Golden Age Continues

World Teams Championship 1990

The English Team were now on a hat-trick and in front of the Aussie home crowd in Sydney. They had a strong team with Suzanne Horner at no. 1, Lisa Opie at no. 2 and Martine Le Moignan at no. 3 against some of Australia's up and coming players. Michelle Martin was now no. 1, Danielle Drady no. 2 and Liz Irving no. 3. Unfortunately, both teams were having injury problems with Opie and Le Moignan both needing treatment and Robyn Lambourne, our original no. 2, out with a groin injury sustained in the individual event where she had reached the semi-finals.[60] Nonetheless, it was still a battle.

Results were:

1. Michelle Martin d Suzanne Horner 9–1, 6–9, 10–8, 5–9, 9–2.
2. Danielle Drady l to Lisa Opie 4–9, 9–6, 6–9, 5–9.
3. Liz Irving l Martine Le Moignan 9–2, 7–9, 9–7, 3–9, 3–9.

England 2–1.

World Teams Championship 1992

This time, were the new kids on the block ready? They were! In the words of Liz Irving 'You little ripper! It's only taken us 10 years!'.[61] Australia had just defeated New Zealand in the final of the World Women's Teams Championship played in Vancouver, Canada. Di Davis, Manager/Coach of this team, had been a playing member of the last team to have won the event in 1983. It was fitting that she had a hand in helping this team to finally get over the line. Liz had been a member of the previous three Australian teams that had been runner-up to England in the finals and she was not to be denied this time. Results, in order of play:

2. Liz Irving d Phillipa Beams 9–1, 9–5, 9–1

1. Michelle Martin l Susan Devoy 5–9, 1–9, 0–9

3. Robyn Lambourne d Donna Newton 2–9, 9–2, 9–6, 9–1

Australia 2–1.

Australia World Champions 1992
Back Row: Di Davis (Manager-Coach), Michelle Martin, Liz Irving
Front Row: Sarah Fitz-Gerald and Robyn Lambourne
(Photo: Courtesy of Squash Australia Annual Report, 1992 Cover)

It had been a long time coming; however, the team was now seasoned and it would be some time before they would be toppled again. Interestingly, the Australian Men had just won the World Men's Team Championship and it was the first time, in the Open era, that both the Men's and Women's Teams event winners were from the same country. In the Amateur era, Australian men (1962–73) and women (1964–80) had dominated with a remarkable run of consecutive wins, before the Team event became Open.

Australia was now the team to beat!

World Teams Championship 1994

The Australian team were again up against their old foes England, in the final. They were not to be denied. Results:

1. Michelle Martin d Suzanne Horne 9–6, 9–2, 9–6

2. Liz Irving d Sue Wright 9–1, 9–5, 9–6.

3. Sarah Fitz-Gerald d Cassie Jackman 9–3, 9–0, 9–4

Australia 3–0

World Teams Championship 1996

The Australian team's run continued; however, it wasn't easy. Results:

1. Michelle Martin l Cassie Jackman 3–9, 9–4, 9–5, 7–9, 7–9.

2. Sarah Fitz-Gerald d Linda Chapman 9–0, 9–1, 10–8

3. Liz Irving d Fiona Geaves 9–4, 9–4, 10–8.

Australia 2–1.

World Teams Championship 1998

Australian team now had a new member, Carol Owens. She had taken the no. 2 spot, behind Michelle and Sarah was now no. 3 and Liz Irving was no.4. Nonetheless, Michelle had a tough battle against Sue Wright of England. Australia emerged victorious. Results:

1. Michelle Martin d, Sue Wright 3–9, 9–3, 9–10, 9–2, 9–5

2. Carol Owens d Jane Martin 9–4, 9–7, 9–1

3. Sarah Fitz-Gerald won the dead rubber against Suzanne Horner 9–6, 9–4. Australia 3–0

8 The 2000s—Change was in the Wind

World Teams Championship 2000

Michelle had retired in 1999 and Sarah was now in the no. 1 spot, with Natalie Grinham, Robyn Cooper and Laura Keating being the other team members. Vicki Cardwell was the Coach. This time the Brits got their revenge, with Sarah the only won to win her rubber.

1. Sarah Fitz-Gerald d Linda Chapman 9–5, 9–0, 9–4.
2. Natalie Grinham l Tania Bailey 1–9, 0–9, 0–9
3. Robyn Cooper l Stephanie Brind 0–9, 4–9, 9–0, 3–9.
England 2–1

World Teams Championship 2002

This time it was our turn again. The matches were played in Denmark and the Australian team was Sarah Fitz-Gerald no. 1, Natalie Grinham no. 2 and Rachael Grinham no. 3—two new weapons!

Sarah Fitz-Gerald d Linda Chapman 2–9, 9–2, 9–0, 9–1
Natalie Grinham d Stephanie Brind 5–9, 9–5, 9–6, 9–3
Rachael Grinham l Tania Bailey (the dead rubber) 6–9, 2–9 .
Australia 2–1

World Teams Championship 2004

Our run was nearly over. The Grinham girls had now fully arrived and they continued to fly the flag! Again, it was against the old foe England in the final.

1. Rachael Grinham d Cassie Jackman 3–9, 9–5, 6–9, 9–1, 9–5

2. Natalie Grinham d Linda Elriani 9–4, 9–7, 9–2

3. Amelia Pittock didn't play the dead rubber.

Australia 2–0

England were victorious in 2006 and the Egyptians in 2008. In 2010, Australia was about to get its final win against their old foe, England under the new point a rally scoring system known as PARS. The results this time were:

1. Sarah Fitz-Gerald d Sarah Kippax 11–4, 11–4, 11–4.

2. Rachael Grinham l Jenny Duncalf 7–11, 4–11, 9–11

3. Kasey Brown d Laura Massaro 11–6, 11–9, 8–11, 11–8.

Australia 2–1

At the time of writing this book (2022), 2010 is the last time that an Australian Women's Team has been World Champion! The competition has

Australia World Champions 2010.
L to R: Sarah Fitz-Gerald, Kasey Brown, Michelle Martin (Coach/Manager)
Donna Urquhart and Rachael Grinham
(Photo: Courtesy of Squash Australia Annual Report 2010, p26)

since been dominated by Egypt in 2012, 2016 and 2018, while England managed to win in 2014.[62] There was no competition in 2020 due to Covid. The changing of the guard has certainly taken place! Full credit must go to the determination of a number of our top players which resulted in Australia winning the Amateur Teams' title nine out of nine times from 1964 to 1980 inclusive and Open Teams' Championships nine out of seventeen times between 1979 and 2010. This was a total of eighteen out of twenty-six events or 69.2%, compared to England seven and Egypt one, up until 2010. It is quite a different story today, where Egypt is the dominant nation, however, they haven't yet matched our record.

During this time the following players represented Australia numerous times, which ensured the continued strength of the teams:

Heather McKay	5	Jenny Irving	5
Barbara Slotemaker de Bruïne	3	Marion Jackman	5
Margaret Zachariah	5	Chris van Nierop	2
Sue King	4	Vicki Cardwell	6
Ann Smith	2	Barbara Oldfield	2
Rhonda Thorne	5	Carin Clonda	2
Jan Miller	2	Di Davis	2
Michelle Martin	6	Sarah Fitz-Gerald	8
Liz Irving	6	Robyn Lambourne	4
Danielle Drady	2	Carol Owens	2
Rachael Grinham	4	Natalie Grinham	3
Amelia Pittock	3	Melissa Martin	2
Kasey Brown	3	Donna Urquhart	2
Robyn Cooper	1	Laura Keating	1
Dianne Desira	1	Lisa Camilleri	1

In some cases, this is similar to representing at 4 Olympics held 4 years apart due to the irregularity of the matches, particularly in the Amateur phase where the matches were irregular. It is also worth noting, that it wasn't until the mid-1980s, when WISPA (World International Squash Players Association) became more organised, that the prize money was sufficient for the players to compete full-time, hence the increased availability of the players.

9 Inspirational Women
(in chronological order)

Betty Meagher (1919–1986)

At a recent Awards dinner held in 2019, Betty Meagher was inducted into Squash & Racquetball Victoria's (S&RV) Hall of Fame (Legend status) as the Pioneer of Australia's Women's Squash in the 1940s and 1950s.The development of the Women's game in Australia only came about through her enormous leadership skills, dedication and passion. She had been made an Honorary Life Member of the VWSRA in 1963. Betty Meagher, who passed away in 1986, had also been inducted as a S&RV Hall of Fame member in 2016 and received the Distinguished Service Award from Squash Australia in 2017.[63]

Betty Meagher was a legend on and off the court. She won the Victorian title in 1946–47 and again in 1949. She then won the Australian Women's Championship in 1946, 1949 and 1950. She was the first Australian woman to travel overseas to London, to play squash. Betty was accompanied by her husband Alan and Gordon Watson. Her achievements here have been outlined earlier in the book; however, it was her observations on how the Women's Squash Rackets Association, which had been formed nearly 20 years earlier in 1934, was run in Great Britain and the facilities available at the courts, that helped form her vision of how this, too, could happen in Australia.

On her return, the opportunity arose for her to purchase the Flinders Lane Squash Courts from Gordon Watson of the Gordon Watson's Squash Academy, which she did for 1,000 pounds. It was her intention to make it the centre of women's squash activities and she decided to combine her career of accountancy with that of squash court management along with her husband Alan and this venture succeeded.[64] In fact, she eventually operated three squash centres Flinders Lane, Elwood and the Station Street courts in Moorabbin, with the able assistance of Alan. Betty and Alan were regarded as the pioneers of public court development in Melbourne' in the 50s and 60s.

She had written on her return from the UK 'I felt that if the women are ever to progress out here, they must have a great many more younger players and a strong organisation behind them.'[65] Her remarkable drive and vision enabled her to form both the Victorian and Australian Women's Associations, in 1952.[66] The VWSRA very quickly had about 70 members and Betty had pioneered the beginning of organised Women's Squash Competition in Australia. In August,1953, a tour to New Zealand was arranged. At this stage, women's squash had grown enormously. There were now Interstate teams' events and there were about 1000 women players throughout Australia. In 1954, an invitation was issued to the British Women's Association to send two players to tour Australia and New Zealand. These players were Janet Morgan, the British Open Champion from 1950 to 1954 and Sheila Speight, runner-up in the British Open in 1954. 'The

Betty playing Mahmoud el Karim four times British Open Champion (1947–50) (Photo: Courtesy of Bev Garfield)

Betty, the administrator extraordinaire, working in her role as Accountant for the Institute of Victorian Photographers. She was organising the Institute's Child Quest to help Junior Legacy. She would later transfer these skills to organise the AWSRA and the VWSRA
(Photo: Courtesy of Bev Garfield)

purpose of the tour was to play in two State and the Australian Championship and to play exhibition matches throughout both countries. It was hoped that the tour would stimulate the growth and interest in women's squash.'[67]

At this stage, the Australians were well below the standard of the British players with Betty, the three-time Australian Champion, being defeated 9–0,9–1,9–0 by Janet in the semi-finals of the 1954 Australian Championships. At the conclusion of the tour Betty stated that 'it was the Australian WSRA's intention to send the Australian Women's Squash Champion every other year to compete in the British Open Squash Championships'. This didn't eventuate for some time, but the seed had been sown!

Playing career

- 1946 Winner Victorian Women's Championship
- 1946 Winner Australian Women's Championship
- 1947 Winner Victorian Women's Championship
- 1949 Winner Victorian Women's Championship
- 1949 Winner Australian Women's Championship defeating Val Watts
- 1950 Winner Australian Women's Championship defeating V. Cox
- 1950 Runner-up in the Hampshire Open (UK)
- 1950 Reached the second round in the British Open being defeated by Betty Hilton*

* *WSRA Handbook* 1950

Awards

- 1963 Life Member of the VWSRA 2016 Inducted into S&RV's Hall of Fame
- 2017 Distinguished Service Award Squash Australia
- 2019 Inducted into S&RV Hall of Fame (Legend Status)

In the words of her compatriot Judith FitzGerald, 'Betty was Women's Squash'. Her vision for Australian women's squash was eventually realised and they did indeed conquer the world in the '60s and '70s and again in the '90s and into 2000—2010. Betty with her energy, vision and drive had set Australian women on their path. An outstanding Aussie!

Judith (Louise) FitzGerald (née Tissot) (1930–2020)

Sadly, Judith passed away in November 2020. Judith was a versatile champion of three racquet sports—badminton, tennis and squash. She represented Victoria in tennis and came under the watchful eye of Australian Davis Cup Captain, Harry Hopman. In 1947, she first stepped on to a squash court and as they say the rest is history.[68]

Judith won her first Australian Championship in 1952 and soon after she was off to see the world with her friend Kay Neville Smith and, in particular, to see the Queen's coronation. While in England, they both competed in tennis tournaments and Judith managed

Victorian Women's Interstate Team 1955 Judy FitzGerald, Betty Meagher, Joan Watson and Val Watts. All Australian Champions during the 40s and 50s.
(Photo: Courtesy of Judy FitzGerald)

to reach the fourth round of the British Open Squash Championships. On her return to Australia (two years later), she won the 1956, '57 and '58 Victorian and Australian Amateur Championships. She was looking to become one of the World's best. She married Edward Graham FitzGerald on 12th February, 1957 and then went on to have six children—Kylie, Mark, Damien, Anthony, Louise and Sarah. This certainly curtailed her playing career, however, she turned her skills to coaching and over the next forty years successfully coached two World Champions, her daughter Sarah and Carol Owens. Between them they won seven World Championships and numerous State and National Championships.

Judith strongly supported Betty Meagher in the formation of the VWSRA and the AWSR A in 1952. In 2002 Judith was inducted into S&RV Hall of Fame. In 2007 Squash Australia presented her with the Distinguished Service Award and in 2015 Judith was elevated to Legend status by Squash Australia.

Playing career

- 1953 Australian Amateur Women's Champion

- 1954 Runner-up in the British Open Plate event, losing to R. Pendered in 5 games

- 1955 Reached the fourth round of the British Open losing to M. Morgan 6–9, 9–5, 9–7, 9–5*

- 1954–55 Won the Isle of Wight Championship defeating R. Byrne ('54) and D. Lange (South Africa–'55) *

- 1955 Won the West of England Championship, defeating R. Nagle*

- 1956–58 Australian Women's Champion

- 1956–58 Victorian Amateur Women's Champion

*WSRA Handbook,1955

Awards

- 2002 Inducted into S&RV Hall of Fame

- 2007 Squash Australia presented her with the Distinguished Service Award

- 2015 Judith was elevated to Legend status in the S&RV Hall of Fame

She will be remembered fondly, by everyone who knew her. I was fortunate to have interviewed her a couple of years before her passing and when I asked her what it takes to become a champion she replied, 'Perseverance, hard work, desire to learn from mistakes, passion, independence of thought and tactical analysis'. She had all of that in spades and she will be sorely missed by everyone in the Squash family. Rest in Peace, Judy. A life well lived.

Yvonne West (deceased–dates unknown) 1960s

Yvonne represented Australia in the first Women's team to travel overseas to play against Great Britain, in 1961. She was selected for this as she had won the NSW Championship in 1960 when she was the first person to defeat Heather Blundell in five games in the quarter finals.

- 1960 Winner of NSW Women's Championship
- 1960 Represented NSW in the Interstate series at no. 1
- 1961 Represented Australia in an unofficial match against Great Britain
- 1961 Played in the British Open and was defeated by Fran Marshall 9–1, 9–0, 9–2.

Aline Smith (deceased–dates unknown) 1960s

Aline represented Australia in the first women's team to travel overseas to play against Great Britain in 1961. She was selected for this as she had won the Victorian Championship in 1960. She acquitted herself quite well in the British Open getting through the first two rounds before losing to M. Gowthorpe 1–9, 3–9, 1–9

- 1960 Winner of Victorian Women's Championship
- 1960 Represented Victoria in the Interstate series
- 1961 Represented Australia in an unofficial match against Great Britain

Jan Tilly (née Shearer)

Jan had been a very keen tennis player and was the no. 1 ranked junior in South Australia from 1955–59. She was ranked four in Australia and was a member of the South Australian tennis team that played in the interstate competition from 1955–58. Each year at the completion of the Australian Tennis Championships and interstate series, selected juniors remained in the city in which they were playing and were coached by Harry Hopman and other local coaches.[69] One wet day in Melbourne, they were taken to the local squash courts to try the game. She took to it like a duck to water and then continued to play both squash and tennis for a few years until squash took over.

After she had won the South Australian squash title in 1960, she was selected to represent Australia in the tour to England to play one unofficial match and play in the British Open. They travelled by sea and the trip took 6 weeks (the mind boggles!) They did jog around the decks to keep fit, which amused the other passengers. They were defeated by the British team of Sheila Macintosh, Fran Marshall and Di Corbett 3–0. The last matches they played were at the Lansdowne Club where Jan managed to win the British Junior Title and get through two rounds in the British Open before losing to Pauline White 9–5, 4–9, 8–10, 6–9.

Playing career

- 1958 Australian Junior Champion
- 1959–61 South Australian Women's Champion
- 1960–62 Represented South Australia in the Interstate series
- 1960–61 Represented Australia in an unofficial match against Great Britain
- 1961 British Junior Champion
- 1961 Runner-up to Heather Blundell in the Australian Women's Championship. Lost 3–1
- 1963–64 South Australian Women's Champion (under married name—Tilly)

Administration

- Served on the South Australian Squash Rackets Association for a number of years in the '60s
- Manager of SA interstate team on at least one occasion

After her squash playing career was over Jan took up golf and attained a single figure handicap. She played pennant for many years and played twice in the Australian Championships. She served as the Associates Captain and was also Associates President at her golf club. She became involved in the promotion of junior golfers through the SA Women's Golf Association.

Jan also took up Badminton, at a later stage and was State Champion in that sport as well. She was what you could call an all-round sportswoman! Well done, Jan!

Heather (Pamela) McKay (née Blundell) AO MBE 1960s–1980s

What a story! So where to begin! Firstly, as noted earlier, Heather was born into a very large family of eleven children—five boys and six girls—Heather was no. 8. Her father, Frank (Francis) was a baker and also had a market garden across the road from their small home in Ford Street Queanbeyan, which no doubt helped to feed the family. He lived to the age of 83 and Dulcie, Heather's mother, lasted even longer until 93. They both even managed to fit in the odd game of tennis well into old age. Perhaps this is from whom Heather gets her resilience and determination. The family was very sporty, excelling in a variety of sports. Of the Blundell girls, Kay was runner-up in the World Masters (Over 60) Tennis Championships, in 1990. She partnered Jan Blackshaw, to win the World Over 50 Doubles Championship, the same year. Her team also won the World Over 60 teams' event. Robyn represented ACT Squash in the interstate series and Australia in master squash against New Zealand. In Hockey she represented the ACT in the interstate series. Heather, played tennis, hockey and a bit of squash! Colleen played ACT Hockey and was a single-figure golfer. Sue represented ACT and NSW in Hockey and at one stage was Vice-Captain of the NSW team. This was just the girls. The boys also excelled in Rugby League, AFL, Basketball and Shooting. This was a very active household. Sport was a good outlet and kept them out of mischief, although no doubt they still got up to some! I think that it was this background that kept Heather very grounded and was the reason she returned to Queanbeyan after her retirement from competitive squash. She'll never be lonely, as I believe they book out the Queanbeyan Community Hall at Christmas time so that the 70+ family can all come—brothers, sisters, cousins, nephews, nieces, aunts, uncles etc, etc!

At 10, Heather took up tennis and at 13 hockey.[70] She was good at them and won prizes in both. She became Queanbeyan Junior and Senior Tennis Champion and played Hockey for Canberra. On leaving school at the Intermediate level, she took a job with the local newsagent. When courts were first built in Queanbeyan in 1959, she started playing squash to get fit for hockey. The court Manageress, Nell McGrath, allowed her to practise after work free of charge. (Court owners take note!). However, her first game had been in Sydney when she was on holidays. After going to the beach, Heather, her sister, Robyn and a friend, decided to have a game of squash at Manly District Park Tennis and Squash Centre. There were two squash courts adjacent to the tennis courts and the complex was run by Jean and Keith Walker, who were to become very familiar names in the squash world for the next 20 years. Now Jean was having none of these teenage girls coming in all scrappy from the beach. They were obliged to buy socks and clean up before they were allowed on to the courts. Little did she-we know.

On returning to Canberra, Heather started playing regularly at the Squash Bowl centre in Civic with some of her hockey friends from the Evergreens Club and from there she was encouraged to play in the NSW Junior Championships in Wollongong. After success there, she was advised by Vin Napier to play in the NSW Championships in Sydney. With the help of her grandmother and mother she entered and won the NSW Junior title in a hard 5 set battle with the no.1 Junior at that time Barbara Baxter, winning 10–8 in the 5th. She had been defeated by no. 1 seed Yvonne West in five games (after leading 2 games to love) in the quarter finals of the NSW Open. A rally which ended up with Heather being hit by the ball made her lose concentration (for once), an experience she didn't repeat! As a result of these performances, she was selected at no.4 in the NSW Women's Interstate Team series to be played in Brisbane.

She was entered into the Australian Senior Championships as she was now 19. As reported earlier, she went on to win the Australian title, defeating the local Queensland Champion Dot Linde in four games. Heather was now Australian Champion and she had been playing for less than one year.

On her return to Queanbeyan, she now had to make a choice. Stay home or move to Sydney to gain more experience. Sydney it was. This was a big move for this kid from the bush. She had to leave her large family and support group to move into the city environment of Sydney. With the help of Spalding, who had agreed to sponsor her, it was arranged that she would work as a receptionist at Bellevue Hill Squash Centre, which was initially managed by Ken Freebury and later by a top NSW player Kay Mansfield with her husband Richard. She boarded at Knight's, just up the road. Vin put her in touch with leading players and coaches. They were generous with their time and advice and John Cheadle, Australian Champion 1957 and NSW Champion 1952, and 1954–58 inclusive, would have a hit with her once a week. In addition, Keith Walker taught her to think more about the game rather than just hitting and hoping! Heather spent the first year in Sydney listening, learning and playing a lot of squash! [71] Staying in Sydney gave her time to refine her skills and to learn what the game was all about. She read Vin Napier's book *Squash the Australian Way*, on a regular basis. 'She was the fastest learner of the game the world has ever known and she never departed from the fundamentals she initially studied and adapted'.[72]

She continued to improve and the following year (1961), won the Australian Championship. In 1962, she won the Australian Championship again, this time defeating a future team-mate Jenny Irving from Victoria 9–1, 9–0, 9–0. Her dominance and consistency were starting to emerge and it was time to take on the world.

With the help of an understanding employer, an enthusiastic and supportive State Association, some helpful sponsors and the locals in Queanbeyan, her new life-style was about to begin. For the next 16 years she would take two months off to visit the UK to play in the British Open. She would play demonstration matches as fund raisers, the AWSRA also provided some money, a cigarette company (!) WD and HO Wills provided funding as did Spalding, her racket sponsor. All monies raised went through the NSWWSRA, so that she could retain her amateur status. They arranged her travel and paid her an allowance.[73]

In 1962, Heather flew to London, not knowing anyone and without even a hotel room booked for the first night. Stepping off the plane, she was fortunately met by Janet Shardlow, a ten-time British Championship winner whose record Heather would eventually beat. This was to become a lifelong friendship and Heather stayed with Janet and her first husband, Joe Bisley and subsequently her second husband, Ambrose Shardlow, during her annual migration. Initially, she was very shy and unsure of herself, however success brought with it the need to speak in public and be available and Heather grew in the process. Janet and Ambrose were vitally important in creating the stability that underlay her success in Britain over the next sixteen years.

Two great champions.
Janet and Heather at the This is your Life *TV Program in 1977*
(Janet was flown out especially for the occasion)
(Photo: Courtesy of Stanberry Photography, Sydney, 1977)

Perfectly poised.
(Photo: Courtesy of Heather McKay)

Heather's first tournament in the UK was the Scottish Championships, which was a baptism by fire. She was playing on courts that were colder than she had ever experienced and she was up against the British no. 1, Fran Marshall in the final. After an epic 5 set struggle she was defeated*. This was her second defeat and she was never defeated again. She was quite pleased that she had taken the British no. 1 to five games but at the same time in a letter to her family wrote 'Don't worry. It won't happen again'! And it didn't! She went on to win the South and North of England titles and when she played Fran a few weeks later in the British Open final she defeated her 9–6, 9–5, 9–4.[74] She was now British Open Champion! She had learned her lesson.

*It is interesting to note, that Heather had only taken two rackets to the courts. She broke both due to the extreme change in temperature and had to borrow a racquet to complete the match! She didn't make that mistake again!

What next? Well, it was back home to represent NSW in the Interstate series, win another Australian title and continue to work on her technique. 'Good technique doesn't break down when you're tired.'[75] She never suffered from the soft tissue and repetitive strain injuries of the modern players, as there were only 4 major championships in the year—the NSW, Victorian and Australian Championships and the British Open. She also attributed this lack of injury to the fact that she had taken up the game so late (18) by today's standards. She also followed strength training and flexibility as part of her

You wouldn't want to be on the receiving end of this!
(Photo: *The Squash Player Vol 1, no. 8*, p30)

fitness regime and she continued to cross-train, continuing to play hockey which was an outside sport and a team sport as well. Heather developed the style of play that was to reap phenomenal rewards. She virtually eliminated unforced errors from her game. She learned what worked for her, playing quite conservatively, with nothing flashy. She also developed the will to take no prisoners on court However, opponents didn't want to cross her or they would feel the consequences.

This lifestyle continued, throughout 1962. She worked as a receptionist at Bellevue Hill Squash Centre. There was no shortage of good players with whom to practice: John Cheadle, Ted Hamilton, her future husband Brian McKay who was a state no. 1 player and many others. Also, a group of top players had started training at Jean and Keith Walker's Tennis and Squash Centre in Manly on Sunday afternoons. Here she not only picked up good coaching tips from Keith, but managed to have excellent hits with leading NSW men and also the leading NSW female players. It was their own AIS!

After winning the Australian Championship again in 1962, and further fundraising events, exhibitions, sponsorship etc, Heather travelled to the UK to win the British Open in early January 1963 defeating Fran Marshall 9–2, 9–4, 9–6 in the final. She had won her second British Open and the time was steadily approaching for an Australian team to spread their wings. Heather travelled back to Australia and followed her normal pattern of playing in the state titles in NSW and Victoria and winning them! It was after winning the Australian Championship again in 1963, that she made the prophetic statement to the leading players at the tournament that it was 'time to knock the Poms off'! This has been outlined earlier in the book, so I won't repeat the details here. Suffice it to say that she got the ball rolling.

The Australian team of Heather McKay (NSW), Jenny Irving (Victoria—Captain), Pat McClenaughan an (NSW) Barbara Baxter (NSW) and Helen Plaistead (WA), pulled off an epic victory 3–2 played over 4 and ½ hours, to secure the first win ever over Great Britain at the soft ball game. In her usual inimitable style, with the scores levelled at 2–2, Heather defeated Fran Marshall in 15 minutes 9–1, 9–0, 9–0. As a result of this match, Great Britain toured Australia, in 1965 to try and get their revenge. Unfortunately, to no avail! (Result Australia 3–0). The full match results have been outlined earlier and in the Appendix. Suffice it to say that Heather won all her matches (in the Test series from 1963–64 until 1972) 3–0 only losing a total of 86 points—an average of 2.5 points per match! She was clearly head and shoulders above anyone except for Anna Craven-Smith who had won 45 of them. In Anna's last British Open final, she lost to Heather 9–1, 10–8, 9–6 to which lasted for 57 minutes! Heather always classified her as her most dangerous opponent. After the British Open final in 1967, Heather stated that 'if she'd lost the third game she'd have been in trouble. I was exhausted.'[76] It must be noted that during throughout her illustrious squash playing career, Heather had also managed to be named in the Australian side in Hockey (1967 and 1971) as well as representing NSW twice and ACT 5 times. She was one active lady.

From 1970–74 Heather had undertaken numerous coaching tours of country areas in Australia as well as travelling to Europe, England and South Africa. She gave coaching classes for elite players as well as beginners and average players. Time now moved on and, in 1974, Heather decided to turn professional. An opportunity had arisen to coach, at the Toronto Squash Club in Canada, which was too good to refuse. Here she undertook individual coaching and, in addition, Brian and her ran the Sports Pro Shop (from 1975–80). Here, she was introduced to Racquetball something she hadn't

Anna Craven-Smith and Heather McKay after the British Open Final 1967
(Photo: Courtesy of Anna Bullock (Craven Smith)

tried before! Needless to say, she became USA Amateur Champion in 1979, and USA Professional Champion in 1980, 1981 and 1984. She also won the Canadian Singles Racquetball Championship from 1980–84, the Canadian Doubles Championship in 1984 and 1985 and was World Masters Champion in 1985. In addition to this Heather was Coach-Manager of the Australian winning team at the World Championships in Toronto in 1981. She also had returned to Australia in 1981 and 1982 to run specialised coaching camps for talented Australian Juniors, with Ken Hiscoe. This was to bear fruit in the next decade.

However, I digress. Whilst Heather was no longer eligible to play for her country in the Teams' events, the British Championships were Open and a World Championship was looming in Australia, in 1976. This was where she showed her true mettle. With very little international Competition, she still managed to win three more British Open Championships (1975–77) losing an average of 9 points per match and she won the inaugural World Championship in 1976, defeating compatriot Marion Jackman 9–2, 9–0, 9–0 in the final. Her only hiccup came in the

World Championships in the 1979 final. Now 38, and with very little match play behind her, she dropped a game to Angela Smith (England) in the semi-finals defeating her 8–10, 9–4, 9–3, 9–1 and again in the final against Sue Cogswell (England), eventually winning 6–9, 9–3, 9–1, 9–4. The writing was on the wall, that it wasn't going to get any easier. Her lack of match practice showed and she was getting older! Perhaps it was time to put her feet up?

No. As you can see from the above, she turned her attention to Racquetball and, in 1985, an opportunity arose to join Geoff Hunt as assistant Coach at the Australian Institute of Sport, based in Brisbane. This was an opportunity to coach the upcoming elite—an offer that also included the warm Queensland weather! After nearly ten years in the cold, Canadian winters, it was a fairly easy decision. This is where the next chapter in Heather's incredible career starts. She was to hold this position until 1998.

Coaching

It was timely, that Heather had been appointed to the AIS. A new wave of talented players were coming through. Australia had won the World Team's event, in 1983 and won the inaugural World Junior Team's event in Ireland. This team included Sarah Fitz-Gerald (Victoria–Captain), Danielle Drady Michelle Martin (NSW) and Sally Ann Robbie (Q) and Margaret Zachariah (Manager). In the senior ranks a number of players had retired and it was time to develop the upcoming players, which eventuated with a vengeance!

The AIS gave the scholarship holders, the opportunity to train full-time under expert coaches, Geoff Hunt and Heather McKay, and they were required to study or work for 15 hours per week [77]. The initial intake included Michelle Martin, Danielle Drady, Sarah Fitz-Gerald, Nikke Solan, Robyn Cooper, Susan Laver and Toni Weeks.[78]

Of these girls, Michelle would win 5 Australian Opens, 6 British Opens and 3 World Championships. Sarah would win 4 Australian Opens, 2 British Opens (runner-up in another 2) and 5 World Opens. Liz would be Runner-

Heather coaching the 1990 Australian World Championship Team in Sydney
L to R: Heather, Daniel Drady, Liz Irving, Robyn Lambourne, Michelle Martin,
Sarah Fitz-Gerald (kneeling)
(Photo: Courtesy of Carol Murray)

Australia's Team at the World Championships 1990
Back Row (L to R): Sarah Fitz-Gerald, Michelle Martin,
Front Row: Robyn Lambourne, Danielle Drady, Liz Irving
(Photo: *Squash Australia 1990 Annual Report*–Front cover)

up in 3 British Opens and Runner-up in the Worlds as well as representing in 6 World Championship teams. Danielle represented Australia in 3 World Championship teams and reached a World No 2 ranking (1991). Robyn represented Australia in 3 World Championship teams, as well as winning the inaugural World Junior Championship, in 1983. She also reached a No 2 ranking (1992). A group of formidable young women who responded well to Heather's tutelage.

Playing career

- British Open Champions 1962–1977
- World Open Champion 1976 and 1979
- Australian Amateur Champion 1960–1973
- Victorian Amateur Open Champion 1961–73
- NSW Amateur Champion 1961–73
- Undefeated for 19 consecutive years from 1962 until her retirement in 1981.
- World Masters Champion (45) 1987 and 1990, 1993 (50) 1995 (50)
- 1963–72 no. 1 player in all Australian Women's Teams during that period winning all her matches 3–0 (at an average at just over 4 points a match). She lost 66 points overall and Anna Craven-Smith won 46 of them!
- 1961–73 Represented NSW as no. 1 player, in all Interstate series. Undefeated throughout winning her matches 3–0, with the exception of losing a game to Marion Jackman in 1972 and 1973.

Heather had been active in Racquetball during her time in Canada. Her results here are equally as impressive!

- 1979 USA Amateur Racquetball Champion
- 1980, 1981 and 1984 USA Professional Champion
- 1980–84 Canadian Singles Racquetball Champion
- 1984 and 1985 Canadian Doubles Champion 1985 World Masters Game Champion

But wait there's more!

In 1967 and 1971 Heather was selected in the All-Australian Team for Hockey. Unfortunately, she could not play, due to her squash commitments and, of course, there's even more!

What about tennis?

- 1998–2018 Won 9 Australian Championship Veterans' Singles titles during this period
- 2001 Part of the Australian team that won World Veterans' Tennis Championships (Over 60). She won the Individual Singles title as well, at this same tournament
- 2002–18 Won 5 Australian Veterans' Championship Doubles titles during this period
- 2001, 2002, 2004, 2009 Represented Australia in the World Veterans' Teams' Championship in her respective age group.

Awards

- 1967 ABC Sportswoman of the Year
- 1967,1969 and 1974 Sportsmen's Association of Australia Walter Lindrum Award (this award is granted to the most outstanding Australian sportsperson for achievement and sportsmanship)
- 1969 Order of the British Empire (MBE)
- 1969 Caltex Sportsman of the Year for NSW
- 1973 Helms Athletic Foundation of California Hall of Fame award. A special medal was struck for squash, in honour of Heather (Kunapipi Vol 23 Issue 1).
- 1975 Voted as Australia's no. 1 Sports representative of the previous twenty years
- 1979 Order of Australia (AM)
- 1979 Winner of the American Amateur Racquetball Championship*
- 1979 American Racquets Athlete of the Year—USA Magazine *Racquets*
- 1980–81 USA Women's Racquetball Player of the year
- 1985 Squash Australia Hall of Fame inaugural inductee
- 1985 Sport Australia Hall of Fame inductee

- 1993 World Squash Federation Hall of Fame
- 1997 USA Racquetball Hall of Fame inductee
- 1999 Inducted into WISPA (Women's International Squash Players Association) Hall of Fame
- 2000 Australian Sports Medal
- 2000 Elevated to Legend Status in Sport Australia Hall of Fame
- 2003 Inducted into International Women's Sports Hall of Fame
- 2005 Squash Australia Hall of Fame Legend
- 2007 World Squash Lifetime Achievement Award
- 2018 Officer of the Order of Australia (AO)
- 2019 Certificate of Special Recognition for being the Greatest Ever Female Squash Player by Squash and Racquetball Victoria
- 2020 Inducted into the Canadian Racquetball Hall of Fame

*This was in the same year that Heather won the World Squash Championship!

Well, what can one say. Australian Squash can consider themselves fortunate, that Heather was spotted in those early days. It is a credit to her, her husband Brian, and various coaches and practice partners, that enabled her to reach her full potential—and she's still going. She just loves sport.

Outstanding!

As an aside, Heather certainly didn't play for the money. In fact, for one of her British Opens she won a thermos flask. Now those were the days.

Jenny Irving

Jenny first started playing squash in 1957. Her earlier sports were tennis, netball, softball and athletics. She had 3 sisters and 1 brother, none of whom played sport. She was coached by Brian Boys from 1962 until 1970. Judy FitzGerald also helped her learn how to get the ball out of the back corners. Her training regimen comprised plenty of time on the court and she did receive some running advice from June Ferguson (Betty Cuthbert's Coach). Jenny did no weight training.

She first came to prominence in 1963 when she toured New Zealand with an official Australian team, that was based on availability, as Manager. Renowned for her dogged fighting ability, Jenny was in the same era as Heather McKay and was runner-up in several Australian and Victorian Championships from 1962–1970. She was an invaluable team member for Australia, representing in the first official touring team to defeat the UK in 1963–64 as no. 2. She lost a closely contested match with the canny Sheila Macintosh in 5 games. She continued to represent in 1965, after the birth of Liz in February, and in 1971 where she won one and lost one. She had contracted food poisoning, so she couldn't contest the remaining rubber. In 1972 Jenny won all 3 of her matches against the UK which were played in Australia. Jenny was also Captain of the Australian Championship team in 1976 that won the international teams' Event. The team comprised Sue Newman of NSW, Chris van Nierop of WA and Margaret Zachariah of Vic. They were victorious 2–1 and Australia had regained their supremacy as World no. 1. Her best individual performance was to be runner-up in the British Open in 1971, where she was defeated by Heather McKay. This feat was to be matched by her daughter Liz in 1988, but more about that later.

Jenny was a Primary School teacher and had the unenviable job of juggling work, home and her squash. In 1972, she moved to Queensland and it did not take her long to make her mark. Post squash Jenny has devoted her time to Masters Squash tournaments, then golf and more recently croquet.

Playing career

- 1962 Runner-up in the Australian Championship
- 1963–64 Represented Australia in the first team to defeat the UK in 1963–64 (playing at no. 2)
- 1965 Represented Australia defeating the UK
- 1968 Runner-up to Marion Hawcroft in the Queensland Championship
- 1969 Runner-up in the Australian Championship to Heather McKay
- 1970 Runner-up in the Australian Championship to Heather McKay

- 1971 Runner-up to Heather McKay in the British Open Final
- 1971–72 Represented Australia defeating England in both Test series
- 1972 Runner-up to Marion Jackman in the Queensland Championship
- 1972 Western Australian Champion
- 1972 Runner-up in the Australian Championship to Heather McKay
- 1974 Runner-up to Marion Jackman in the Queensland Championship
- 1974 Runner-up in the Australian Championship to Heather McKay
- 1975 and 1977 Queensland Champion
- 1976 Captain of the winning Australian team at the World Championship international match[*]
- 1978–79 Queensland Senior Champion
- 1981 Australian Over 40 Champion
- 1982 Queensland Over 40 Champion
- 1980 British Open Champion Over 40
- 1987 World Master's Over 50 Women's Champion

She also has the remarkable record of representing four different states in the Interstate series—Victoria 1961–65, NSW 1967–71, WA 1972 and Queensland 1973–76! A record that probably won't be matched.

Jenny has shown outstanding dedication to the sport, evidenced by her longevity—25 years playing competitively at a high level. Well done.

Note: Unfortunately, Jenny lost many of her records in the floods in Queensland so there may be some omissions!

[*]The official World Teams Matches didn't commence until 1979.

Pat McClenaughan (Trish Faulkner)

Pat McLenaughan was born in Sydney and is the daughter of St George Rugby Union player Terry McClenaughan. He later served as Team manager for the Wallabies. Pat excelled in tennis and squash and in 1963 won the Australian Girls' Doubles title in tennis, and the Australian Junior Squash Championship. Her other achievements are listed below.

- 1961–3 NSW and Australian Junior Squash Champion
- 1964 Member of Australian winning squash team which defeated Great Britain in a gruelling 4 and ½ hour match. Pat won a critical match defeating Anna Craven-Smith, 10–9, 7–9, 5–9, 10–8, 10–8
- 1965 Her attention moved to tennis and she reached the Quarter finals of the French Open partnering Fay Toyne. In the singles she reached the third round.
- At Wimbledon, she reached the third round in the singles. She also excelled at doubles reaching the Quarter finals of the French Open (1965) and the third round at Wimbledon (1973)
- 1970s–2022 In the US Open, Trish reached the third round in the singles. She had married Englishman, Roger Faulkner, by then, and moved to live permanently in the US—initially in Detroit and later in Florida.

Trish established herself as an outstanding tennis coach at the Ballenisles Country Club, in Florida. She was awarded the US Professional Tennis Association's Professional of the Year Award in 2013

As an aside, in 2001, Trish won the 55 years and Over World Tennis Championship (played in Perth) whilst Heather McKay won the 60 years and over World Tennis Championship at the same venue. The two old squash team mates met up. Squash and tennis seem to go together!

Trish Faulkner
(Pat McClenaughan)
(Photo supplied)

Barbara Slotemaker De Bruïne (née Baxter) AM

Now for the easy part. After researching and writing the profiles of all these outstanding women, writing my own story is comparatively easy, as I have all the facts at my fingertips. Like many of the other Australian representatives, I have always been involved in sport. My mother had been an A grade tennis player and one of the first women lifesavers at Bondi, in the 1930s and 40s. To channel my energy, she enrolled me in swimming lessons where I was spotted by Bruce McDonald, coach of Gary Chapman who was a gold medallist at the Olympics in Melbourne in 1956. I was 8 at the time and he asked me to swim 8 laps, which I did! Looking at my grandchildren now, it was quite an achievement. Anyway, to cut a long story short I went on to be coached by Harry Gallagher who was Dawn Fraser's Coach and Frank Guthrie who was Lorraine Crapp's coach. I ended up winning all my swimming events at the School District Carnival and the Combined High Diving, for which I was coached by Lesley Thickness, an Australian representative in the 1948 British Empire Games.

The discipline that was involved in competitive swimming such as getting up at 4am, on the train at 5.00am, in the pool at 6am and training again in the afternoon from 4.00pm—6pm to swim a total of 120 laps at the age of 9–12 made me realise what it takes to be successful. This, together with being in the company of exceptional Olympic gold medallist swimmers such as Jon Hendricks, Johnny Devitt, Murray Rose, Dawn Fraser and Lorraine Crapp, instilled in me the drive for the pursuit of excellence. As John Newcombe said in a recent interview, 'If you are surrounded by champions, you're encouraged to become a champion!'

At age 12, I announced to my parents I was giving up swimming as I was sick of the early starts and following the black line and I was going to take up tennis. This was the era of Hoad and Rosewall and we used to be glued to the radio listening to the Davis Cup and Wimbledon. There was a tennis court at the end of the street, so it was much easier to access than the swimming pool and my mother used to play there every Wednesday afternoon. Again, Mum paid for coaching lessons and it wasn't long before I was representing the district in the under 16 division in the Irene Mathews Cup and the Under 19 division in the Angus and Coote Cup. To compete in these, I had to ride my bike, with no gears or helmet in those days, around the Parramatta District. I was also selected in the Under 14 Squad at White City to receive additional coaching from Nancy Dalton. I had spent hours in the backyard with a copy of the magazine Sporting Life, which had frame by frame shots of Lew Hoad playing forehand, backhand, serve etc. So, I drew a chalk line on the garage wall at the height of the net and put numbered boxes from 1–6 above the line of the net. I'd got this idea from reading Maureen 'Little Mo' Connelly's book. I then called out a number and had to hit the ball into it. This was excellent training to transfer to squash.

Squash didn't come into the picture until 1958. I was 17 and courts were just starting to be built in Sydney. Like many of the other players in this book, we used to go down to the courts when tennis was washed out. I was fortunate in that John Luscombe, an Englishman and owner of the courts, spotted me and, as mentioned previously, he arranged coaching which set me on my way. I played in the Australian Junior Championships at Royal Sydney Golf Club in 1958 and reached the semis. I'm not boasting as there were only 4 in it! Bev Meagher defeated me and won the title. I was in limbo for a while, as I was studying at Sydney Teacher's College and a career in squash was not even considered.

However, as mentioned earlier in the book, my court owner persisted, arranged coaching with Kevin Kennedy and Vin Toohey for technique, Brian Marsden (Manager of the Australian Weightlifting team to Tokyo, in 1960) for weight training and June Ferguson, who was Betty Cuthbert's Coach, for sprint and endurance and I started to make my mark.1960 saw me reach the semi-final of the NSW Open and I was runner-up to Heather in the NSW Junior Championships.1961 saw me goof about and not really commit as I was settling into a career as a teacher, however when I wasn't selected in the NSW State team to go to Adelaide for the Australian Championships, even though I had beaten the no. 4 player twice in the State 1 competition, I thought 'Right. I'll show them what I can do!' Failure often brings success. It was this disappointment and the fact that the next Interstate series would be held in Perth, that led me to state 'I will beat everyone in NSW to under 10 points in the Comp so they can't leave me out!'

I strictly followed the equivalent of a periodised weight training of today. I trained at the oval under June Ferguson's watchful eye (I was a hopeless runner) and spent hours perfecting my strokes. When I felt lazy, I'd get Mum to get out the car and instructed her to drive at 10mph (16km). I would then run in FRONT of the car, which forced me to get over my lethargy! Crazy! Other schemes involved playing at club practice with a diver's weight belt on and two tracksuits, like handicapping a horse, so that when I played in normal squash gear and no weights, I was so much faster. Being 5'11' (177cms) speed wasn't my strong suit! Running knee deep in surf and back along the soft sand, also did wonders for my fitness and the strength in my legs. You shouldn't get tired in a squash match as fitness is something within your control. However, the outcome was achieved! I did beat everyone in NSW to under 10 points, except Heather, of course. I was runner-up to Heather in the NSW Open, having defeated Helen Michel from Victoria in the semi, and was selected in the team to go to Perth as no. 2. On this trip, I also was selected to play for Australia against New Zealand. Quite an honour, however, in those days, things weren't quite as organised and I still remember Bev Meagher running up to me and saying as I was about to go on court 'I think you'll need one of these' as she used safety pins to secure the Australian badge, onto my shirt!

I was fortunate in that there were several very good coaches in Sydney: Fred Barlow for tactics, Keith Walker, Jean's husband, for boasts, Kevin Parker, based in Newcastle but not too far away, for patterns, and Dardir, an Egyptian who had been brought to Australia by Doug Croft, (Manager of the Bondi Waverley Squash Club), for disguise, deception and nicks. You can learn from everyone, and these coaches were amongst the best. It also helped that the top NSW players, both men and women, used to congregate at Jean and

Keith Walker's courts in Manly on Sunday afternoons to practise. It was our own mini AIS with Ken Hiscoe, Dick Carter, Cam Nancarrow and other top men players together with Heather McKay, Pat McClenaughan, Yvonne West and Thea Moore. It was a fun time. Good habits had been formed and things started to happen.

In 1963 I was ranked no. 2 in NSW and reached the semi-finals of the Australian Championships in Melbourne where I was defeated by Jenny Irving. It was at these Championships that the Australian women, at Heather's instigation, decided to take on the world and a makeshift team was formed to travel to the UK, as described earlier. I raised my funds through a gambling night and a Melbourne Cup raffle, ably supported by my Parramatta Club members. There was no financial assistance in those days! We were given official status for one match and defeated the UK 3–2 in a marathon 4 and half hour match which has been described earlier. I elected to stay on in the UK and found a job at Fred Perry sportswear, which gave me access to Wimbledon and the international Squash and Badminton matches. Watching Abou Taleb win the British Open in 1963,1964 and 1965 and his deception and disguise were mesmerising. I was also taken under the wing of Nazrullah Khan who was coaching at the Lansdowne Club. He taught me to hit the ball harder and also had magic drops, lobs and disguise and put the final touches to my game. Heather came over to defend her British Open title at the end of 1964 and made me quite homesick, as she was so fit and tanned. After living in England with the sun rising at 10am if you were lucky and setting at 3.00pm, it was time to go home. We travelled together back through the US and played the American hardball Doubles Game in Philadelphia, which was great fun. We played for 5 hours and managed to beat all challengers!

Now it was back to work! Did I really want to do this? I knew that I hadn't played at my best in the UK due to the long sea voyage. I knew that I still had petrol in the tank! I made the decision to move into an apartment in Bellevue Hill across the road from where Heather worked. Then the fun started, a bit like the Rocky movie! We had a hell run in Cooper Park which required hill running, sprints on an oval for 50 metres, netball courts for 10 metre sprints and then 100 stairs, 2 at a time 3–4 times, to finish off. I would meet Heather at 7.30am in the morning for this and then we would go back to the courts and do routines and play until she had to start work at 9.00am. There's nothing like practice with the best female player in the World to improve your game! I shed the excess weight I had put on in the UK and 1966 proved to be my best year. I was runner-up in the Queensland and NSW Championships and semi-finalist in the Victorian and Australian Championships, this time meeting Marion Hawcroft from Queensland. My Australian ranking rose to no. 3. Again, we approached the AWSRA to see if we could organise a tour to the UK. The British had come out to Australia in 1965 and had played a series of Test matches which Australia won 3–0. It was time to take them on again. The AWSRA stated that there was no money, the usual story. I said 'make me Secretary of the AWSRA and I'll find the money', which I did! By door knocking I raised $6000, a lot of money in those days, and was given a free airline ticket by UTA (Air France) for Heather and reduced fares for the other 4 girls. The team was Heather no. 1, Marion Hawcroft of QLD no. 2, me at no. 3 and Marlene Tierney of SA no.4, with Australian Junior Champion from Victoria Robyn Kennedy at no. 5. We were all able to fly this time and even had $500 pocket money! It was a close tussle, however we managed to defeat Great Britain 2–1 with Heather as our knockout punch. During my playing career I earned the nickname 'Boom Boom', because I hit the ball so hard, thanks to Naz Khan. I came back to Australia from that trip, feeling that I had fulfilled my potential and so I moved to Canberra in 1967 to get away from squash, resume my teaching career and start my university studies in Education.

Initially, I did play some squash, however, I did not find it to be challenging. I won the ACT Squash Championship in 1968 and then lost interest as I took up other activities including bushwalking, tennis, scuba diving and gliding. It was so nice to be outdoors. I met my husband Chris at University in 1968. We married in 1971, built a house, had two sons, studied and lived a normal

Practising at Parramatta, a young Barbara.
(Photo: Courtesy of Barbara Slotemaker de Bruïne)

married life. I had escaped, or so I thought! Then came a phone call from ACT Squash in 1983 and my life changed direction completely! 'Would you like to take the ACT Women's Squash team to Darwin?' At that stage, our two boys David (5) and Michael (3) were taking up a fair bit of my time as I was teaching full-time and was pretty-well flat out. I said to Chris 'I haven't been to Darwin. Should I go?' He replied 'Why not?' which meant that he would be managing the household and the kids. A great support. At that stage ACT Squash was not strong and they usually played for the wooden spoon with Tasmania or Northern Territory. On my return, I was offered the position of Part-time Coaching Director on the huge salary of $10,000 per annum. In teaching I was earning $40,000 as I was a Level 2/ Master teacher. Fortunately, we had paid off our mortgage and we thought this would be useful to give us a bit more time over the next couple of years. I could get leave from the Department of Education and I would be able to put into practice all the skills I had learnt during my international career. It was a challenge!

I undertook the Part-time ACT Coaching Director's position, which was located at ACT Sports House in Hackett. This was a position I held from 1984–88. In addition, I undertook a degree in Sports Studies at the University of Canberra studying part-time, which was completed in 1988.

Playing career

- 1960 Runner-up to Heather McKay in the NSW Junior Championship losing 10–8 in the 5th
- 1960 Semi Finalist in the NSW Championships
- 1962 Semi-finalist in NSW Championships
- 1962–63 Represented NSW (no. 2) at the Australian Championships in Perth and Melbourne
- 1962 Selected to represent Australia v New Zealand in Perth
- 1962 Semi-finalist to Heather McKay in the Australian Open
- 1963 Semi-finalist to Heather McKay in the Australian Open
- 1963–4 Represented Australia in the first team to defeat the UK 3–2
- 1965–66 Represented NSW (no. 2) at the Australian Championships
- 1966 Runner-up to Marion Hawcroft in the Queensland Championships
- 1966 Runner-up to Heather McKay in the NSW Championships
- 1966 Semi-finalist to Marion Hawcroft in the Australian Championships
- 1966–67 Ranked no. 3 in Australia
- 1966–67 Represented Australia in the Test series against Great Britain. Australia won 2–1
- 1967 Semi-finalist in the North of England Championship having defeated England's no. 2, Fran Marshall, 0–9,9–5,9–1,10–8 in the quarters
- 1967 Quarter finalist in the British Open, where I was defeated by Fran Marshall

Administration

- Secretary of the AWSRA in 1966. Fund raised ($6000) for the Australian Women's Team to travel to England for a three Test series.
- Conducted a Squash in Schools program which resulted in many schools

from both Primary and Secondary levels being introduced to the game of squash from 1984–88

- ACT Squads were successful on many occasions at the Green Shields and improved results at the Australian Championships
- Numbers of Level 1 Coaches rose from 7 in 1984 to 37 in 1988 (ACT). Over 100 players attended courses
- Conducted the first Level 2 Course in Australia in 1987. Coaches from all over Australia and Overseas attended—13 in all. Lecturers were obtained from the University of Canberra and Geoff Hunt attended from the AIS
- Attained Level 2 Coaching Accreditation

In 1988, after completing my degree in Sports Studies. I became the National Coaching Director—a position I held until 1992. Achievements included:

- Funding of $250,000 was granted from the Australian Sports Commission for the NCD position, AIS Satellite Coaches, National Coaching Conferences (the first time these had been held) National Coaching Committee meetings where the ASC provided funding for at least one coach to attend and Funding for State Coaching Directors' meetings
- Development of Resources such as the Aussie Sports Manual and video, Level 2 manual, Heart Health Skills video
- Establishment of the Australian Squash Rackets Association of Coaches (ASRAC) in 1990, which later became the Professional Squash Coaches Association of Australia (PSCAA) in 1992. Membership reached 500 in 1990.
- Establishment of a National Coaching Newsletter
- Commencement Annual State Coaching Directors' Workshops
- Biennial Coaches Conferences established Brisbane, Canberra, Adelaide
- 1988–93 National Coaching Committee membership
- 1988–91 Sports Committee membership
- 1988–91 International Coaching Committee member

- 1991 Coordinator of the National Sports Research Program
- 1991 Attendance at the Inaugural International Coaches Committee in Hong Kong
- 1991 Attendance at AIS Coaches Camps
- 1992–4 Planning of the AIS Talent Development Camps
- Conducted the inaugural Level 2 Coaching course in New Zealand with Butch Gifford (NZ)

In addition, throughout my term as National Coaching Director (1988–91) the number of NCAS Level 1 Coaches Australia-wide rose from 214 (1987) 657 (1988) 795 (1989), 511 (1990) and 593 (1991) *. The number of NCAS Level 2 Coaches rose from 4 (1988) 31 (1989) 30 (1990) 41 (1991).

* The fall in numbers was due to the implementation of the updating policy, whereby coaches no longer coaching were archived or taken off the current register.[79]

After I resigned from the NCD position in 1992, to resume my teaching career, I still kept my hand in and the following outlines what happened:

Coaching

Whilst being NCD, I had still coached at the ACT level. Here are some of the results:

- In 1976 BC (before children!) I coached Leanne Aust to win the ACT Championship and the Australian Under 16 Championship. I didn't coach for a while once the children arrived (1976 and 1979)
- As ACT Coaching Director, I coached ACT players Kellie Cuschieri who became no. 1 in Australia (Under 19) and Scott Spillane became no. 6 in Australia (Under 19). Both became AIS scholarship holders in 1988.
- Whilst NCD, Kellie Cuschieri became an ACT Academy of Sport Scholarship holder 1990–91
- Howard Johns became no. 1 in Australia (Under 19) in 1988 and became a part-time AIS Scholarship holder and a part-time ACT Academy of Sport Scholarship holder (1991)

Australian Women's Team 1966–67
Top to Bottom: Marion Jackman (Qld) Marlene Tierney (SA) Heather Blundell (NSW)
Robyn Kennedy (Vic) and Barbara Baxter (NSW)
(Photo: Courtesy of Barbara Slotemaker de Bruïne)

- Toni Weeks became the no. 3 ranking (Under 17) in NSW in 1989 and an AIS Scholarship holder in 1990. She later reached no.19 in the World.
- Whilst teaching, I was selected as ACT Coach to the Australian Championships in Alice Springs where I coached Stewart Boswell to win the ACT's first Australian Junior Age title in the Under 15 (1993). He went on to win his age-group until 1997. He also won the NSW and Victorian Under 15 in that year. In 1996, he became ACT Sport star of the Year, Runner-up in the World Junior Championships, was a semi-finalist in the British Junior Championships and winner of the Scottish

Junior. He was an AIS Scholarship holder from 1995–2009 and an ACT Academy of Sport Scholarship holder in 1996. He is now National Coach at the Gold Coast, 2021

- Tim Manning was runner-up in the Australian Under 15 Championship in 1992 and became an AIS Scholarship holder in 1993
- Laura Keating won the Australian Under 19 Champion in 1998 and was selected in the Australian Junior Team to the World Championships in Rio de Janeiro in 1997, where she was defeated in 5 in the quarter-finals by the eventual winner. She was a part-time Scholarship holder at the AIS 1996–97. She achieved a ranking of no. 39 in the World and in 2000 she represented Australia at the World Championships Teams event held in Sheffield, England.
- Peter Hughes reached a national ranking of no. 6 in the Under 19 in 1999
- Coached Christine Nunn from 2001–2006. Australian Champion (2018) and winner of 10 titles on the WISPA Circuit plus a gold medal at the World Championships in Doubles 2018. Her career high ranking was no. 1 in Australia and no. 36 in the World. Member of Australian team for the Commonwealth Games in 2018. AIS Scholarship holder
- Coached Sam Sergo to the no. 1 ranking in the Under 19 Boys (2019). He was runner-up in this event that year.
- James Lloyd reached the ranking of No1 in Australia (Under 19) and reached the semi-finals of this event in 2020. He has been invited to train under Stewart Boswell at the National Camp at the Gold Coast
- Charlie Carey was Runner-up in the NSW Under 17 Boys and semi-finalist at the AJC 2020. Currently ranked 1 in the ACT Under 19

Awards

- 1993 ACT Squash Coach of the Year
- 1993 Australian Squash Coach of the Year
- 1993 International Consultant Coach
- 1994–2001 AIS Satellite Coach
- 1995 ACT Squash Coach of the Year
- 1995 PSCAACT Female Squash Coach of the Year

- 1995 ACT Coach of the Month (December–All Sports)
- 1996 ACT Female Coach of the year
- 1997 ACT Coach of the Month (August–All Sports)
- 2000 Awarded Australian Sports Medal
- 2002–2004 AIS Mentor Coach
- 2004–5 Head Coach of National Talent Squad (Under 15) Canberra
- 2006 Attained NCAS Level 3 Coaching Accreditation (the only female coach in Australia to do so)
- 2008 Life Member of Squash ACT
- 2010 Awarded Distinguished Services Award from Squash Australia for over 50 years of Contribution as a Player, Coach and Administrator
- 2014 Committee Member of High Performance Review Committee
- 2014 Chairperson of Selection Committee for Coach of World Women's team to Canada
- 2022 Awarded the Member (AM) of the Order of Australia (General Division) for significant services to squash as a player administrator and coach.

Publications

- 1978 Contributed to *Squash Rackets* by Henry Macintosh, Pelham Books, Ltd
- 1991 Heart Health Skills Video
- 1991 Aussie Sports video
- 1991 Produced Aussie Sports manual
- 1993 Produced three chapters in Level 2 Manual
- *The Golden Age of Australian Women's Squash 1962–2010*

It's all been great fun and broadened one's life considerably.

Helen Muir (née Plaisted)

To me, Helen's real claim to fame was her win in the first successful Australian Women's team to defeat Great Britain in 1964. At the time she was ranked no. 8 in Australia but she defeated Great Britain's no. 5 player, Pauline White, in 5 hard games. I was waiting in the wings to go on and we didn't think Helen

Helen with her cheeky grin and never say die attitude.
(Photo: Courtesy of Helen Muir)

would win, but she had other ideas! The scores were 10-8, 4-9, 4-9, 9-5 9-5. Helen's tenacity and superior fitness won through. I have learnt more about Helen while writing this book and I can now see why she should never have been underestimated! Here's her story.

During her school years at Perth College, she excelled at many sports, most notably at tennis.[80] She represented WA at the Wilson Cup, the Interstate Teams' competition for U19 tennis players. She then moved to Melbourne to further her tennis career. In 1961, whilst waiting to practise tennis, Helen was talked into having a game of squash with the aim of improving her fitness and reflexes. She loved squash and had a natural aptitude for it. Helen continued to play squash whilst still playing tennis. Her main strengths were her hand-eye co-ordination and fitness. Helen was selected in the WA State Squash team in 1962 and the next year won the WA Squash Championship. She again won from 1965–1968.

Whilst on the tour of Great Britain in 1963-4, Helen reached the third round of the British Open and managed to take the first game from the no.4 seed, Anna Craven Smith, eventually going down 6-9, 9-1, 9-3, 9-1. She then continued with the main purpose of her tour and that was to play tennis. She did play on the centre

Helen with her Hall of Fame Award (2017) after being made a Life Member of WA Squash (2017)
(Photo: Courtesy of Helen Muir)

court at Wimbledon in the Mixed Doubles, which must have been a wonderful experience. Her partner was Brian Tobin and they played against Abe Segal and P. Haygarth from South Africa. Earlier, I mentioned how Helen was selected in the Australian Team. It was a spontaneous decision taken by the players to rope together whoever was available. It was very fortunate that Helen was, as she secured a vital rubber, ensuring that we had every chance of defeating Great Britain for the first time.

On her return to Australia, Helen continued with squash, reaching three quarter-finals and one semi-final in the Australian Championships. On each occasion, she came up against Heather.

She continued playing A Grade pennant, winning with the Claremont Cottesloe and Mosman Park clubs.

Administration

Full of energy, Helen was also a player who put back in. She helped pioneer the Women's State Grade teams at Claremont Cottesloe Club in 1965, winning several pennants. She started the Golden Open in Kalgoorlie, which to this day is one of WA's best tournaments. Working with Del Mazzuchelli, Pat Torpy and others, she started Squash News in the early 1970s. It was distributed to thousands of Western Australian squash players four times each year.

Coaching

- Coached St Hilda's School and Kalgoorlie Country Week teams. She also coached many students in squash at the Claremont Cottesloe Clubs.
- Lectured in the Squash Unit for Physical Education at the University of Western Australia.
- Established the Helen Muir School of Tennis and Squash in Kalgoorlie
- Trained the Mens' and Ladies' Kalgoorlie Country Week teams

Business

Helen and Margaret Court opened a boutique in 1966, called Sports Spot in Claremont. They sold sports clothing to the squash and tennis players, selling the famous Fred Perry brand.

Awards

- Helen was inducted into the WA Squash Hall of Fame, in 2017.
- Life member of WA Squash 2017

Marion Jackman (née Hawcroft)

Marion first represented in an Invitational Australia Team, in 1963 as a Junior, touring in New Zealand and playing a number of matches against the New Zealand team. The Australian team included Heather Rhead, Bev Meagher, Jenny Irving, Marion Jackman and Di Bruce.

So, from little things big things grew.

Marion's family was very supportive of her squash as they were of her sister Barbara, who played tennis at Wimbledon and reached the quarter finals losing to Olga Morozova. I still remember the big hitting wall that was in their backyard. No doubt, Marion honed many of her squash skills there as well. She was also fortunate to have been coached by the Egyptian, Dardir, who taught her to boast magnificently, a great weapon. Marion had a nickname 'Fairy Feet'

Invitational Australian Team to New Zealand 1963.
Left to right: Heather Rhead (Q), Bev Meagher (Vic), Jenny Irving (Vic),
Marion Hawcroft (Q) and Di Bruce (Vic)
(Photo: Courtesy of Bev Garfield (Meagher)

because you couldn't hear her coming up behind you on the court. Another useful weapon. Marion did find time to get married to David Jackman in 1969 and had two children Peta Louise (1978) and Juliann Maree (1979). She now has two grandchildren Finn aged 10 and Austin aged 8.

Marion played at no. 2 for Australia in Australian teams in 1965 and in the first official Australian Touring team in 1966–7 and again in 1971, 72 and 75. The last time Marion represented, she was no. 1, after Heather McKay had turned professional. She had a very successful result winning all of her matches 3–0 and Australia defeated Great Britain 3–0. The tide had turned well and truly and the flag was still being flown without the amazing Heather McKay.

Marion turned professional at the age of 34, just before the inaugural World Championships held in Brisbane in 1976. During her career she won 11 consecutive Queensland Championships from 1964 to 1974 and won the Australian Amateur Championship in 1974. She also travelled to South Africa in 1975 and won the Zambian and Kenyan Open Championships in that year. As a Senior player she won the inaugural Over 35s Senior Championship in 1980. One of her highest achievements was reaching the final of the inaugural World Women's Championship in 1976, losing to the invincible Heather McKay in straight games. However, no doubt winning her first Australian title in 1974 and managing to take 3 games off Heather McKay during her career, was also up there! These games were won in the 1968 Australian Final (9–0, 9–3, 3–9, 9–6) in the Interstate series in Queensland in 1972 (9–7, 6–9, 9–5, 9–5) and in 1973 (9–6, 9–0, 6–9, 9–1). She eventually retired from competitive squash in 2003.

Playing career

- 1963–1974 Represented Queensland at the Australian Teams Championships
- 1964–72 Captain of the Queensland team at the Australian Teams Championship
- 1965, 67, 71, 72 and 75 Represented Australia defeating England in all 5

Australian Champion 1974, Marion Jackman
(Photo: Courtesy of Queensland Hall of Fame Profile 2006)

Test matches

- 1966 Runner-up to Heather McKay in the Australian Championship
- 1967 Runner-up to Heather McKay in the Australian Championships
- **1968 Runner-up to Heather McKay** in the Australian Championships (lost 3–1)
- 1964–1974 Won the Queensland State Championships
- 1971 Runner-up to Heather McKay in the Australian Championships
- 1972 In the Interstate series took a game off Heather McKay
- 1973 Runner-up to Heather McKay in the Australian Championships
- 1973 Captain of the Queensland team that won the Interstate series for the first time
- 1974 Captain of the Queensland team that won the Interstate series
- 1974 Won the Australian Amateur Championship (Heather had turned professional)
- 1975 Won the Zambian Open Championship
- 1975 Won the Kenyan Open Championship
- 1975 Runner-up in the British Open to Heather McKay
- 1976 Runner-up to Heather McKay in the inaugural World Championship
- 1980* Won the inaugural Over 35 World Master's event
- 1980 and 1982 Represented Queensland at the Australian Teams Championships

Awards

- 1971 Nominated Queensland Sportswoman of the Year
- 1973 Nominated Queensland Sportswoman of the Year
- 1974 Nominated Queensland Courier Mail Sportswoman of the Year
- 2000 Awarded the Australian Sports medal in 2000
- 2006 inducted into the Queensland Squash Hall of Fame

Her other interests, apart from grandchildren include, travel, music, gardening, tennis and home activities.

Marlene Tierney

Marlene was from South Australia and first started playing squash after a tennis cancellation, like many other squashies. Her boyfriend and future husband Trevor Tierney suggested they play once a week, which snowballed into playing more often. 'The court owner watched us play and suggested that we should play competition', and that was how Marlene's career got started. Marlene used to be assisted by a no.1 A Grade male player at the time. She also mentioned being inspired by seeing Heather McKay play and her aspiration was to be 'half as good as her.' She felt that the main contributor to her success was her husband Trevor, because whenever they played, they were very competitive.

She first represented Australia in an Australia v New Zealand International in 1966. She had an outstanding record in South Australia, winning the SA title from 1965–72 and 1975. Marlene also represented SA in the Interstate

Nina Walker (L) presenting Marlene (R) with her Hall of Fame Award in 2013
(Photo: Courtesy of Marlene Tierney)

series consecutively from 1962–70 and again in 1972, 1974 and 1975. She was selected to represent Australia in the team to tour the UK in 1966–67. Marlene was the only unseeded player to reach the British Open quarter finals in 1967, defeating Sylvia McClure of Scotland 9–3, 9–2, 9–0. For her achievements she was awarded Sportswoman of the Month for SA in 1967 and was inducted into South Australia's Hall of Fame in 2013. She retired from competitive squash in 1975. Her nickname was 'Swinger' due to her walk.

Her other sporting interests were tennis and later golf, where she won the State B Grade golf in 1977. She also played in the A grade pennant where her team from the Grange Golf Club won the pennant for the first time in 36 years. Perhaps the greatest award you can receive is the praise of others and I have included some comments from a friend and former team-mate on Marlene's contribution to the game we have all loved. On collecting Marlene's Hall of Fame award, Nina Walker said:

> 'I was very happy to oblige as we had been team members and became good friends and fortunately, still are. Marlene was a wonderful captain and mentor to all in her team and we have many happy memories of playing together. Marlene probably won't tell you this, but on her return from the UK trip, she offered to teach young players the game. Marlene felt she wanted to give back to the sport, which I feel is admirable and shows the kind of person she is. Some of us joined her on a Sunday morning at these coaching clinics where, of course, even managing to keep the ball warm and bouncing was an effort with real beginners. Marlene was wonderfully patient and giving to each of her 'clients'—a real unsung hero, I feel. She's a wonderful person who is very modest and a great role model for both the sport and life.'

Good on you, Marlene.

Robyn Howard (née Kennedy)

Robyn was discovered by Joan Morey in 1962. Joan was a highly respected squash administrator and S&RV Life member.[81] Robyn, was an outstanding junior tennis player at the time, who was training with Kerry Melville, now Reid, under Keith Rogers, Margaret Court's Coach. Robyn thinks Margaret was probably her inspiration, until Joan spotted her and whisked her away to squash. She had never seen the game played before, but under the guidance of Brian Boys, Robyn became virtually an overnight sensation.

Playing career

- 1964–66 Winner of three Victorian Junior Championships. The first she won after only playing for approximately 16 months
- 1965 member of the Australian Junior Women's team to tour New Zealand
- 1966 Winner the NSW Junior Championship.
- 1966 Winner Australian Junior Championship. She won this despite suffering a hamstring injury in the semi-finals. She competed in the final with her leg heavily strapped and playing against medical advice.
- 1966 She was the first junior to win all three major Junior Championships in the same year—the Victorian, NSW and Australian.

- 1967 Member of the Australian Women's team which defeated the United Kingdom, 2–1.
- Played State One Interclub Women's pennant, mainly in the Number One position for four clubs (Albert Park, Alma, Balwyn and Kooyong), winning several Premierships

Robyn Howard (née Kennedy)
(Photo: Courtesy of S&RV, 2019)

- Represented Victoria 5 times at the Australian Amateur Team's Championships.
- A Victorian selector

Robyn was also heavily involved in the administrative side of the sport at the Victorian Squash Rackets Association headquarters, which was then located in Albert Park. She also worked at Alan Minchington's Oakleigh Squash centre.

She was also a very effective Public Relations Officer of the Victorian Squash Rackets Federation for four years.[82]

In 2019, she was awarded Life membership of Squash and Racquetball Victoria for her services to squash.[83]

Robyn is married with 2 sons, Shaun and Scott, who are both outstanding police officers. Scott is also the proud father of three children, aged 8, 7 and 6. Robyn now works part-time as a receptionist at a medical practice.

Robyn's one of those people that would give you the shirt off her back! She is always willing to pitch in.

Bev Johnson

Bev was a top player who emerged in the 1960s, when Australian women were dominant on the World scene. She was formerly an A Grade tennis player and like many of us, turned to squash when tennis was washed out. She was 17 when she started playing and was immediately hooked. She was small

in stature, so her speed of movement was an attribute that was to take her to the heights of the game. In 1963, she played in an Australian Junior Team against New Zealand. She

Heather and Bev after the British Open final in 1968
(Photo: Courtesy of Bev Johnson)

NSW winning team 1968.
Back (left to right) Jenny Irving, Heather McKay,
Sue Newman
Front (left to right): Mavis Nancarrow,
Bev Johnson.
(Photo: Courtesy of Bev Johnson)

travelled overseas and lived in England from 1965 until early 1968. This enabled her to develop her game, having been coached by Nazrullah Khan and she certainly made her mark as an individual being runner-up to Heather McKay in the British Open in 1968. It was unfortunate for her that no international events took place until 1971, as by then she had turned professional. As a result, she was ineligible to play for Australia because of her professional status and her residential qualifications. If a team had been selected between 1968 and 1970 and these two circumstances had not arisen, she would probably have made the team as she had beaten some of the team members that had been selected. It was just one of those things and no doubt, in hindsight, she may have done things differently.

Playing career

- 1960 started playing State Grade in NSW.
- 1963 Represented in the Australian Junior Team to play against New Zealand
- 1965, 68 and 69 Represented in the NSW team for the Interstate series.
- 1965 Runner-up to Heather McKay in NSW Championships
- 1965 Runner-up to Fran Marshall in the Scottish Open
- 1960–70s represented Queensland in the Interstate series
- 1966 Won the Midland Open, West of England and North of England Championships whilst living in the UK.

- 1967 Semi-finalist in South of England Championship
- 1967 Won the Surrey Championships
- 1968 Runner-up to Heather McKay in the British Open. Unfortunately for her, Heather was in brilliant and ruthless form and Bev was defeated 9–0, 9–0, 9–0. She made one unforced error. Still, it was an achievement in itself to reach the final.
- 1968 Semi-finalist in NSW Championships
- 1968 Highest Australian ranking—no. 4
- 1969 Bev turned professional
- 1969 Runner-up to Heather McKay in NSW Championships
- 1971 Runner-up to Heather McKay in NSW Championships
- **Coaching career**
- Coach of the NSW Women's Team for the Interstate series. They won the Teams' event
- 1992 Coach of the Queensland Junior team to the Interstate series
- 1994 Coach of the Brisbane region 1 and 2 Teams for the Queensland Junior Age Titles
- Coached various individuals—Kym Johnstone, Carin Clonda and Bradley Hindle

Qualifications

- 1992 Completed NCAS Level 1 Accreditation
- 1993 Completed NCAS Level 2 General Principles at the Queensland University
- 1993–94–5 AIS Satellite Coach.
- 1993 A Level Referee for the Queensland SRA
- 1993–4 Member of the PSCAA (Professional Squash Coaches' Association of Australia)
- 1993–4 Completed NCAS Level 2 Coaching Accreditation

Awards

- 2000 Awarded Australian Sports Medal

Just a note with regard to the photo below—the NSW winning team comprised Heather McKay, no. 1 in the World, Jenny Irving, Runner-up in the Australian and British Open and Australian representative, Sue Newman, future Australian and British Open Champion and Australian representative, Mavis Baker, future Australian representative and Bev, runner-up in the British Open. So, you can see how difficult it was to make the Australian representative team. The NSW team was good enough to be an Australian team.

She gave it her best shot and did contribute to the development of many players during the '90s.

Well done, Bev.

Margaret Zachariah

A diminutive player, Margaret was a great mover and the match was never over until the ball had bounced twice on the last rally. Her perseverance, endless hours of practice and will to win were characteristics that were rewarded, with her becoming Australian Champion in 1977 after the retirement of the incredible Heather McKay. Her story and contribution to squash, both during and post career, are an inspiration to all those elite players out there when the day comes and they finally decide to hang up the racket.

Margaret started playing squash socially in her teens on summer holidays when it was raining. Her life changed when she agreed to play a school friend, who was then being coached by well-known Victorian coach Brian Boys. He happened to see Margaret play and suggested to her that he thought that she could make a reasonable player. Her favourite sport at that time was A Grade Netball, the sport that she most enjoyed in school competitions. She had a few lessons in squash and after a severe neck injury in Netball, she had a break and then decided to give squash a go. Margaret started off in C Grade, and after a few more lessons played A Grade, no. 4 for Balwyn and quickly moved up to no. 2 in the team.

The Australian Women's Team 1985
Back Row (L to R): Jan Miller, Margaret Zachariah, Di Davis,
Front Row (L to R): Tracey Smith, Carin Clonda
(Photo: Courtesy of Jan Miller)

Margaret's friend Lyn White was selected in the Interstate Victorian team in 1966 to play in the Australian Championships. Margaret decided to enter in the Australian Championships, to both play and observe with another friend Susan Gedye (née Ritchie). They were being played in Brisbane that year. This gave her the opportunity to see how the top players played and she was hooked. Not long afterwards, she was invited to travel to New Zealand in 1966 with the Australian Under 23 team. She had only been playing for about 10 months. She enjoyed the experience. On her return she continued to play A Grade pennant and eventually earned her place in the Victorian Team at no. 3. She then represented Victoria from 1968–1977 inclusive and from 1979–82 inclusive.

Margaret was a trained diagnostic radiographer and didn't see squash as a career path. In those days there wasn't much money to be won. She had saved money at work so was able to pay her own way for all international travel, which was required as part of the Australian teams in 1975, 1976, 1977 and 1978. When she won the Australian Championship in 1977 and become the no. 1 player in Australia, she was given an airline ticket to travel to the US. The teams were billeted on many of their trips; however, hotel accommodation was recommended after the 1975 trip as it gave the players more opportunity to relax.[84]

Every squash player's training program is fairly unique; however, Margaret's was even more special. As she worked full-time, she had to make time to practise. She would practise 6 to 7 times per week after 10pm on weekdays, when the courts were available. The club was called the 'Night Owl Club at Balwyn' and she would train with the men and boys doing individual drills and fitness work, which provided her with the challenge that she needed. Weekends were spent having coaching and again, playing against the men. She also ran, skipped went to the gym and stretched when court time was not available. Her job as a radiographer was also very physical requiring lifting, pulling and pushing patients and equipment constantly, which added to her overall fitness.

Highlights of her career were being selected in the Australian team in 1975 which toured Sweden, the UK and Canada. In the Test series against England, which Australia won 3–0, Margaret only dropped one game in winning her 2 matches. Playing in the 1976 International Women's Team Championship, Margaret won her crucial rubber 3–0 in Australia's 2–1 defeat of England. She toured again in 1978 to USA and the UK and was Captain of the Australian team, however she injured her foot whilst on tour and subsequently had to have an operation. She did represent Australia again in 1980. Brian Boys, the National Coaching Director was the Captain and Manager. The tests were played in Perth, Sydney and Brisbane. Australia won the series 2–1

Playing career

- 1968-77 Represented Victoria at the Australian Championships(in the Teams and Individuals). Eleven of the 14 years played were as No 1

- 1971,74-75 Tasmanian Champion
- 1974-76 and 1979 Victorian Champion
- 1975-76 Represented Australia in the Teams' event
- 1976 Third in the inaugural World Championship
- 1976 No 1 Amateur in the World
- 1976 Member of the World Championship team, winning the deciding rubber 3-0
- 1977 Australian Champion
- 1977 Irish Open Championship
- 1977 Won the Hard Ball Championship in Boston, at Harvard defeating Sue King in the final
- 1978 Runner-up to Barbara Maltby in the Hard Ball game in Cleveland, Ohio
- 1977-78, and 1980 Represented Australia in the Teams' event
- 1979-82 Represented Victoria at the Australian Championships
- 1981 Runner-up to Vicki Cardwell in the British Open final
- 1981-83 World Open Master's Champion Over 35
- 1982 Scottish Open Champion

Manager

Margaret kept up her involvement in Squash and was:

- 1984–1996 Australian Selector
- 1985–92 Coach at the National, (Senior and Junior teams) State and grass root levels.
- 1985 Manager-Coach of the Australian Junior Women's team to Ireland for the World Open Championships, Winner 2–1 v England
- 1985 Manager of Australian Women's Team to Ireland for the World Open—runners-up
- 1986 Manager-Coach of the Australian Junior Women's team to New Zealand—runners-up. to England with New Zealand finishing third. This was the Vic Belsham Triangular series

- 1989 Manager-Coach of the Australian Junior Women's team to New Zealand for the World Junior Championships—runners-up
- 1990 Manager of the Australian Women's Team Mazda World Open, Sydney—runners-up
- 1991 Manager-Coach of the Australian Junior Women's team to the World Championships, Norway—finalists
- 1992–2011 Honorary Secretary of the Australian Squash Racquets Association of Coaches (PSCAA)

Coaching qualifications

- NCAS Level 1
- 1985 NCAS Level 2 Coach

Awards

- 1974 Hall of Fame—Victoria Squash Federation for squash playing, squash titles held, Australian Team member, Coach and Manager of Australian Teams, Australian Selector, Secretary of the PSCAV from 1983–2011 and PSCAA 1992–2011
- Life member of the Professional Squash Coaches' Association Victoria
- Life member of the Victorian Squash Federation. Now Squash and Racquetball Victoria (S&RV)
- 2000 Australian Sports Medal
- 2001 Vicsport Volunteer Administrator of the Year—The International year of the Volunteer—for contribution as Honorary Secretary of the Victorian and Australian Squash Coaches Associations
- 2005 Life member of PSCAA
- 2007 Life Member of Squash Australia
- 2018 Victorian Hall of Fame Legend Status

Administration

- 1983–2011 Honorary Secretary of Victorian Squash Coaches Association
- 1984 On the Committee for the organisation of the Australian Championships

- 1985 Assisted in the organisation of the Squash Section Australia Games —Melbourne
- 1985 Represented Australia at the World Women's meeting in Ireland
- 1988–92 Represented Australia on the ISRF Committee
- 1992–2011 Honorary Secretary of the Australian Squash Coaches Association (now PSCAA)
- 2001 Assisted at the International Squash festival Conference—Melbourne
- 2006 Squash Specific Volunteer at the 18th Commonwealth Games—Melbourne

Chris Van Nierop

Chris now lives in Queensland and is a trained nurse and PE Teacher. She represented Western Australia from 1970–76 and was WA Champion 1973–76. In addition, she was an Australian representative to New Zealand in 1974 and Great Britain in 1975. She reached the quarter finals of the British Open in 1975 and attained the rank of no. 3 in Australia. The epitome of her career would have to be representing Australia in the winning 1976 International Team. In the final against England, Sue King had lost an epic 5 game battle 10–8, 9–7, 7–9, 3–9, 3–9 against Sue Cogswell. Chris won her match at no. 2, defeating Angela Smith 4–9, 10–8, 9–5, 9–2. It was left to Margaret Zachariah to claim victory for the Aussies. She took mere minutes to convince the gallery that the Aussies would claim victory and she was untroubled to defeat Therese Lawes in three games 9–6, 9–2, 9–2.[85] The rubber was decided and Australia became International Champions. What a way to finish!

Lyle Hubinger

Originally from Perth Western Australia, Lyle started playing squash in 1964 and soon started her quick rise to the top under the coaching of Aub Amos, the fitness guru of the time. She was a hard-hitting left-hander and in 1965–66 she toured New Zealand with an unofficial Under 21 Australian team. She was all set for State representation when she broke her leg in a car accident and she was out for 12 months. Undeterred, she represented

Queensland from 1969–75 and was runner-up to Marion Jackman in the 1970 and 1971 finals.[86] Lyle also represented Australia in the highly successful Australian team in 1975, She then moved to South Australia, where she became South Australian Champion in 1976. She was a school teacher before turning professional in 1977. She bears the distinction of being the first woman to win a professionals' only tournament and was a founding member of the Women's International Squash Players' Association (WISPA), in 1978. Other professional Australian players who joined Lyle as founding members were Barbara Wall, Marion Jackman and Sue King. The game today would be very different if not for the initiatives of these professional players who made it happen.

Australian Team to New Zealand 1974
Left to Right: Lesley Chapman (Vic) Lyle Hubinger (Qld)
Anne Smith (Vic) Chris van Nierop (WA)
(Photo: Courtesy of Anne Smith)

Lyle also played in a Rest of the World Team National Mixed Tournament, in various locations in Great Britain in 1979–80. Her partner was an Egyptian, Ahmed Safwat. He was the reigning British professional champion and reached the semi-finals of the British Open in 1976. This was the second tournament of this type. The first was played in 1978 and was won by Jonah Barrington and Sue Cogswell of Great Britain. This was certainly an innovative move and offered considerable prize money, though not equal. The men's winner received GBP2000 and the women GBP1400. Work that one out!

Lyle was part of the fabric that instigated change and moved the game forward. Well done, Lyle.

Playing career

- 1965 Represented Australia in an Under 21 touring team to New Zealand.
- 1968–1975 Represented Queensland in the Interstate series
- 1974–78 Australian representative to New Zealand
- 1975 Australian representative to the UK
- 1975 Reached the Quarter finals of the British Open
- 1976 South Australian Champion
- 1976 Runner-up in the Victorian Championship
- 1979 Ranked no. 4 in Australia

Anne Smith

Anne 'was something of a late bloomer on the Australian Women's Squash scene.'[87] She had played netball until she was 20 and then stumbled on to squash and took to it like a duck to water. She played 1st Grade pennant in Victoria for 14 years from 1968 to 1981 and her team won the Pennant 10 times during this time.[88] She first represented Victoria in 1968, however it wasn't until 1977, when she was the mother of three young children, that she enjoyed her greatest year winning the Victorian, Tasmanian and North Queensland Championships against the finest players in Australia. She reached an Australian ranking of no. 4. Below are some of her career highlights:

- 1968–81 Represented Victoria in the Australian Interstate Team's event
- 1974 Represented Australia against New Zealand winning her match 3–0
- 1977 Represented Australia against New Zealand
- 1977–78 Victorian Champion
- 1977–78 Tasmanian Champion
- 1977 Northern Territory Champion
- 1978 Represented Australia in the International series in Great Britain. Australia won 2–1
- 1978 Ranked no. 4 in Australia
- 1979 Quarter finalist in the World Open losing to Heather McKay 9–2, 9–5, 9–4
- 1979 Ranked no. 8 in the World

After the World Championships, she returned to Australia and began playing in the Masters' events. Listed below are her achievements in these events:

- 1979–82 Victorian Over 35 Masters' Champion
- 1982 Runner-up to Jenny Webster in the inaugural Over 40 World Masters' Championship
- 1983–87 Victorian Over 40 Masters' Champion
- 1983 and 85 Australian Over 40 Masters' Champion
- 1985 New Zealand Over Masters' Champion
- 1988–92 Victorian Over 45 Masters' Champion
- 1989 Australian Over 50 Masters' Champion
- 1993 Victorian Over 50 Masters' Champion

Anne Smith
(Photo: Courtesy of Anne Smith)

At the age of 50 Anne ruptured her Achilles tendon and never played squash again. Her family are active in sport with both her sons Graham and Mark playing State Grade. Graham also plays VFA football with Oakleigh and basketball with Monash. Her daughter Leanne is not at all interested, having been dragged off to 'this match or tournament'. Her husband Vic has supported her throughout her squash career, often left holding the baby. Anne is still active with tennis and aerobics.

Sue King (née Newman) OAM

Sue was the first Australian woman to raise the Aussie flag at the British Open after Heather had turned professional and taken up a coaching position in Canada and was unavailable. In 1978 she defeated an up-and-coming young player, Vicki Hoffmann in straight games 9–4, 9–7, 9–2. Vicki's turn would come in 1980. This was a just reward for Sue's perseverance as she had finished 3rd in the British Open in 1973 and 1975 and was runner-up to Heather McKay in 1976, losing 9–2, 9–4, 9–6 in the final. Also, in 1976 she was 4th in the first World Open Championship held in Brisbane Australia, losing to Marion Jackman in the semi-finals 9–1, 9–7, 9–3. She subsequently lost in the play off for 3rd position to Australian Margaret Zachariah in a tremendous tussle, 7–9, 10–8, 9–5, 8–10, 9–7. For those young players out there with high aspirations, this is a prime example of Rome wasn't built in a day and you need to pursue your dreams and have self-belief, to achieve at the highest level!

Sue King
(Photo: Courtesy of British Open Championship Programme 1979)

British Open Champion 1978
(Photo: Courtesy of *Australian Squash News*, 29th March, 2009)

Sue first became involved with squash when her father built the Moorefield Squash Courts in Kogarah, Sydney in 1957. Unlike many other children brought up in family-owned squash courts, she initially resisted the urge to play. Instead, she earned pocket money by sweeping the courts at the end of the day's play. She only started playing when a patron challenged her to a game of squash after she had beaten him in the greatest number of bounces on a pogo stick! From then on, she was hooked! Her other interests until then had been horse riding and swimming. [89] In 1963 at the age of 13 she started playing C Grade squash and in 1965 won the NSW C Grade Championship. It wasn't long before she won her first major titles, winning both the NSW and Australian Junior Championships in 1968. She won the NSW Amateur Championships from 1974–1976 and the Australian Amateur Championships in 1975 and 1976 after Heather McKay turned professional.

With the encouragement of Haydn Daly and Fred Barlow (both well-known squash coaches, in NSW), Sue pursued squash as a career. She toured Britain and Ireland (in the early 1970's) and reached the final of the British Championship, in 1976, losing to Heather McKay (see earlier). Sue became a professional, in 1977 and won the British Open in 1978 (see earlier).

Throughout her playing career (and beyond), she was sponsored by Dunlop-Slazenger and Stellar from 1967–1997. She also managed to involve herself in administration and served on the AWSRA from 1970–76. She had to resign from this position when she turned professional. In November, 1977 she initiated and helped form the NSW Junior Squash Rackets Association. The Committee was established in 1978. This occurred whilst she was still playing at the highest level. She was very keen to encourage junior players to ensure that they were given every opportunity.

In addition, she was a delegate for Australia at the WSRA's inaugural meeting in Birmingham, England, in 1978, regarding the future of the World Women's Championships and Women's Professional Squash. It was later, that same year, that she helped found the first Women's Squash Players' Association (WSPA). Other professional Australian players on that Committee were Marion Jackman, Barbara Wall and Lyle Hubinger. Great Britain players that were also on the Committee were, Fran Marshall, Angela Smith and Irene Hewitt (Ireland). All of the Committee were recognised National and International ranked players.

Sue continued with her role in administration, on completion of her elite competitive days, and from 1989–1992 she was Chairwoman of the Junior Committee of NSWSRA. She also was a State selector and the Committee introduced a State Junior Tournament Circuit and a Computer Point System. In 1992, she completed a Level 1 Sports Administration Course conducted by ASSA and as an indication of her desire to improve, she also completed, in 1992, the Coaching Principles component of the Level 2 Accreditation, developed by the Australian Coaching Council (ACC).

Her involvement in coaching, however, was where she really made her mark.

- 1967 toured New Zealand with two other junior girls
- 1976 gave exhibitions and coached juniors with Marion Jackman in the NSW country areas
- 1977–78 Coach of NSW Junior Squads and Manager of the State team to the Australian Championships
- Conducted a Coaching tour at Whyalla, Port Augusta and Port Pirie Squash Centres in South Australia.

- 1981 Took three Juniors from Moorefield Junior Club to England for two weeks.
- 1983–89 Coached at various locations throughout Sydney
- 1989 was involved with the USA Youth for Understanding Sporting exchange of 14 boys.

Subsequently, with the assistance of the USA coach, Donald Mills, Sue took a team of five girls and twelve boys on a tour of the United States. This visit developed a whole new world for Sue and her young charges.

From 1991–1993 tours took place both in Australia and the United States through the Youth for Understanding program. Sue took teams to the U.S and hosted them in Australia. It was a wonderful opportunity and there was considerable exchange of ideas, with all teams having to adapt to the different playing conditions, as the American courts were narrower and they played with a harder ball. You didn't want to get hit with it!

In 1997, Sue toured the US, playing exhibitions and her hosts, Carol and Fred Weymuller were very keen for the U.S to adopt the wider courts and the softer ball used in Europe and Australasia. Sue, felt that her involvement had helped influence this development. Now the USA plays most of the major tournaments on the British sized courts.

On her return to Australia, in 1999, she continued to be involved with local teams and organised another tour for the USA Junior team which visited Australia. In 2000, she toured the USA for 4 weeks as Coach-Manager with nine junior players. She continued coaching NSW juniors, in her immediate area, from 2000 until 2009. Some of her charges, have been highly ranked, in the Australian Junior Age Championships.

Playing career

- 1968 NSW Junior Champion, Australian Junior Champion
- 1969–72 NSW Under 23 Champion
- 1971–76 NSW Representative
- 1973 Welsh Open Champion

- 1974–76 NSW Amateur Champion
- 1975-76 & 78 NSW Open Champion
- 1975–76 Australian Amateur Champion
- 1975–76, and 79–80 Australian Team Representative
- 1976 Irish Open Champion
- 1976 Scottish Open Champion
- 1976 Runner-up in the British Open Championship to Heather McKay
- 1978 British Open Champion. Defeated up-and-coming player, Vicki Hoffmann 3–0
- 1979 Captain of Australian Women's team to the first World Women's Team's Championship
- 1980 South of England Open Champion
- 1980 NSW Open Champion

Awards

- 1999 Awarded the Order of Australia Medal (OAM) for services to squash–playing administration and coaching
- 2000 Awarded the Australian Sports Medal in recognition of services to squash
- 2009 inducted into Squash Australia's Hall of Fame

Sue attributes her success to her parents, Ron and Shirley, her husband, Steve, her daughter, Eloise and many loyal friends who have assisted her and provided support throughout her career.

PS Her nickname was TT (see Quiz).

Barbara Wall

Barbara learnt to play squash in the squash centre that her parents, George and Enid, together with partners, had built. This was one of the first centres in Western Australia, where people could walk in off the street, pay their money and have a game. Squash was booming in Australia in the 1960s and if you wanted to practise, you could only get a game if someone was running late or cancelled.[90] Barbara's father George was a great influence on her. He was a great strategist, who had studied the tactics of visiting international players, including Hashim Khan and Mohamed Dardir Ali El-Bakary, when they visited Perth in the 50s–60s.

Barbara was originally a tennis player, but opted to play squash as she felt it provided many more opportunities to travel interstate and play national tournaments, which was a big attraction for a teenager living in Perth in the late 1960s. She turned professional in 1973. This was brought about because she ran a coaching school in Perth and managed the courts where her father was co-owner and this affected her amateur status. This meant that she was not eligible to play in tournaments, which were strictly amateur. In her early 20s, she did think of retiring but changed her mind after driving to Sydney in 1976, a return journey of almost 8000kms, to watch the Australian Championships. The British team members, who were on tour there, advised her that she could play in British tournaments as they were Open. This had occurred as Heather McKay had turned professional in 1974 and the sport wanted her to keep on competing. Here was Barbara's chance. How far could she go?

Barbara thought that playing squash, would be a great way to see the world. Obviously, a risk taker, she sold everything and travelled to England to play in tournaments there. Her gamble paid off and she was the first unseeded player to reach the final of the British Open in 1977. Heather, playing in her last British Open, won 9–3, 9–1, 9–2. At least it wasn't a whitewash and Barbara kept the champion on the court for 27 minutes—longer than most.

Barbara inducted into WA Hall of Fame in 2012
(Photo: Courtesy of WA Squash Hall of Fame Program)

Barbara v Heather in the British Open Final in 1977
(Photo: Courtesy of Barbara Wall)

She stayed on in England. There she put on weight. She stated that she 'waddled into the quarter finals' in the British Open in 1978 and was soundly beaten by another up and coming Australian, Rhonda Thorne. Fortunately for her a South African professional, Alan Colburn, told her that she would never achieve her potential unless she lost weight and applied herself.[91] This comment could be applied to many talented players out there who don't realise that the hardest opponent you'll ever play is yourself. Self-discipline is the key.

Anyway, undaunted Barbara returned to Australia later that year and contacted Shirley de la Hunty (née Strickland), a three-time Olympic track and field gold medallist, who then spent 12 months helping Barbara with her fitness training and her speed work. Barbara lost three stone (approximately 19kg). She undertook a strict regime of skipping, based on different rally lengths—short, sharp and fast, long for endurance, and track work. Was she ready?

In 1979, Barbara returned to the UK to play in the British Open. She was seeded no. 8 and was definitely an outsider. Heather had retired but Sue King and Vicki Hoffmann were in the mix, as well as Great Britain's Sue Cogswell and Angela Smith who were not to be underestimated. In fact, Australia had 7 of the first 9 seeds including, Rhonda Thorne no. 5, Lyle Hubinger no. 6, Anne Smith no. 7, Barbara Wall no. 8 and Margaret Zachariah no. 9. An Aussie had to be in with a chance.

As Barbara was seeded no. 8, she did not have the easiest of draws. Let's see what transpired. Her first match was against Irene Hewitt from Ireland and she won 9–3, 9–1, 9–5. no worries there. The next was against Great Britain's no.3 Teresa Lawes and Barbara won 9–1, 9–6, 6–9, 10–8. That was a bit more of a tussle. Now she was up against an Aussie, the no.1 seed, Sue King.

Could she do it? Yes, she could. Barbara, benefitting from her fitness regime and new-found confidence, defeated Sue 9–0, 9–6, 9–5. Unfortunately for Sue, she had just received news of a family bereavement which preyed on her mind. This, however, should not detract from Barbara's superb performance. Her next match was against no.4 seed Angela Smith. Barbara, with an exciting blend of power and touch play took the ball early and volleyed purposefully in the best Australian tradition. She moved Angela around with deft angles and neat drops. Angela was never given the opportunity to find any rhythm or control, such was her opponent's relentless onslaught.[92] The resultant score was 9–4, 9–4, 9–7 to Barbara and she was through to the final. The other Aussies had fallen by the wayside, so Barbara was up against Sue Cogswell of Great Britain. Would a Brit take the coveted British Open crown—the first since 1962?

It would appear so, as after a shaky start, Sue won the first two games 10–8, 9–6. However, Barbara had other ideas. She became more relaxed as she realised that she had nothing to lose, whereas Sue began realising she had everything to lose. Good psychological lessons here. Barbara made only two unforced errors in the third game which she won 9–4. At that time the scoring system was such that you could only win points when serving. There were 19 changes of serve however, in the end Barbara only lost 4 points and won the game 9–4. The scores were now level! As Barbara gained in confidence with each stroke, Sue's resistance crumbled as her morale was shattered. Barbara became British Open Champion by winning the final game 9–3. An Aussie still flew the flag. The Brits would have to wait a bit longer to win their Championship.

Barbara had managed to continue the tradition of having an Aussie win the British Open. She had followed in the footsteps of Sue King 1978 and prior to that, the illustrious Heather McKay, British Open Champion from 1962 to 1977. It hadn't been an easy ride however, and Barbara's story hopefully will be an inspiration to other young players out there who are just starting their careers. 'If at first you don't succeed, try, try again.'

As a post-script to this match, Barbara revealed when I interviewed her that she had broken a string in her racket in the final game. As she had such momentum going, rather than go off court to change the racket, thereby giving Sue a chance to regroup, she played on! She knew that her game was based on touch and that the broken string wouldn't affect her drop-lob game. She was right. Len Steward commented on the final 'Two games down. Well even the larrikins in your Cheer Squad had shut up. My God girl... your readiness to risk all and pull off so many brilliant winners under such pressure and on such a big stage, was simply breathtaking. (Not to mention that your skills really opened my eyes to the inadequacies of my own, low risk attritional game). Definitely one of the best and most exciting matches that I've ever seen.' [93] There's a lesson there.

She became a founding member of WISPA (Women's International Squash Players' Association) in 1978.

Playing career

- 1969–71 Western Australian Amateur Champion
- 1977 Runner-up in the British Open Championship
- 1978 Irish Open Champion
- 1979 Western Australian Open Champion
- 1979 South African Champion of Champions
- 1979 Belgium Open Champion
- 1979 NSW Open Champion
- 1979 British Open Champion
- 1979 no.1 in Australian Team at the World Championships

Awards

- 1979 Caltex Sports Star of the Year
- 1979 Berlei Sportswoman of the Year
- 1979 Lindy Sports Star of the Year
- Member of Western Australia's Institute of Sport Hall of Champions

- 2009 Inducted into Squash Australia's Hall of Fame
- 2012 Inducted into the Western Australian Hall of Fame

Post competition

Barbara's playing career was brought to a halt when she had to have an operation on her right foot for a troublesome spur and repair to damaged ligaments. She was still involved however, and when she returned to WA, she organised the first under age squash tournament—the Coca Cola Junior. This proved to be the breeding ground for future Australian representatives in Dean Williams (Australian Champion, in 1977) and Robyn Friday (World Junior Champion in 1983).

She also became heavily involved in the Life Be in It Program. Her idea was to create a squash club in Australia that would welcome people from all walks of life. She included the disabled, the socially disadvantaged, the lonely, the good players, the bad players, the serious players, the social players and she looked after them. This club became the largest squash club in Australia. In 1988, she introduced the characters: Barry Backhand, Debbie Dropshot, Barbie Boast, Sally Serve, Franky Forehand, Larry Lob, Vicki Volley and Sammy Smash, as part of a major initiative to launch across Australia. Over 120 centres were to become involved.[94] She certainly had put back into the sport.

She has now retired, after running a successful Real Estate business, and is living in Blackheath in the Blue Mountains. She plays golf, bushwalks, does photography and generally enjoys life. Her bubbly personality still shines through.

Vicki Cardwell (née Hoffmann) BEM

And then there was Vicki. She is one of those characters, who once met is never forgotten. She is what one of my friends called me once—a wazziwig— What you see is what you get! There are no frills on Vicki and she is what you call a True-Blue Aussie. Very patriotic, she played her squash with a passion, which is still with her today.

Vicki has always been involved in Sport and trained to be a Physical Education teacher from 1973 to 76 in Adelaide. She excelled at a number of sports at school including softball, tennis, netball and athletics. She taught at two Secondary Schools in South Australia throughout 1976–80. A left hander, Vicki had her first squash experience at age 12 when her club tennis was rained out and her sister, age 23 and number one player in their team, decided to child mind her little sister at the local squash courts. Vicki first played competition squash at age 13 with Findon High School before going off to play netball with club team Grevillia her first year at Teacher's College. She decided to play squash competitively for fitness training. After immediate success in the C grade competition, the President of College Squash Club, David Falk, contacted the Secretary of Squash Racquets Association South Australia, who was coach of the Junior State tennis team in which Vicki was number 1 player, saying that he thought she had some Squash potential. At the time, efforts were being made to send a Junior State team to the Australian Squash Championships, for the first time in 5 years. She would be selected if she made the semis in the State Junior event. Vicki entered 'simply because it was just down the road from where she lived'. She reached the final and this made her eligible for selection to compete in the 1973 Australian Championships, at which she would be inspired by Geoff Hunt, Mohibullah Khan, Qamar Zaman and Heather McKay. 'Seeing the way they hit the ball, made me feel there was something in this game for me.' [95] There certainly was.

Vicki, at the age of 18, decided to stop tennis and netball to concentrate on squash and commit to squash training and competition. She was usually on the court at least 5 times

World Open Champion 1983
(Photo: Courtesy of Vicki Cardwell)

Vicki in her last competitive game—the Australian Open 1997. Note the racquet, shirt and shoes (Photo: *Squash Courtside*, 1997, p37)

a week, as well as off court training every day. Movement and relentless effort and determination to get to the ball, were her strengths throughout her career, which she maintained while addressing other weaknesses in her game.

In 1974 she was named in the Senior team for South Australia and went on to represent South Australia from 1974–1983 and Victoria in 1984,1986 and 1987. In 1974 Vicki was selected in her first national representative team in the Under 23 Australian team against New Zealand. In 1977, she was selected in her first Australian Senior team against New Zealand in a test series. She also won her second South Australian title, having previously won in 1976. In 1978, Vicki became Australia's number 1 player.

In an article Vicki was described as a 'small but gutsy blonde......On court, she is amazingly fleet of foot with plenty of sting in her left-handed shots. She is an excellent match player with amazing determination—often defying the laws of gravity to reach a shot'. It is this determination that took her to the World Open title in 1983, 20 National titles in 7 countries, including 8 Australian titles, 4 successive British Open titles in 1980, 81, 82 and 83, and 28 State titles in Australia. She was also an Australian team representative in Australia, New Zealand, England, USA, Canada and the Netherlands including representing as a player, selector, manager, captain and coach. Some of these roles occurred when she was a player as well.[96]

It was in her first British Open victory in 1980 when Vicki arrived. Always meticulous in her preparation, Vicki was known for the strenuous exercises and skipping which made up her rigorous warmup, however in the 1980 British

Open she discovered that the squash shoes that she had gone to great lengths to break in, had been mistakenly left behind during a warm up tournament in Abbeydale. In the final, with her toes poking through her old shoes (which she trusted to survive the tournament), she completed the job in 30 minutes, defeating Sue Cogswell of GB 9–5, 9–5, 9–3. The Aussies had retained the British crown for the 19th straight year. 'Vicki's tactical nous, and refusal to give up on a ball, won the day. If she cannot reach a ball in the orthodox way, she will first throw herself at it and if she can't reach it, then she'll throw her racket at it'.[97] Such is her determination. Some of her team-mates felt that the shoes had helped her focus, as she didn't think they'd last out a long match. There was still more to come. A lot more.

Later that year, Vicki was a member of the winning Australian team with Margaret Zachariah and Sue King to play Great Britain, comprising Sue Cogswell, Lesley Moore and Barbara Diggens, in a test series in Australia. This series travelled to three capital cities: Perth on 31-8-80, Sydney 4-9-80 and the third test was played in Brisbane on 12-9-80. Vicki had to miss the First Test, due to an elbow injury. Unfortunately, Australia lost that match 2–1, however with Vicki recovered, they won the next Test 2–1. Vicki went down to Sue Cogswell on this occasion, however she rallied in the third and final test and with the scores levelled at 1 all, played a fine Captain's knock to defeat Sue Cogswell 9–7, 10–8, 9–5 and Australia had defeated Great Britain again.

1981 had its highs and its lows. The highs were winning the British Open and the World Team Championship. The lows were a 2-year ban from representing Australia in Team's events in international competition and a significant fine for a misdemeanour. It hurt her 'pride, her pocket and her reputation, but it didn't damage her self-belief'.[98] Vicki maintains the punishment far exceeded the misconduct and would have failed to survive a legal challenge had she decided to expend emotional energy on an appeal. This transgression occurred after losing to Rhonda Thorne in the World Women's Final in an epic 10–8, 4–9, 5–9, 9–7, 7–9 that lasted 1 hour and 57 minutes playing time. It is still the longest recorded match in the Women's game. Nonetheless, in typical Vicki fashion she refocussed and in 1981 was part of the winning team 1981 that defeated Great Britain 2–1 to become World Champions, avenging their loss in the 1979 World Championship event. The scores were Rhonda Thorne d Angela Smith 9–1, 9–6, 9–0, Vicki Hoffmannn d Lisa Opie 9–5, 9–6, 9–7, Barbara Oldfield lost to Sue Cogswell 8–10, 9–3, 9–4, 7–9, 9–10.

Restricted now to individual events, in Vicki was undeterred and won the 1982 Australian Open Championship and the British Open defeating Lisa Opie of the UK 9–4, 5–9, 9–4, 9–4 in the final. She repeated this performance in 1983, defeating Lisa again 9–10, 9–6, 9–4, 9–5. In addition, she won the World Women's Open, winning all matches without the loss of a single game and defeating her nemesis Rhonda Thorne in the final 9–1, 9–3, 9–4. She was now undisputed Number 1 in the World.

Vicki retired from international squash to start a family after winning the World Championships in 1983. Josh was born in 1985 and Sarah in 1991. She retained her involvement in squash as Captain-Coach of the World Women's Squash Team in 1989 and Coach in 1990. They were runner-up to England on both occasions. Vicki continued to compete at the Masters level winning the World Open Over-35 Masters in 1990, the World Open Over-45 Masters in 2001 and the World Over-55 Masters in 2010. She also won 5 Australian titles and 4 British Open Over-35 titles. She also continued to play in the Australia v New Zealand test series and defeated her successor to the British Open, Susan Devoy, in 2 out of the three matches in 1984. Vicki was again victorious in 1987, defeating Susan, who by then had won 4 British Opens, in the World Teams Championship semi-finals where Australia played New Zealand. Her fighting qualities shone through. To show her longevity, she was also Coach of the Australian Junior Teams in 2011, 2013 and 2014. She officially retired from competitive squash in 1997 when she played in her last World Masters Open. Forever the sentimentalist, to mark her final game she wore the same shirt and wielded the same antiquated racket that she used when she won the World Title 14 years earlier.

Playing career

- 1978 Australian Amateur Champion
- 1979 Australian Open Champion 7 times—1979–80, 1982–84, 1988–89
- 1979 Represented Australia at the World Teams Championships in England. England won 3–0
- 1981 Represented Australia at the World Teams Championships in Canada. Australia won 2–1
- 1981 Victorian Women's Open Champion 1981, 1982–3, 1986–9
- 1983 World Open Champion.
- 1980–83 British Open Champion
- 1983 Ranked no. 1 in the World
- 1987 Represented Australia at the World Teams Championships in New Zealand. Australia finished 3rd
- 1989 Represented Australia in the World Teams Championships in the Netherlands. England won 2–1
- 1990 Coach of the Australian team at the World Teams Championships in Sydney. England won 2–1
- 1990 World Over 35 Champion
- 2001 World Over 45 Champion
- 2010 World Over 55 Champion

Awards

- 1980 and 1981 Australian Sportswoman of the Year—Sportswoman Association of Australia
- 1981 Awarded the Order of the British Empire Medal for her services to Squash
- 1981 Australian Female Athlete of the Year—Confederation of Australian Sports (Channel 7 TV)
- 1982–3 Australian Sportsman of the Year Finalist (only female finalist in 1983 award)
- 1985 Inducted (in inaugural intake) to the Sport Australia Hall of Fame

- 2005 Inducted (in inaugural intake) to the Squash Australia Hall of Fame
- 2005 Inducted into the Victorian Squash Federation Hall of Fame
- 2008 Inducted as a Legend (in inaugural intake) into the Squash (South Australia) Hall of Fame
- 2010 Inducted (in inaugural intake) into the South Australia Sport Hall of Fame
- South Australian Sportswoman of the Year 5 times
- News-Caltex Sports Star of the Year 3 times
- South Australian Lindy Award twice.

Administration

- 1984–87 Appointed to the Australian Sports Commission
- 1984 Appointed as Squash Australia selector (resigned 1988)
- 2006 Board Member Victorian Squash Federation
- 2013—2015 Board Member Squash Australia

Vicki has led a very full life, ably backed by her husband Ian, who she married in 1982. Her son and daughter have competed on the PSA tour, with Joshua achieving a career high ranking of 148. Sarah has continued to pursue a squash playing career, having represented Australia at World Team Championships and Commonwealth Games. She has a career high world ranking of 41, thus far. Vicki has retired to Adelaide, South Australia but continues to coach, develop, encourage and support club players to be their best. Furthermore, Vicki stands out amongst the top players as she has the knowledge of and respect for the past players and the History of the Game. In an article in this magazine *The History of the Women's Game*, she stated that 'I unashamedly believe that the top 10 players are no faster, fitter, stronger or better than past champions, however I do believe conditions, equipment and training methods have improved and provided players with more opportunities and incentives to travel and compete at international level. The lighter weight equipment and larger string area also require less effort and the pace of the game has, therefore, quickened and matches are of shorter duration.'[99] It is refreshing to see a player who has such respect for the History of the Game.

Vicki (in the words of Frank Sinatra) 'did it her way'. No doubt, 'regrets she had a few, but then too few to mention'. Vicki is the epitome of to thine own self be true and it ain't over yet!

Rhonda Thorne (née Shapland)

The highlight year for Rhonda, was surely 1981. She won the big three: the Queensland Open, the Australian Open and the World Open. In the World open final, she defeated fellow Aussie, Vicki Hoffmann, in 5 gruelling sets 8–10, 9–4, 9–5, 7–9, 9–7. This match still holds the record for the longest World Women's Championship match in history, lasting 1 hours and 57 minutes. So where did it all begin?

Rhonda was born on 6th February, 1958. Her father Bernie was a top swimming coach and her mother Dorothy, ('Tuppy'—as everyone knows her) represented Queensland in squash in 1963. She has two brothers, Brian and Chris. It was always going to be a toss-up as to which would be her preferred sport. She had her first hit of squash when she was ten at Bell Street Courts in Toowoomba. At this stage, she was a top swimmer and had represented Australia when she was 13 in a swimming meet against West Germany held

in Sydney. When she was 11 her parents moved to Brisbane. She started playing squash at Sandgate and was fortunate to come under the tutelage of Aub Amos. Her future sport was chosen. Now Aub, as anyone who met him would

World Champion 1981
(Photo: Courtesy of Rhonda Thorne)

Rhonda in full flight!
(Photo: Courtesy of Rhonda Thorne)

know, was the Percy Cerutty of squash. His first impressions of Rhonda were that she was a really good-looking, happy, easy going and mature natured girl, a little on the plump side. Aub practised with her and taught her the importance of determination and hard work. In Aub's words, 'Rhonda was one of the best pupils I ever had and I've had some top-notchers.' She always did as she was asked, never whinged or complained and, above all, she never cheated on a set workout, which is a vital ingredient of champions'. [100]

She used to catch a bus to training from Redcliffe, a 20-minute ride, then walk ¼ mile to the court 4–5 times per week, demonstrating extraordinary keenness for a youngster. This soon resulted in success, with a win in the 1972 Australian Junior Championships (AJC). She lost the 1973 AJC due to lack of preparation however, learning the error of her ways, she subsequently went on to win the AJC in 1974,1975 and 1976. At this stage, there were no U13, U15, and U17 Championships and she had started winning at 14 in the Under 19 division. Her success in the 1974 AJC resulted in her selection to tour New Zealand in 1974, with Dean Landy of NSW, Dean Williams of WA, Steve Bowditch of NT, Steve Lawson of Qld as well as Di Grose of SA, Sue Heaney of Vic and Vicki Hedge of Qld. A few of these names would subsequently feature in the Senior ranks at international level.

In 1975, Rhonda got her first job as a dental nurse and she then moved to Fiveways Squash Centre where she came under the influence of Marie Donnelly, whose son John had won the Australian Junior title and her other son Mike had won the Australian Amateur title. She was in the right environment to further her career. She started to watch her diet, avoiding fats, sugars or anything artificial. Off court training increased and included running 4–5 miles 4–5 times per week. She worked on 440m sprints, with up to 16 repetitions at a speed of 80–90s per repetition. Skipping played a big part, 3 times per week for 20 minutes. Her training varied according to the time of year and the number of tournaments that were on the calendar.

Her style of play evolved. As Aub didn't consider speed to be her strength, he worked on her stroke production and her shot selection so that she could work her opponent. Other factors were the role models that were available throughout her career. Qamar Zaman, was her favourite male player. She also rated Heather McKay as the best female player that she had ever seen. Marion Jackman, Australian Amateur Champion in 1974, was small and light on her feet (her nickname was Fairy Feet) and had a beautiful boast. Watching her play enabled Rhonda to see that size was not a factor, but controlling the ball *was*! In addition, in 1979 she married Ross Thorne, who later became the no.4 ranked male player in the world. It was this union that had the most influence on her career and they became constant training partners and touring companions.[101]

Rhonda was on her way and in 1975, she progressed from the Junior ranks to membership of the Queensland Women's team for the Australian Championships in Sydney. She was first selected as a senior player for Australia in 1977, touring New Zealand. She went on to tour America and Great Britain in 1978 with the Australian Women's team and again in 1979 to Great Britain. In 1980 she was part of the Australian team to defeat Great Britain 2–1. She won 2 of her 3 rubbers 3–0. She went on to Captain the two winning teams in 1981 and 1983 and during her time as Captain, Australia never lost a series to any country and they remained undefeated. She was ranked in the World Top 10 from 1979–84 and was no. 1 in the World 1981–2.

Playing career

- 1972–76 Queensland Junior Champion
- 1972–76 Queensland Junior representative
- 1972, 1974–76 Australian Junior Champion (record number of wins by any Junior–still stands)
- 1974–75 Australian Junior representative
- 1976 Youngest Competitor in the inaugural World Open Championships held in Brisbane
- 1977–83 Queensland Open representative
- 1977–84 Australian Open representative
- 1978 Represented Australia on a tour to the US and Great Britain (as the Reserve)
- 1978–82 Queensland Open Champion
- 1978–83 Captain of the Queensland Women's Open Team
- 1979–80 British Open semi-finalist
- 1979–84 Ranked in Top 10
- 1980 Represented Australia as a playing member on the tour to the US and Great Britain
- 1981 Australian Open Champion
- 1981 World Open Champion (Toronto, Canada)
- 1981–82 Ranked no.1 in the World
- 1981–83 Captain Australian Women's Open Team. During her time as Captain, the Team remained undefeated
- 1981 and 1983 World Open Teams Champions
- 1983 World Open Runner-up
- 1984 Founding member of WISPA (The Women's International Squash Players' Association)
- 2019 Attended the 35th Anniversary of WISPA

Other titles

- South African Champion
- New Zealand South Island Champion

- Scottish Open Champion
- North of England Open Champion
- East of England Open Champion
- Monaco Open Champion
- 1977 London Open Champion
- 1977 Ontario Champion
- NSW Open Champion South Australian Open Champion Northern Territory Open Champion
- AUDI World Cup Champion (3 times—Mixed Team's Event) with Qamar Zaman and Dean Williams.

Awards

- 1982 and 1984 Sport Australia Award
- 1984 Queensland Sportswoman of the Year (all sports)
- 2000 The Australian Sports Medal
- 2005 Inducted into the Queensland Hall of Fame
- 2006 Inducted into Squash Australia's Hall of Fame
- 2006 In her birth city of Toowoomba, Queensland the Rhonda Thorne Park Oval honours her achievements in the sport of Squash

Administration

In an administrative role, she was one of the driving forces in the creation of the Women's International Squash Players Association (WISPA) that was established in 1984. This evolved to further the interest of professional women squash players. This also involved developing a World circuit of major squash championships. The success of this visionary players' group has culminated in the securing of financial sponsorship for the World Women's Squash Circuit that now provides approximately $A2 million annually. Rhonda retired from international Competition in 1985 and remained involved in the game becoming Vice President of ASRA, in 1987.

She traded her racket for the world of business as Queensland Account Executive for Amcor Australasia in the packaging paper division. She is now happily married to Geoff Clayton and has two boys, Robert and Wade. They live on the Sunshine Coast in Queensland.

Her demeanour on and off the court made her a first-rate Ambassador for Australian Squash.

Well done, Rhonda.

Barbara Oldfield

Barbara was born in Busselton, WA and didn't start playing squash until she was 20; in today's terms, a late starter. However, like many squash players at that time who had previously played tennis, she had attained other skills that could be transferred to squash, especially volleying. This skill is not as prominent in today's game.

Barbara started playing squash with some of her brothers at the Broadway Squash Club in Nedlands (WA Squash Hall of Fame, 2014). In 1971 she was introduced to Pennant squash by Lorraine and Carol Webster (who was soon to marry Steve Wall—three times WA Champion) and their Mum, representing

Western Australian Squash Hall of Fame 2014
Left to Right: Di Davis, Barbara Oldfield, Ken Watson, Cath Bellemore and
Debra Majteles
(Photo: Courtesy of Western Australia Hall of Fame, 2014)

Scarborough Squash centre. She made rapid progress and in 1976 was selected in her first WA Interstate team with Chris van Nierop, who became an Australian rep, Marg Prout and Di Diedrich. By 1978 she was ranked no. 2 in WA, after Barbara Wall (winner of the British Open in 1979) who defeated her in the 1978 WA final. She was runner-up again in 1979 and then won three State titles in 1980, 1981 and 1982.

In 1980, Barbara was selected to play for Australia in a one-off test match against Great Britain in Perth. She had earned her Australian badge. Later that year, she travelled to England and made the last 16 in the British Open. She was now hungry for more. Barbara was not to be denied and was again selected in the Australian team in 1981 to play in the World Teams Championship held in Toronto, Canada. Full credit to her, as she had to overcome a serious back injury on the way. The Coach of this team was Heather McKay and the other team members were Rhonda Thorne, World no. 1, Vicki Hoffmann, World no. 2 and Rae Anderson from Victoria. In the final against Great Britain, Rhonda and Vicki won their respective matches 3–0, however Barbara had a marathon struggle with Sue Cogswell losing 8–10, 9–3, 9–4, 7–9, 9–10. She was knocking on the door of reaching the highest levels of World Women's Squash and the team was World Champion, avenging their defeat by Great Britain, in 1979.

In 1982, Barbara again played in the British Open, together with Di Davis and Cath Bellemore. This time the Women's Championships were played at the same time as the Men's event. It was to packed crowds at the Churchill theatre in Bromley, south of London. The court was prefabricated, with wooden walls front and side, and a glass back wall, erected on the stage and the referees were sitting in the stalls. A bit different to today, eh? Barbara played Rhonda Thorne in the quarter-finals. It was an epic battle and extremely physical, resulting in many bruises, lets and strokes. In an upset win, Barbara prevailed winning 9–0 in the fifth game. Unfortunately, she found it hard to sustain this form in the semi-final against Lisa Opie of Great Britain and lost 9–7, 0–9, 3–9, 9–10. In the fourth, Barbara had several game balls at 9–8 and 9–9 but couldn't quite finish it off. Still, she'd gone further than she ever had before and I'm sure it's a result, of which, she's still very proud. Barbara had achieved a World ranking of no. 5 and Australian ranking of No.3.[102] She played in South Africa (unofficially) on her return to Australia, accompanied by Rae Anderson.

Part of Barbara's success story was her outstanding fitness. When tested at the AIS in Canberra it was revealed that she had an exceptional Max VO2 (oxygen uptake capacity) and could virtually run all day. She had sound technique and a good all-round game. From my observations when I saw her play in Perth in 1982, she was a thinking player with good tactical nous.

Unfortunately, her career came to a halt in 1983 due to an ectopic pregnancy rupture and then, just as she was regaining her strength, she had an ovarian cyst rupture which further weakened her. It was game over. Her life direction changed course after her retirement from squash and her focus turned to Bible Studies during 1984–85. Barbara is still involved with this calling and preaches at the Ministry run by former World Champion tennis player Margaret Court. She did however play the odd game of squash and represented WA again in 1988, where the team was Runner-up.

From information given to me by Barbara, her enthusiasm for the game still shines through. She is 'so grateful to have played this magnificent game, at a high level and to have made so many friends along the way, from all over the World. It was such a delight to represent my State and Nation.'

To all the young ones out there, that's what it's all about. If you love the sport and give it your all, the rest will follow. Not everyone becomes World Champion, but the journey of trying is what makes it all worthwhile.

Playing career

- 1978 and 79 Runner-up in WA Championships
- 1980, 81 and 82 Western Australian Champion
- 1980 Represented Australia in a match against Great Britain in Perth
- 1981 Ranked no. 1 in WA
- 1981 Ranked no. 3 in Australia

- 1981 Member of the winning World Australian Championship team
- 1982 Semi-finalist at the British Open
- 1982 Ranked no. 5 in the World
- 1978–81 Represented WA in the Interstate series, at the Australian Championships (winning in 1981)
- 1983–84 Member of the winning WA Interstate team, at the Australian Championships
- 1988 Represented WA in the Interstate series, at the Australian Championships (they came 2nd)

Awards

- 2014 Inducted into the WA Squash Hall of Fame

Administration

Worked as WA Squash Development Officer for a period, where she developed and implemented the Champion of Champions Schools event, developed and delivered certification and accreditation courses for coaches and conducted coaching courses[103].

Dianne Davis

Di was in the next wave of players that came through, just before the retirement of Rhonda Thorne in 1985. She had represented Western Australia from 1979 and won her first Western Australian title in 1983. This resulted in her being selected in the Australian Women's team for the 1983 World Women's Teams Championships, which were played in Perth. The other team members were Rhonda Thorne of Queensland, Carin Clonda of NSW and Jan Miller of South Australia. As reported earlier, this team won the World Championship beating England in final 2–1. Di was on her way.

Playing career

Now for the beginning. Di started her squash career fairly late, aged 25. She had moved to Perth and was playing A Grade tennis at Royal Kings Park. Playing squash was easier to fit in with raising her two young children.

She started at Dianella Club in C Grade and was soon encouraged by the eccentric court owner, Ron Jacques to play in the much harder night pennant competition. Good results followed and she was soon playing A Grade.[104] In 1979, she was selected in her first State team. She worked hard on her fitness and under the tutelage of Ken Watson, improved her squash technique. In 1981, she indicated her improvement by defeating Sue Cogswell in the first round of the Australian Open. Sue had been runner-up to Barbara Wall in the British Open the previous year. The Western Australian Women's team were also achieving what was once thought impossible. They won the Australian Interstate series in 1981. Ken Watson was the coach responsible for their amazing improvement. 'He had recognised in our group the potential to build a really strong core of players'. [105] The team comprised Di Davis, Barbara Oldfield, Debra Majteles and Cath Bellemore—a team of considerable potential. There were some outstanding results. Day 1, playing against Queensland, Di Davis defeated Marion Jackman, a former Australian Champion, in 4 games, Cath Bellemore won in straight games against Robyn Prentice, a future World Master's Champion, and Barbara Oldfield took two games from Rhonda Thorne, the Australian Champion that year. The match had been decided. They continued with their winning run defeating South Australia 3–1, with Barbara managing to get two games from Vicki Hoffmann. Against NSW they won 3–1 with Carin Clonda from NSW, a future Australian team representative, the only winner defeating Debra Matjeles in 5 games. So, to the hardest match against Victoria! Barbara defeated fellow Australian team member Rae Anderson to only 8 points. Di Davis conceded only 10 points in defeating former Australian Champion Margaret Zachariah. Lesley Chapman of NSW defeated Debra Majteles of WA 3–1, however, as Debra had won the first game, the match had been decided. WA were the Australian Team Champions. Thrilling times. They were later joined by Lorraine Meuleman and Robyn Friday and Western Australia went on to win 5 more Australian Teams' titles in 1983, 1984, 1985, 1986 and 1987.[106]

Di decided to look further afield to gain international experience and in 1982 travelled to the UK to play in the British Open and other tournaments. She reached the last 16 and this was the spur that led her to even greater heights. She also worked hard on her own game and won the 1984 and 1985 Western Australian titles. Di was again selected in the Australian Team to play in the 1985 World Championships in Ireland. The other team members were Jan Miller of SA and also Captain, Liz Irving of Qld and Carin Clonda of NSW. Unfortunately, Liz Irving suffered a serious back injury prior to the tournament and withdrew. [107] Tracey Smith of Victoria was sent as a replacement. Liz's withdrawal no doubt weakened the team as she was Australia's no. 2 player. Di, playing at no. 3, still managed to win her match 3–1 against England. She played to a set plan and avenged her defeat by Alison Cummings in the Individual Championships. However, Carin Clonda lost as did Jan Miller. As a result, Australia finished third in this tournament and England defeated New Zealand in the final. Di was recognised as the Senior Player of the series. The Ulster Women's Squash Rackets Association presented her with a Waterford Crystal Vase. In the Individuals, Di had a good run and again reached the last 16. [108] Later that year, she reached the final of the Australian Championship, losing to Jan Miller of South Australia. She had become no. 2 player in Australia.

Shortly after winning her fourth Western Australian title in 1986, Di moved back to Melbourne and wasted no time in being in selected for Victoria in the interstate series. She was a very determined, extremely fit and slightly unorthodox player, and this playing style made it very difficult for her opponents. [109] Di also managed to win the World Over 40s master's title in 1990. She didn't sit still for long.

Coaching

In 1980, the Watson Davis School of Squash was set up in partnership with Ken Watson. She thrived in her coaching role, even though she was still competing. Ken was a great mentor and coach and her game improved considerably during 1980–86. This experience gave her an excellent platform for the next phase of her squash career.

After moving to Melbourne in 1986, Di was appointed the inaugural Coach of the Victorian Sports Institute. She attained her NCAS Level 2 Accreditation, became a PSCAV Instructor for Level 0, 1 and 2 Courses and moved into the role of AIS Satellite Coach. She ran Talent Identification days and co-ordinated and assessed Level 1 Coaches. In 1990, with Vicki Cardwell acting as administrator and Di as the coach, a Girls in Squash pilot programme was conducted aimed at increasing the number of girls that played squash.[110] This programme received a special commendation from the Prime Ministerial Women's and Sports Awards. Di also served on the Professional Coaches Association of Victoria Committee from 1987 until 1992.

Di was very active in grassroots development, becoming Squash in Schools— Skills Programme Co-ordinator for the Eastern region of Victoria. In this role she:

- Organised Coaches to attend classes held for schools in squash centres in her area
- Promoted squash to school children in the region
- Set up After School and weekend coaching programmes for these new players in the clubs
- Ran promotional school yard programmes for Primary Schools in the region
- Presented In-service courses for teachers in the region

In addition, in her spare time (!), she was personal coach of several World Class Female players including Liz Irving (World no. 4, 1992) Sharon Bradey (World no. 18), Amanda Hopps (Australian Under 19 Champion (1988) and Meaghan Bell (Australian Under 17 Champion (1989).

But there was still more to come!

1992 saw Di appointed as Manager-Coach of the Australian World Women's team comprising Michelle Martin, Liz Irving, Robyn Lambourne and Sarah Fitz-Gerald. It was game on as, at this point, Australia hadn't won the World Team's event since 1983, when ironically Di was a member of the winning team. They were not to be denied, and in the final defeated New Zealand, who had beaten England in the semi-finals, 2–1. The Australian

Team was World Champion again! These girls had benefitted from the tutelage they had received at the hands of Heather McKay and Geoff Hunt at the Australian Institute of Sport in Brisbane, as well as from their own personal coaches. They were to dominate for 12 of the next 14 years, that is, from 1992 until 2004, only losing in 2000 to England. Di was their coach for the World Championships 1992, 1994, 1996 and 1998 in which they won every time. The only team change was Carol Owens, who became World Open Champion in 2000 and 2003, replacing Robyn Lambourne from 1994–1998. A phenomenal run. Di was also appointed Coach of the Australian Women's team in the inaugural Squash Commonwealth Games event held in Kuala Lumpur in 1998. This time the girls achieved the following: Michelle Martin gold in both the individual and in the Mixed Doubles with Craig Rowland, Sarah Fitz-Gerald silver in the individual, Rachael Grinham and Robyn Cooper silver in the Women's Doubles and Sarah Fitz-Gerald and Carol Owens bronze in the Women's Doubles.

During this period Di was also Coach of the Australian Junior Women's teams in 1993, 1995, 1997 and 1999. They won in 1993 and 1995. However, the tide started to turn after that, with the emergence of strong Junior teams from Egypt and England. There was a future champion in the Australian side,

Rachael Grinham, who won the British Open in 2003, 2004, 2007 and 2009 and the World Championship in 2007. Di had had a dream run and had made an enormous contribution to the performance of Australian players on the World stage.

Chris Sinclair awarding Di Davis the Distinguished Service Award, on behalf Squash Australia
(Photo: Courtesy of Chris Sinclair)

Life was never still for Di and she moved to South Australia in 1994. She soon became Head Squash Coach at the South Australian Institute of Sport and imparted her knowledge there. She held that position until 2000 and many highly talented players emerged under her guiding eye.

From a family perspective, one of Di's sons, Byron, became Head Coach at the AIS in 2003, after Geoff Hunt went overseas. He retained that position until 2013. He had formerly carried on from Di in setting up programs in South Australia. Her knowledge had been passed forward. They say in life you need to know when to pass the baton. Di was wise enough to do that.

Awards

- 2011 Received the Distinguished Service Award from Squash Australia
- 2014 Inducted into Western Australia's Hall of Fame

Jan Miller

Jan came from South Australia and was always in Vicki's shadow, as she was residing at that time in Adelaide. As a result, Jan didn't manage to win a South Australian Championship, however, she did represent South Australia in the Interstate series from 1980–85. Jan was first selected to represent Australia in 1983 in Perth. Other members of the team were Rhonda Thorne (Captain), Carin Clonda and Diane Davis. She lost her match in this final to Angela Smith (GB), but it was a dead rubber as Rhonda and Carin had already won their matches. Australia won the World title 2–1. In 1984, she represented again in the Trans–Tasman series against New Zealand. The team was Vicki Cardwell (Captain), Jan and Mary-Jo Reid. She acquitted herself

Australian Champion 1985 Jan Miller
(Photo: Courtesy of Jan Miller)

well, playing in the no. 2 position winning all of her matches, with the loss of only one game. Australia won the series 3–0. At the end of this series, she was ranked at no. 6 in the World. The magazine article described Jan's style as play as 'Aggression. It starts with a vicious serve and only ends when the last shot is played. A bright future is predicted'.[111]

Well, Jan proceeded to live up to that expectation. In 1985, Jan won the Australian Championship defeating Di Davis in straight games, in the final. She had been a semi-finalist twice previously and this time she had a clear run, as Vicki Cardwell was out having her first child Sarah. Needless to say, Vicki was in her corner helping her devise a game plan that would secure her the title. It worked to perfection and Jan kept the Australian title in South Australia. Vicki had won it the previous 5 years. To indicate Jan's level of play, she had to defeat Rae Anderson, a former Australian rep, Danielle Drady, a future Australian rep and Carin Clonda, an Australian rep. She only dropped one game en route to the final, and that was to Cath Bellemore of WA. In the same year, Jan was selected to represent Australia at the World Championships in Ireland, where she was ranked in the Individual at no.4, behind Sue Devoy (NZ), Martine Le Moignan of England and Lisa Opie of England. She was the only Australian ranked in the top 8 seeds; such had the landscape changed. England had 4 ranked players and Scotland 2.

Jan attributed her success to being fit. She had a good volley and mental toughness. She perceived that 'if a match goes for an hour and a half, it is unlikely that your opponent will maintain their form over the whole of that period. It is a matter of hanging in there until their run has come to an end'. She was a goal setter and set herself the following goals: win the Australian Championship—tick, make the top six in the World—tick (she made no. 4), and qualify for the Australian team to play at the World Championship—tick. To achieve this, she had to put her career in accountancy on hold and have long periods away from her husband, Andrew. No doubt there have been more goals that have been achieved since she retired from squash.[112]

Playing career

- 1980–85 represented South Australia
- 1983–85 South Australian Institute of Sport scholarship holder
- 1983 Member of Australian World Championship team
- 1984 Member of Australian team to defeat New Zealand winning all of her matches
- 1984 Winner of Bridge and of Allan and Essex Open
- 1985 Australian Champion defeating Di Davis in the final in straight games
- 1985 Member of Australian team to World Championships in Ireland. Australia finished third.
- 1985 Reached quarter finals of British Open
- 1985 Runner-up to Sue Devoy in the Irish Open

Awards

- 1984 Award of Merit presented by the South Australia Minister for Sport and Recreation for winning the Bridge of Allen and Essex Open
- 1985 Sport Australia Awards—Certificate of Outstanding Performance

Jan managed to fly the flag for a brief period, before her life took off in another direction. She fulfilled her dreams!

Carin (Alexia) Clonda

Carin was born in Sydney in the suburb of Manly to an Estonian mother and a Romanian father.[113] There were 8 siblings. She was introduced to squash at the age of 13 and began to play competitively, winning the Australian under 16 Championship after only playing for two years. In 1978, she started to dominate the Junior Age groups winning the NSW and the Australian Junior Women's Championships in the Under 15, Under 16 and Under 17 Age groups. In 1979, she became the de facto Under 19 World Junior Champion, when she won the British Junior Women's Open, there being no higher Championship in that age range. No Australian Woman has won the British Women's Under 19 since then and Jan Shearer was the only Australian player to win the title previously and that was in 1961, the year that Carin was born.

*Left to Right: Carin Clonda (NSW),
Jan Miller (SA) Di Davis (WA)
and Rhonda Thorne (Queensland)*
(Photo: Courtesy of Jan Miller)

In that same year, she was diagnosed with chronic asthma and took eighteen months off to undergo respiratory treatment and was in and out of hospital for 18 months. She gained 56 pounds in weight due to the heavy regime of treatment. Throughout her professional playing career, she travelled with a nebuliser and a squash bag full of medications. Fortunately for her, drug testing wasn't around in those days. Dubbed the worst asthmatic elite athlete in Australia by the Head physiologist at the AIS, the asthma was chronic and life threatening. Carin did go down to the AIS, three years later and taught a number of the elite athletes the Buteyko Breathing Technique, which she had learnt in 1996, and this had turned the debilitating asthma right around for her.

In 1979, she decided to come out about her sexuality and she was the first female professional squash player to do so. She had experienced considerable hostility, although more from outside the squash community than within it, and that determined many of the aspects of her character in life. In the years to come she was forthright, open, determined and persistent on and off the court. A force to be reckoned with.

In 1982, she won two NSW tiles on the same day. Firstly, in the final of the NSW Open she defeated Sue Devoy from New Zealand, who went on to win the British Open 8 times from 1984–1990 and again in 1992. Carin was 2–0 down in this match before she fought her way back to win in 5. An hour later she defeated Liz Irving in the Under 23 final, winning in straight games.

*Alexia in action**
(Photo: Courtesy of Alexia Clonda)
*Note: Carin changed her name to Alexia
in 2014, hence the changed names in the
photographs above which were taken
after this.*

One of Carin's playing career highlights would have to be defeating Martine Le Moignan of England in the 1983 World Teams Championships played in Perth. World no. 2 Rhonda Thorne had won her rubber defeating world no. 6 Lisa Opie 2–9, 9–6, 5–9, 10–8, 10–8—a real cliff hanger. When Carin, who was not ranked in the top 10 in the world, defeated world no. 4 Martine Le Moignan 9–4, 9–5, 9–1, it was quite the upset and Australia had won the World Teams' Championship. Jan Miller lost to Angela Smith 6–9, 4–9, 9–6, but this was a dead rubber.

The other highlight for Carin would have been reaching the semi-finals of the World Open in 1983, by defeating Martine in the quarter-finals 9–3, 9–7, 5–9, 9–4. This, no doubt gave her some confidence going into the Teams' event. These two outstanding performances meant that she achieved a World Ranking of no.5. She had sound technique, played a creative game and was capable of beating any player in the world when on her game. Sometimes her mental approach let her down and she became anxious and tightened up, which triggered her asthma. No doubt today's sports psychology techniques would have helped her, but there was nothing of that around in those days.

Playing career

- 1975–79
  - ~ NSW U15, U16 and U17 Champion
  - ~ NSW Junior Teams representative

- ~ Australian Junior Teams Representative
- ~ Captain NSW Junior Teams
- ~ British, Australian and NSW Junior Champion
- 1981
  - ~ NSW U23 Champion
  - ~ NSW and Australian Top 10
  - ~ Quarter finalist in Australian Open
- 1981–86
  - ~ NSW Open Teams Captain
- 1982
  - ~ ACT Open Champion
  - ~ NT Open Champion
  - ~ NSW U23 Champion
  - ~ Semi-finalist in Australian Open
  - ~ Semi-finalist in Scottish Open
  - ~ Quarter finalist in British Open
  - ~ World ranking no. 16
  - ~ Australian ranking no. 4
  - ~ NSW ranking No1 (until 1986)
- 1983
  - ~ Quarter finalist Scottish Open
  - ~ Quarter finalist Irish Open
  - ~ Last 16 British Open
  - ~ Semi-finalist in World Open
  - ~ NSW Open Champion
  - ~ Semi-finalist Victorian Open
  - ~ Semi-finalist Queensland Open
  - ~ World Ranking no. 5
  - ~ Australian Ranking no. 3
  - ~ NSW ranking no. 1
  - ~ Australian representative 1983–85

- 1984
  - ~ Semi-finalist French Open
  - ~ Semi-finalist NSW Open
  - ~ Semi-finalist Swedish Open
  - ~ Semi-finalist Victorian Open
  - ~ Semi-finalist Dutch Open
  - ~ Semi-finalist ACT Open
  - ~ Runner-up Belgian Open
  - ~ Runner-up Finnish Open
  - ~ Runner-up WA Open
  - ~ Warwickshire County player
- 1985
  - ~ Last 16 World Open
  - ~ NT Open Champion
  - ~ Alice Springs Open Champion
  - ~ Semi-finalist Australian Open
  - ~ Semi-finalist German Open
  - ~ Runner-up in WA Open
  - ~ Quarterfinalist NSW Open
  - ~ Quarterfinalist French Open
  - ~ World Ranking Top 16
  - ~ NSW representative
  - ~ Australian representative
- 1986
  - ~ Last 16 French Open
  - ~ Runner-up in Swedish Open
  - ~ Quarter-finalist in Spanish Open
  - ~ World ranking top 20
  - ~ Australian ranking top 16
- 1987 Played in World Open
- 1989 Played in NSW Open

A more recent photo
(Photos: Courtesy of Alexia Clonda)

•   1990
~   Winner NSW Classic Open
~   NSW ranking no. 4

Carin certainly fits the slogan 'Have racket. Will travel.' However, in her post playing career she also left her mark despite considerable medical issues.

Carin has been plagued by health issues all of her life, which could certainly fill a medical dictionary.[114] In 1988, she underwent surgery to remove a tumour from her leg. Later, in 1989, she had a spinal fusion, which held the risk of permanent paralysis. She then experienced chronic fatigue syndrome, which resulted in damage to her immune system, worsening her asthma and increasing the risk of infections. Later, she incurred a hip injury after a fall and the recurrence of her tumour.

Miraculously, at the age of 46 in 2007, Carin reached the quarter-finals of the Australian Closed Championship, with wins over 3 of Australia's top 20 players, all half her age. Unfortunately, that wasn't the end of the occurrences of poor health. In 2009, Carin underwent two hip replacements, which failed and led to metallosis (metal poisoning). In 2016, she suffered a series of heart episodes, caused by a 75% blockage of a major artery with a cardiac stent having to be inserted. In 2017, Carin contracted septicaemia, which paralysed her and required emergency surgery. In addition, she had to have revisionary bilateral hip replacements. Despite all of this, she has been incredibly active in a number of fields.

Administration

During her time as NSW Squash CEO and Director (2005–2009) she secured a:

- Department of Health and Ageing Grant of $127,000 for a Schools Get Squashed Program in NSW Primary Schools. This enabled the purchase of 3 portable inflatable mini squash courts, which could be taken to schools, shopping malls and other venues, for the promotion of squash
- NSW Government Grant of $90,000 for renovations at Thornleigh Squash Centre
- Sponsorship of $5000 for the 2008–9 NSW Open
- Sponsorship of $3000 for the 2007–2008 for the NSW Junior Age Championships
- Sponsorship of $1000 for the 2009 NSW Junior Age Championships
- Sponsorship of $5000 for the 2009 Australian Junior Age Championships
- 1982–89 NSW Asthma Foundation Voluntary promotional work (Community announcements, media interviews etc.)
- 1982–83 NSW Women's Squash Rackets Association—Committee member (Publicity Officer)
- 1983 Foundation member of WISPA
- 1985 Chairwoman of WISPA
- 1985–86 Representative on the Australian Sports Commission National Athlete Award Scheme
- 1985–89 Women's Committee member of the International Squash Rackets Federation
- 1986–89 NSW Selector
- 1986–89 ASRA—Australian Selector
- 2000 Volunteer Sydney Olympics
- 2002 Sports Forum Co-ordinator for World Asthma Awareness Day initiative by the Institute of Respiratory Medicine (IRM)

- 2002 Gay Games VI Squash Working Group Coordinator/ Manager
- Coordinator for Sydney Harbour City G squash—a gay squash group that plays twice weekly in Sydney

Carin also oversaw the promotion of squash at the Royal Easter Show in 2009, where an inflatable mini squash court was set up in Sports Alley, attracting over 3,000 school age children to come 'n try squash. In all, over 100,000 people were exposed to the game of squash. The Squash Exhibition display won 2nd prize in the Sports Category. Carin also brought back David Palmer, twice World Champion and three-time British Open Champion, to help in the Royal Easter Show promotion and then secured an article for David Palmer in the June issue of *Inside Sport*.

The ability to effectively juggle the role of CEO and Director of NSW Squash, whilst dealing with health issues, including monthly hospital visits for medical infusions for a compromised immune system, was well and truly put to the test at this time. She also had a bout of pneumonia and the previously mentioned bilateral hip replacements, with the necessary rehabilitation from these. Carin continued to hold the fort and prepared for her role as Tournament Championship Director of the Australian Junior Championships in September, 2009 and the World Masters Games event in October. In 2009 there were record entries at the NSW Open and NSW Junior Age Championships, largely due to Carin's ability to network, promote and enthuse people to participate in the game of squash.

Carin also secured a spot for Squash (and took part in) a prime television viewing programme on Channel 7, 10 Years Younger in 10 Days. The segment highlighted that anyone can achieve, and Squash came across as a great sport to play for anyone of any standard. This segment certainly reached a wide audience, which attracted not only an interest in squash itself, but also gained attention for the sport to be played as part of one's overall health and fitness and lifestyle management.

Awards

- 1984 Sport Australia Award for Outstanding Performance in the Australian Women's Team
- 1985 NSW Department of Sport and Recreation Sports Scholarship Award Certificate
- 2000 Australian Sports medal for Services to Squash over 20 years.

Carin's life has been the epitome of where there's a will there's a way and to thine own self be true. She has been a highly driven, passionate and motivated individual who has openly displayed her love of squash and also injected into the sport so much of her time, ability and funds, in her endeavour to move the sport forward. She has been an outstanding example to the next generation to give it your all.

Robyn Lambourne (née Friday)

Robyn had a younger start than many other earlier Australian representatives, first playing the game at the age of 10. [115] This was probably because by then, squash was an established sport and she hadn't taken up tennis first. Growing up in Perth's eastern suburbs, Robyn found herself at the Swan Districts Squash Centre on Saturday mornings, where leading Western Australian Coaches Bill Lawton and Alan East, were helping promote the sport in the district.[116] The group boasted a number of promising youngsters. The first tournament that she entered was the Coca Cola State tournament. This tournament was organised by former British Open Champion

World Junior Champion 1983
(Photo: *Squash and Fitness News*, June,1991 p9)

Barbara Wall. Robyn was runner-up in that event and many more before she started winning her age events. Robyn stated 'that Barbara had a huge influence on my squash career. Not only was she a fantastic player, but the amount of time and effort she put into Western Australian Juniors was enormous. She was a huge hit with everyone with her infectious smile and genuine concern for all the players, parents, helpers and sponsors'.[117] Robyn had been fortunate that other female players of Barbara's calibre were around at that time, such as Di Davis, Barbara Oldfield and Chris van Nierop. They were achieving success at international level. Ken Watson, who with Di had started the Watson-Davis School of Squash in 1980, also had a major influence on her career. The culture in WA was ripe for an up-and-coming young player.[118]

Robyn did not disappoint. She responded to the initiative of a National Junior Championship and in her mid-teens won consistently in her age group. In one year, she won the Western Australian Under 15, 17 and 19 Age group in the same tournament. She travelled interstate, for the Cheezels National tournaments and eventually won the Under 17 in the South Pacific Under Age Championships. Her representative career with Western Australia started at the age of 14, playing in the Australian Junior Championships (Under 19). This was not unlike Rhonda Thorne. The Australian Age Championships didn't start until 1982. A highlight was being selected in 1981 to represent Australia in the Junior team to go to England for six weeks. The other team members were Robyn Belford, Michelle Toon and Wendy Williams. The team played a Junior three test series against the UK, but without success. Even so, the ASRA deemed the tour to be a success due to the experience gained by the girls.[119]

This was just a taster for Robyn. In 1982 and 1983, she was selected in the Australian Junior Team to play against New Zealand and the *piece de resistance* was when she won the World Junior Championship held in Perth in 1983. She defeated fellow Aussie, Helen Paradeiser 10–8, 9–2, 9–3 in the final. She said 'It was a wonderful experience to win in front of a home crowd and indicated that WA was up with the rest of the world'. She was on her way—or was she? They say 'life wasn't meant to be easy'! Let's see what happened.

In Robyn's words: 'My first year out of Juniors in 1984 was a disaster! I had trouble with my feet, ending up having to wear orthotics, without which I couldn't play. I also had to have my appendix out. This gave me breathing space to see what I really wanted to do.' Decision made, she started on the international circuit in 1985 when she played in the British Open. She was also the recipient of a $1500 Sports Talent Encouragement grant from the Australian Sports Commission. This funding was provided to assist athletes to become world-ranked, in the immediate future. Robyn continued with her career, undergoing a strict training regime. This included jogging, swimming, aerobics, gym work and on court circuit training as well as match play. In 1987, she won her first Western Australian title, was unbeaten in the Interstate series at no 1, and was Runner-up in the Australian Open. She was then selected in the Australian team to play in the World Championships in New Zealand. The other team members were Vicki Cardwell (Captain), Sarah Fitz-Gerald, Michelle Martin and Robyn. She won all her matches playing at no. 2, including a win against world no. 3 Martine Le Moignan. The team did not win the Championship, losing 2–1 to England in the final, however, they had demonstrated that they would be a force to be reckoned with in the future. They weren't quite ready at this point in time.

Other overseas tours with the Australian team followed with World Championships in Holland, Sydney and Vancouver.[120] Her first venture to the British Open saw her reach the last 16 and she later added two Canadian Open titles and one New Zealand title. When she returned home, she received the backing of the WA Institute of Sport, with fellow—Australian player and former Australian Champion Dean Williams being appointed as her coach under a scholarship arrangement. Ken Watson also continued to play a coaching role with Robyn after he moved to Scandinavia in 1989, coaching her at the British Open that year and at the World Championships and a number of British Opens in the 1990s.

In 1990, when the World Championships were played in Sydney, she came very close to winning the title, but it was a bridge too far. She lost in the semi-final to England's Martine Le Moignan (British Open Champion, in 1989)

9–4, 0–9, 9–5, 5–9, 9–10. In the 1991 British Open Championship, she had a chance, as Susan Devoy had been defeated in the quarter finals by England's Sue Wright. This inspired Robyn to defeat fellow Aussie and world no. 2 Danielle Drady. She was now in the semi-finals up against the conqueror of Sue Devoy, Susan Wright. She made a great start and led 2–0, lost the next two games, was looking good in the fifth, but eventually was defeated. Lisa Opie of England went on to win the title, defeating Sue Wright 6–9, 9–3, 9–3, 9–3 in a rare all England final. In the Teams' event, unfortunately for Robyn and Australia (our No. 2) she had pulled a groin muscle in the Individual event and could not play. The team lost in a tight tussle (reported elsewhere) to England 2–1.

Robyn competed again in the British Open in 1992, reaching the semi-finals. It had taken a while, and in the same year Robyn was part of a winning Australian Team at the World Championships in Canada. By then, Robyn was ranked No 2 player in the World. The team comprised Robyn No 1, Liz Irving No.2, Michelle Martin No.3 and Sarah Fitz-Gerald No.4. Di Davis was Coach/Manager. In the final they played New Zealand which had upset the English team in the semi-finals. Liz Irving gave Australia a great start defeating Phillipa Beames in the first rubber 9–1, 9–5, 9–1. The next match saw World Champion Susan Devoy defeating Michelle Martin 9–5, 9–1, 9–0 and then it was up to Robyn to win her match and decide the Championship. After a tentative start, she defeated Donna Newton 2–9, 9–6, 9–2, 9–1. The girls had been through the school of hard knocks and had emerged as World Champions. It had been 10 years since Australia had previously won and Di had been a player in that team. A fitting result.

Robyn had married Andie Lambourne in 1987 and this had given her a stable base from which to pursue her career. But now family life started to take precedence and four children and a husband became the focus of her life. After 12 years living in the USA and England, where her husband was working, she returned to Australia and is now living in Perth. Her interests are exploring Outback Australia, with its uniqueness, white wine and boutique gin, of which Australia has a wonderful collection to sample and of course, family life!

Awards

- 1984 Australian Sports Award—Young Australian Female Athlete of the Year
- 1987 Player of the series trophy at the Australian Interstate Series—Undefeated at no. 1
- 1988 WA Senior Sports Star of the Year
- 1990 Winner of the Barbara Wall Perpetual Trophy in the Westpac State Closed event
- 1990–91 WAIS Athlete of the Year
- 2014 Inducted into WA Squash Hall of Fame

Playing career

- 1983 World Junior Women's Champion
- 1981, 82, 83 (Junior) represented Australia
- 1987, 89, 90, 92 (Senior) represented Australia
- 1987, 89, 90, 91,92 Western Australian Champion
- 1987 Undefeated in the World teams Championship, playing at no. 2 for Australia. This included defeating World no. 3 Martine Le Moignan of England.

World Champions 1992
Left to Right: Robyn Lambourne (WA), Sarah Fitz-Gerald, (Vic), Michelle Martin (NSW), Liz Irving (Qld) and Di Davis (Coach–Vic)—a truly Australian blend
(Photo: *The Belsham years 1976–92*, p82)

- 1987 Quarter finalist World Open
- 1987 Runner-up in Australian Open
- 1988 Quarter-finalist in World Open
- 1988 Quarter-finalist in British Open
- 1988 Winner ACT Open, Queensland Open
- 1988 Semi-finalist in Australian Open
- 1988 Semi-finalist in New Zealand Open
- 1988 Quarter-finalist in Singapore Open
- 1988 Runner-up in Judy Traviss Open (Toronto)
- 1988 Runner-up in Canadian Open
- 1988 Winner Squash Ace Grand Prix (Germany) defeating Martine Le Moignan (World no. 3)
- 1989 Winner ACT Open, NT Open, WA Open
- 1988,89,90 Western Australian Closed Champion
- 1990 Semi Finalist in the Australian, New Zealand, Singapore and World Open
- 1991–92 Semi-finalist in British Open
- 1992 No.1 member of Winning Australian team at the World Championships

Highest ranking

- 1991 no. 1 in Australia
- 1992 no. 2 in the World

Robyn was in a tough generation with many high achieving women, including, Vicki Cardwell, Michelle Martin, Sarah Fitz-Gerald, Danielle Drady and Liz Irving. It wasn't easy. She did almost achieve her dream of becoming World No.1, with 1991 and 1992 being the pinnacle of her career. In 1991 she was ranked No.1 in Australia and No.2 in the World. In 1992 she was a member of the Australian team winning the World teams' event. She won the deciding rubber in 4 games and Australia had reclaimed the World title after an absence of 7 years.

Robyn had a motto that she had read in the book *The Power of One*. 'If someone wants something badly enough, nothing in the world can stop them. First with the heart and then with the head'.

A supporter (Jean) gave her the following to put in her squash bag in 1983.

Winners Creed

If you think you are beaten, you are.
If you think you dare not, you don't.
If you'd like to win, but you think you can't,
It's almost certain, you won't.
Life's battles don't always go
To the stronger or faster man.
But sooner or later,
The man who wins,
Is the man who thinks he can!

There's a lesson there for all the young ones out there. Well done, Robyn. You gave it your best shot.

Liz Irving

Liz, more or less, grew up on a squash court. I still remember her being tied to the top railing in the spectator area at Bellevue Hill Squash Centre in Sydney, whilst her mother Jenny, runner-up in the British Open 1971 and Australian team representative from 1963–64 until 1972, was practising down below. Needless to say, Liz went on to represent Australia from 1983–1998 and was also runner-up in the British Open in 1988, 1993 and 1994, and the World Championship in 1993. Her highest World Ranking was no. 2 in 1998.

She first started playing when she was four and took to it like a duck to water, however Jenny encouraged her to play other sports such as tennis and she didn't really start concentrating on squash until she was 12. By then she reached the semi-finals of the Under 15 Australian Junior Cheezels tournament and she was playing D1 fixtures. She quickly moved up to C1 and whilst Jenny did give her some advice when she asked for it.[121] She also

Liz in full flight
(Photo: Courtesy of PSA World Tour, 2018)

gained valuable information on tactics, theory and how to create situations to play winning shots, from Keith Walker. After their move to Queensland, Liz sometimes went to the Queensland coach Rita Paulos for further tips. By the time she was 16, she had committed to squash, and in 1983 she became Australian Under 19 Junior Champion when she defeated that year's World Junior Champion Robyn Friday. She was then selected to represent Australia in the Trans-Tasman match against New Zealand, which they won. She also won the New Zealand Championship. In 1984 (aged 19), she managed to defeat Rhonda Thorne, the 1981 World Champion, in a Melbourne tournament and was ranked in the top 15 in Australia. During 1985–87 she was out periodically with a back injury, which wasn't resolved until she was recommended to a Scottish doctor, who fixed the problem without surgery. What a relief! She still managed to win the Dutch, Scottish and Queensland Opens and in 1987 was semi-finalist in both the World and British Open Championships. [122] Fully recovered, she came back with a vengeance and was runner-up in the British Open to Susan Devoy in 1988. She was then ranked no. 2 in the World.

By 1989, Liz had been selected in the Australian Team for the World Championships held in the Netherlands. The team reached the final, losing

2–1 to England. Liz, playing at No.1, went down to the World Champion Martine Le Moignan 3–9, 2–9, 10–8, 4–9. In 1990, Liz represented Australia playing at No.3 and this time she again played Martine and was defeated in 5 hard fought games 9–2, 7–9, 9–7, 3–9, 3–9. Australia was defeated 2–1 by England, however, the tide was about to turn.

In 1991, Liz was defeated by Michelle Martin in the final of the Australian Championships 16–17, 15–12, 15–11, 15–12 in a close tussle. Not long after this Liz started a periodised weight training program, under the direction of Vince Powell from 1992 to 1995 and later, whilst at the AIS with Ian King. She also saw various sports psychologists throughout her career for psychological training. These strategies paid off and Liz was Runner-up in the World Open to Michelle Martin in 1993, Runner-up in the British Open in 1994 and 1995 and No. 2 in the World. She was in the top 5 from 1985–1998. She was a member of the winning Australian team at the World Championships from 1992–1998, winning all her matches between 1992 and 1996 in straight games. Liz was a risk taker and played with a lot of flair. She was a great athlete with a wide array of shots, however on critical points her shot selection often let her down, as she found it hard to play percentage squash. She had the opportunities but couldn't quite reach the elusive No.1 ranking. Still, she had a marvellous career and was in the top 10 from 1985–1998 which was the third longest stretch by any player, male or female.

After Liz finished her international career, she established a coaching school in the Netherlands in 2003–4. One of her pupils, Vanessa Atkinson who she coached from 2000–2004,

Liz with Nicol David—a great team (Photo: Courtesy of PSA World Tour, 2018)

won the World Championship in 2004, defeating Natalie Grinham in 3. Word got around and Nicol David (Malaysia) approached Liz to see if she would coach her. Well, they clicked and Nicol went on to win 8 World titles. Firstly in 2005 and then consecutively from 2008–2012 and 2014. She also won the British Open 5 times in 2005–2006, 2008, 2012 and 2014. Interestingly, Liz helped her psychologically. She felt that Nicol lacked aggression and lacked physicality in the way she played. It certainly worked, as the results speak for themselves.

Liz coached for 20 years in the Netherlands and has demonstrated quite a business acumen. She brought into Amsterdam the first F45 Functional Training Centres which are boutique fitness centres. Also, she has developed a Squash App called Squash Lab Communities, which is being rolled out to Squash Federations and Squash Associations globally. It is currently about to be distributed in Queensland, Northern Territory, South Australia, Victoria and ACT with further states to follow. It is designed to help new players learn to play and to make a connection between coaches and clubs and is very interactive. You can make court bookings, contact coaches, find out what tournaments are on etc. It is the first app of its kind and other sports, for example, cricket, and volleyball are expressing an interest.

She is planning to establish another base in Australia to be closer to family and also to develop her businesses here.

Liz has been an outstanding athlete, who represented Australia over a long period of time. Her induction into Squash Australia's Hall of Fame in 2010 was a fitting reward for her dedication to the game.

PLAYING CAREER

- 1981–2 Queensland Junior Under 19 Champion
- 1981–83 Represented Queensland in the Australian Interstate series
- 1983 Australian Junior Champion
- 1983 Won the NZ Junior Women's Championship

- 1983 Represented Australia in a test series against NZ prior to the WISRF World Junior Championships. Australia won both tests.
- 1983 Won the NZ Junior Women's Championship
- 1983 Represented Australia in the winning (unofficial) World Junior Teams Championships in Perth
- 1985 Ranked no 2 in Australia
- 1986 Queensland Champion
- 1986 Dutch Open Champion
- 1986 Scottish Open Champion
- 1986 Runner-up in the Australian Open to Lisa Opie (UK)
- 1988 Runner-up in British Open to Susan Devoy
- 1988 Ranked no. 2 in the World
- 1991–93 Queensland Champion
- 1991 Irish Open Champion
- 1991 Runner-up in the Australian Open to Michelle Martin
- 1992–1998 Member of the Australian winning team at the World Championships
- 1993 Runner-up in the World Open Championship to Michelle Martin
- 1993–94 Runner-up in the Australian Open to Michelle Martin losing 13–15, 8–15, 5–15
- 1993 Won the Welsh Leekes Classic defeating Martine Le Moignan
- 1993 Runner-up in the Hong Kong, New Zealand and Guernsey Opens
- 1994–95 Runner-up in the British Open Championship to Michelle Martin
- 1995 Runner-up to Lisa Opie in the Australian Open
- 1995 Won the Welsh Leekes Classic defeating Michelle Martin
- 1995 Won the Malaysian Open
- 1994–5 Ranked no. 2 in the World
- 1997 World Mixed Doubles Champion (partner Dan Jensen)
- 1997 Malaysian Open Champion
- 1983–98 Represented Australia (in Junior and Senior Teams) except in 1985–7 when she was out with injury

Awards

- 2011 Inducted into the Squash Australia's Hall of Fame

Administration

- 1992–93 Member of WISPA

Michelle (Susan) Martin OAM

Michelle was born into a very sporting family. She was the fourth of six children and her older brothers, Brett and Rodney also went on to become top professional players. Her parents Dawn and Bob had built the Engadine Squash Centre below their family home and Michelle was introduced to the game of squash when she was three.[123] She often played squash with her family after school and at the age of 8, won the Under 13 NSW Junior Championship.

Her mother, Dawn had been a very handy tennis player and had won an Australian Junior doubles title and was a Junior finalist with John Newcombe in the Mixed Doubles. It was inevitable that Michelle together with her brothers, Rod and Brett, also became A grade tennis players. Asked where the talent came from in her offspring, Dawn replied 'it must have come from us, because

1994 World Champion played in Guernsey
(Photo: PSA World Tour)

they all have it! It's just born in you'[124] It certainly was! Michelle was World Open Champion 1993, 1994 and 1995, British Open Champion 1993–1998 inclusive, Australian Champion 1991, 1993–1996, and 1998–1999. A fantastic record. Her brother, Rodney was World Champion in 1991, Australian Champion 1990, 1992 and 1993, whilst Brett was Australian Champion in 1994 and 1996. All three of them represented Australia in winning teams throughout the 1990's. An amazing family.

Their uncle, Lionel Robberds, who was to take over the role of coaching Michelle, was an Olympic rowing cox and Commonwealth gold medallist. He was also a QC and he took up squash when he no longer had any time for rowing. He was twice runner-up in the Australian Championships (squash) and captained the Australian World Championship Men's team to South Africa, in 1973. He was just the man Michelle needed to have in her corner, to fulfil her potential, but more of this later.

The family moved to Brisbane in 1980 and there Michelle attended Everton Park State High School. She continued playing squash and won the Australian Under 19 Junior Championship in 1985. By now, the Australian Institute of Sport's squash unit had been established and Michelle came under the tutelage of world champions Geoff Hunt and Heather McKay. She worked in the banking industry and began her professional squash career in 1987, touring overseas with other AIS members Sarah Fitz-Gerald and Danielle Drady. They became known as the 'Terrific Trio' and were a breath of fresh air on the Women's scene.[125] She then represented Australia in the first of six World Women's Teams Championships from 1987–1998 (they were held every two years). Initially she played in the No. 2 position in 1990 and 1992 and then she was elevated to no.1 in 1993 and kept that position until 1998. The team was runner-up to England in 1990. Then began an incredible run of consecutive victories for the Australian team from 1992 until 1998 and Michelle played a very important part in these victories. However, I'm getting ahead of myself.

*Commonwealth Games gold medallist
defeating Sarah Fitz-Gerald in 1998*
(Photo: Courtesy of Squash Pics.com 1998)

In 1990, Michelle was considering giving up the sport due to lack of progress. Her World ranking had been steady at no. 6. Then her uncle Lionel Robberds began coaching her, providing her with a rigorous training program of running, gym work and physical drills, which he knew was required to perform at the elite level. Within six months of following this training programme, she was the 1991 Australian Champion. She was to win this title 6 more times from 1993–1996 and again in 1998 and 1999. Her confidence in her game grew and after 2½ years of solid work with Lionel, Michelle was on her way. She was No. 2 in the World behind Susan Devoy. When Susan retired in 1992, Michelle became No.1 in 1993. After a shaky start in her first tournament in Wales as World No1, where she lost to Liz Irving in the final, she settled herself and won the British Open without dropping a game. 'The sleek long striding Martin, ran down balls that would have beaten her before, covered the court with ease, bounced up and down on the T and hit good clean drives. Using the Martin magic, she varied the pace by lobbing and dropping winners, but was always prepared to steady herself when needed. She read her opponents easily and calculated her shots.'[126] Michelle went on to win the British Open five more times from 1994 until 1998.

Her next target after winning her first British Open was the World Open Championship to be played in South Africa. This time she avenged her earlier loss to Liz Irving, winning 9–2, 9–2, 9–1. She won again in 1994, defeating Cassie Jackman of England 9–1, 9–0, 9–6 and again, in 1995, where she defeated the new kid on the block Sarah Fitz-Gerald 8–10, 9–2, 9–6, 9–3. This one of the many highlights of Michelle's career. One of the others, which she stated was the best of them all, was in the inaugural Commonwealth Games in 1998 in Kuala Lumpur. Michelle went on to win two gold Medals. The first was in the singles, when she defeated the top-seeded Sarah Fitz-Gerald 9–0, 9–6, 9–5. This was the very first gold Australia had won in squash, and for Michelle, it was a dream come true! She then combined with Craig Rowland to defeat the top seeds, Simon Parke and Suzanne Horner from the UK 15–4, 15–7. These were the only gold medals won by Australia at this tournament. As her coach and mentor said 'I don't take the credit for one moment. She is the one who has to do it. All I've shown her is how to do it!'

Well do it, she did! It also helped to have her brother, Rodney as a coach and training partner! He helped her win the Singles gold medal at the Commonwealth Games in Kuala Lumpur in 1998. Michelle also credited her successful career to the influence of Heather McKay and Geoff Hunt at the Australian Institute of Sport. 'Without them I would never have had the same opportunities.'[127] Michelle ranked Sarah Fitz-Gerald as her toughest opponent. 'The matches were always tough, both physically and mentally and we both played fast-paced squash and volleyed well. The toughest match against her was in the World Open in Germany in 1998. I was 2–0 down, came back to 2–2 and led 8–2 in the fifth only to lose it. If only the point a rally scoring system was in place, then.'[128]

In 1995, she was inducted into the Squash Australia Hall of Fame. In 2000, Michelle was awarded an Australian Sports medal and in 2001 she was inducted into the Sport Australia Hall of Fame and the Australian Institute of Sport Hall of Fame. In 2013, she was awarded the medal of the Order of Australia (OAM).[129]

She retired in 1999 to become a mum, however she still found time to contribute to squash at the national level. She was Manager/Coach of the Australian Women's Junior teams in 2003 and 2007 and Senior Teams in 2004, 2006, 2008 and 2010 at the World Championships. The Senior teams were World Champions in 2004 and 2010. She was also an Assistant Coach at the Australian Institute of Sport in 2007. Michelle was also a Board member of Squash Australia from 2014–19.

Playing career

- 1985 Australian Under 19 Champion
- 1991 Australian Open Champion
- 1993–96 Australian Open Champion
- 1993–1998 British Open Champion
- 1993–1995 World Open Champion
- 1993–1995 Ranked no. 1 in the World (March 1993–October1996)
- 1996 and 1999 Represented Australia in the Teams' event at the Squash World Cup
- 1998–1999 Ranked no. 1 in the World (November1998–December1999)
- 1998–1999 Australian Open Champion
- 1987, 1990–1998 Represented Australia at the World Teams Championships playing at no. 2 in 1990 and 1992 and no. 1 thereafter. The team won in 1992, 1994, 1996 and 1998.
- 1998 Represented Australia at the Commonwealth Games in Kuala Lumpur. Won gold medal in the Singles and gold medal in the Mixed Doubles, playing with Craig Rowland
- 1998 and 1999 Winner of the World Grand Prix Championship
- 2003–2010 Manager and Coach of Australian Junior and Senior Teams at international events

Awards

- 1993
  - ~ Sportsmen's Association of Australia—Walter Lindrum Award
  - ~ Australian Sports Hall of Fame—Female Athlete of the year
  - ~ Young Achiever of the Year—Sports
  - ~ ABC Sport Australia Award—Best Female Athlete
  - ~ Caltex Queensland Sports Star of the Year
  - ~ NSW Sportswoman Association—Sportswoman of the Year
- 1994
  - ~ NSW Sports Federation—Athlete of the Year
  - ~ NSW Sportswoman Association—Sportswoman of the Year
- 1995
  - ~ Inducted into Sports Hall of Fame NSW—Sporting Achiever Award
  - ~ NSW Sportswoman Association—Sportswoman of the Year
  - ~ Inducted into Squash Australia Hall of Fame
- 1996
  - ~ Dawn Fraser Medal for Outstanding Achievement
- 1998
  - ~ NSW Sports Hall of Champions.
  - ~ Australian Institute of Sport Athlete of the Year (Brisbane unit)
  - ~ Australian Sports Hall of Fame—Best Team
- 1999
  - ~ Australian Institute of Sport Athlete of the Year (Brisbane unit)
- 2000
  - ~ Australian Sports medal
- 2001
  - ~ Inducted into World Squash Federation Hall of Fame
  - ~ Inducted into Sport Australia Hall of Fame
  - ~ Australian Institute of Sport 'Best of the Best'
- 2005
  - ~ Squash Australia Hall of Fame

- 2006
  ~ Australian Institute of Sport's 21st Anniversary—one of the best athletes over the past 21 years
- 2009
  ~ Queensland Hall of Fame
- 2011
  ~ Upgraded to Legend Status in Squash Australia Hall of Fame
- 2013
  ~ Awarded the Order of Australia (OAM) for her services to Squash

On court and off, Michelle has been an exemplary role model for all squash players both in Australia and globally, portraying a wonderful respect for the game. She has been an absolute credit to squash in particular, and sport in general, not only in Australia but wherever squash is played throughout the World. Excellent work!

Danielle Harte (née Drady)

Danielle was born in Sydney and is a Maori Australian from the Ngati Maru tribe. Her mother, Prue Drady migrated to Australia in 1961 from the Watene family, Matai Whetu marae, near Thames on the Coromandel Peninsula on the New Zealand's North Island. She became interested in squash as a young child, when she started tagging along with her mother to her twice weekly social squash gatherings at a local club. In 1978, she won the Queensland Under 12 Championship and in 1981 she was defeated in the final of the Australian Under 13 Championship by her future team-mate, Sarah Fitz-Gerald.[130] Her coach

during this developmental stage, was Bob Parker from Labrador, in Queensland.

Danielle Harte (Drady) in action
(Photo: Courtesy of Gold Coast Hall of Fame,1999)

In 1985, she joined the Australian Institute of Sport under the tutelage of Geoff Hunt and Heather McKay. This further developed her game and as Heather McKay stated, 'at the AIS players learn how to become professional athletes, how to manage themselves as squash players, how to train and prepare for a major tournament and to react mentally'.[131] This experience resulted in her being selected in the Australian Junior team to compete in the World Junior Championships in Ireland in 1985. This proved to be a steep learning curve for her and whilst she did not play so well in the Individual Championship, due to nerves according to Margaret Zachariah's Manager's Report, she made amends in the teams' event and won all of her matches playing at no. 2.

In 1986 Danielle won the Australian Under 19 Championship and in 1987 she turned professional. She became part of the Terrific Trio, along with including Sarah and Michelle, to tour England and she steadily climbed the World rankings from no. 22 to no. 3 in 1990. She was a semi-finalist in the 1989 British Open, runner-up in the 1989 and 1990 Australian Open, runner-up in the 1989 New Zealand Open, runner-up in the Singapore Open and winner of the Canadian Open in 1989. In 1989 she represented Australia at the World teams Championships in the Netherlands. Australia was defeated by England 2–1. Danielle, playing at no. 2, was defeated by Suzanne Horner 5-9, 9-4, 6-9, 9-5, 5-9. Liz Irving had earlier lost in 4 to Martine Le Moignan so again, it was not to be! In the Individual event, Danielle was one of 5 Australians that reached the quarter finals! Only Sarah and Liz went through to the semis.

In 1990, the World Championships were held in Sydney and Australia was in with a good chance. We hadn't won the title since 1983. Danielle was Captain of the team, comprising Robyn Lambourne, Liz Irving and, Michelle Martin. Unfortunately, it wasn't our time and the team lost to England 2–1 in the final with Danielle going down in 4 to Lisa Opie. Michelle won a hard-fought match in 5 against Suzanne Horner and Liz lost in 5 to Martine le Moignan—so close! At this stage of her career, Geoff Hunt described Danielle as a good 'all-rounder, with every facet of her game being sound'.[132] By 1991, she had achieved a World ranking of no. 2 and she had her sights set on the World no. 1 ranking.[133] She flew to England to prepare for the US circuit under Coach Mike Johnson, when disaster struck! The day before leaving for the US she snapped her Achilles tendon in a practice match. The injury required immediate surgery and this ended any chances that she had of obtaining the No1 World Ranking and virtually finished her career.

While Danielle continued to win tournaments, including the Western and South Australian Opens, squash took a back seat after her marriage to Phil Harte, her manager, in 1996. The birth of their daughter Tayla also gave her a different focus in life. She did win the 1998 World Pro-Am, however her playing career was over and between 2010 and 2015 Danielle and Phil established the first squash and fitness academy at the Emirates Golf and Country Club in Dubai. She now spends her time between Sydney, the Gold Coast and Dubai. They run Harte International. She also does freelance photography and contributes to an international lifestyle and travel magazine *Classic Lifestyle*.

Australian representatives at the World Open 1990
Back row: Michelle Martin, Robyn Friday, Liz Irving Front Row: Danielle Drady and Sarah Fitz-Gerald
(Photo: Courtesy of *Squash Australian Annual Report 1991*, p13)

Playing career

- 1978 Queensland Under 11 Champion
- 1981 Runner-up in Australian Under 13 Championship to Sarah Fitz-Gerald
- 1985 Australian representative in the World Junior Championships in Ireland
- 1985 Selected for the AIS training squad
- 1986 Won Australian Under 19 Championships
- 1987 Turned Professional and played on the World Circuit
- 1998 Won NSW Open
- 1989 Sem-finalist in the British Open
- 1989–1990 Runner-up in the Australian Open
- 1989 Runner-up in the New Zealand Open
- 1989 Runner-up in the Singapore Open
- 1989 Won the Canadian Open
- 1989 Represented Australia in the World Teams Championship (Netherlands) England won 2–1
- 1989 Reached Quarter Finals of British Open
- 1990 Captain of the Australian team in the World Championships (Sydney) England won 2–1
- 1991 Ranked no. 2 in the World
- 1991 Ruptured her Achilles, which effectively ended her professional career.
- 1998 Won World Pro-Am Championship
- 1999 Inducted into the Gold Coast Hall of Fame

Sarah Fitz-Gerald (AM)

Sarah was fortunate to have an Australian Squash Champion for a mother! Judith FitzGerald was a pioneer of the Women's game, in the 1950s and won 4 Australian Championships in 1952 and 1956–58. Judith was also one of the few women that travelled overseas to play, reaching the fourth round of the British Open in 1955. Sarah was one of six siblings. There were three boys and three girls in the family and she was the youngest. The sisters played tennis and the boys played football, amongst other sports. 'The family needed a squash player' however she was the only one who seriously pursued a career in squash.[134] She was introduced to the sport at the age of 8 and also enjoyed Netball, Tennis and Gymnastics, where she reached Level 5. Sarah first started entering tournaments in Victoria when she 10, but won her first trophy aged 8 in an in-house event. It didn't take her long to make her mark and she won the Australian Under 13 in 1981 defeating Danielle Drady in the final. She won the Australian Under 15 in 1983, the Australian Under 17 in 1984 as well as the Australian Under 19, in 1984. She was 16 at the time.

On the World stage she started to make her presence felt, being runner-up in the World Junior Championship in 1985 to Lucy Soutter of England and she was a Captain of the winning Australian Junior Team in the inaugural World Junior Teams Championship played in Ireland. This team became a force to be reckoned with in the future. They were Sarah, Danielle Drady, Sally Anne Robbie and Michelle Martin. They defeated England 2–1.[135] Sarah lost to Lucy Soutter 3–0, Danielle defeated Tracey Cunliffe 3–1 Michelle defeated Senga Macfie 3–1. Sally Ann Robbie did not play as she was ill.[136] In 1987 Sarah was ready to commit to a career of playing squash and travelled overseas to play on the circuit and she toured with Danielle Drady and Michelle Martin—the Terrific Trio. It was tough going, and took some time for her to find her way. However, it did start to bring rewards as she won the World Junior Championships in 1987, defeating Donna Vardy of England in straight games.[137] She was also Captain of the Australian Junior Women's Team, which included Amanda Hopps, Angela Johnson and Shannon McNamara. Heather McKay was Manager-Coach. They lost 2–1 to England in the final. In 1989 she reached the semi-finals of the World Individual event being defeated by Martine le Moignan, who went on to win the final, defeating Sue Devoy 4–9, 9–4, 10–8, 10–8. She was learning the ropes and her road to the very top, was about to commence! She turned professional in 1998.[138]

In 1990 the World Championships were held in Sydney. Here was Australia's chance to shine! On this occasion, the members of the Australian team were Danielle Drady, WISPA No. 3, Robyn Lambourne WISPA No. 5, Liz Irving

Sarah—World Champion 1996 in Petaling, Malaysia
(Photo: Courtesy of stuff.co.nz)

WISPA No. 6, Michelle Martin WISPA No. 8 and Sarah Fitz-Gerald WISPA No. 9. Surely, this time we could do it? Australia hadn't won this event since 1983! Vicki Cardwell was the Coach and Margaret Zachariah was the Manager, however, it was not to be. This was another lesson in the school of hard knocks. In the Individuals, Robyn Lambourne lost in 5 in the semi-finals to Martine le Moignan, Sarah lost in 5 to Lisa Opie, runner-up in British Open Champion in 1982–84 and in 1986, a very experienced player. She needed to win this match to be selected to play in the Australian Team, however this match helped her realise that she could compete at the top level. In the Teams event, both teams were plagued by injury and in Australia's case, Robyn Lambourne couldn't play due to a pulled groin muscle. The result was 2–1 in England's favour. Michelle had a great start defeating Suzanne Horner in 5. However, Danielle Drady lost in 4 to Lisa Opie and Liz Irving lost in 5 in a marathon of five hard games. The tide was about to turn and the Aussie Squash Squadron was about to make its mark!

Sarah was a member of the winning Australian team in the World Championships, which had an amazing run from 1992–2002. They won 5 out of a possible 6 times. This has been reported elsewhere, however, the fact that Sarah represented for 12 consecutive years illustrated the consistency and level of commitment of her performance. It took some time for her to emerge from the shadow of her team-mate, Michelle Martin, who dominated the World scene at this time. Michelle was World Open Champion from 1993–1995 and British Open Champion 1993–1998. Sarah was runner-up to her in the World Open in 1995 and the British Open in 1996,1997 and 1998. When I asked Sarah 'What changed that helped you overcome her?' She replied 'I was just really pissed off! I was playing to defend and not to win'. Underlying all of this, was an intensive periodised training programme, which meant fitness wasn't an issue. This included weight training, particularly for her knee , massage 3 times per week, skipping, ghosting, routines, technique sessions 3 times per week and pressure sessions 2–3 times per week. They say a champion leaves no stone unturned. This was certainly the case with Sarah, and it paid off.

She became World Open Champion in 1996 defeating Cassie Jackman of England 9–0, 9–3, 9–4. In 1997 and 1998 she became World Open Champion again, defeating her nemesis, Michelle Martin 9–5, 5–9, 6–9, 9–2, 9–3 in 1997 and 10–8, 9–7, 2–9, 3–9, 10–9 in 1998. It was never going to be easy against Michelle! It would take some time for Sarah to regain the World Title, as she was out with an injured knee , which required surgery in 1999. She did make the semi-finals in 2000, however, and won the World Title in 2001 against Leilani Joyce (NZ) 9–0, 9–3, 9–2. She won again in 2002 against Natalie Pohrer (Grainger) of England 10–8, 9–3, 7–9, 9–7. She also won the British Open in 2001 defeating Carol Owens 10–9, 9–0, 9-2 and again in 2002 defeating Tania Bailey of England 9–3, 9–0, 9–0. Sarah was ranked no. 1 in the World in 1996, 1997, 2001 and 2002. She had certainly emerged from Michelle's shadow.

Sarah also represented Australia at the Commonwealth Games. In Kuala Lumpur in 1998 she was a silver medallist to Michelle Martin in the Individual event. She also won a bronze medal in the Women's Doubles with Carol Owens. It was after these Games that Sarah suffered a meniscus tear and underwent knee surgery in December, 1998 and May, 1999. However, you can't keep a good girl down! She recovered (see other results) and in 2001–2002 she was British, Australian and World Champion and she won the gold medal at the 2002 Commonwealth Games in Manchester defeating

Carol Owens, who was now playing for New Zealand, in the final. She retired from squash in 2003 following a stellar career!

During her career, Sarah also had problems with a sway back, which often gave her trouble. However, with the help of Geoff Mackay, an Australian physiotherapist who also worked with the Australian cricket team, the Australian Davis Cup team and the Carlton Football Club team, she managed to continue with her squash career.

As with most players, there are many people who contribute to their success. Sarah's case was no exception. She attributes coaching, by first of all her mother, Judy, then Bruce Alexander, Victorian State Coach, Roger Flynn VIS Coach, Geoff Hunt and Heather McKay at the AIS, Mike Johnson, coach for 15 years at her English base in Caversham in Reading, the legendary Jonah Barrington, Malcolm Willstrop, from Pontefract, Yorkshire and Mike Way, based in Canada but from Nottingham UK, all played a role. Mike Walton was her Manager in the UK, which took away some of the pressure, whilst Greg Hutchings handled the Australian contracts. A Sports psychologist, Ken Way, brother of Mike Way, from Leicester Football Club, also helped her overcome her early lack of ambition and helped her establish her goals. Initially, she was happy to be in the top 10 with no definitive self-belief or goals.[139] This attitude certainly changed and helped her reach the top of the Women's Squash

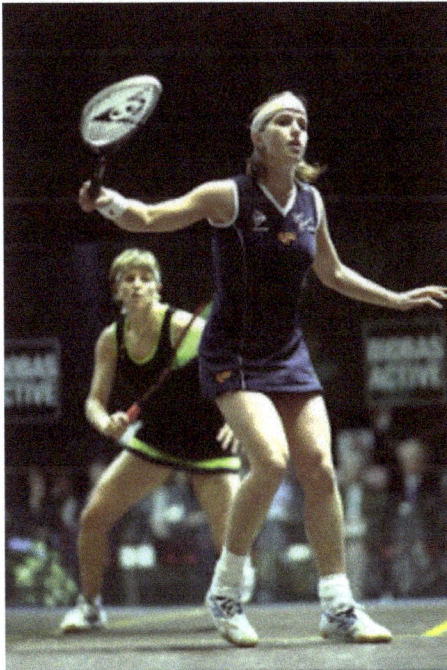

Sarah defeating Carol Owens in the 2001 British Open final
(Photo: Courtesy of Squash Pics, 2013)

World. Sarah also believes that her 'hard work, dedication, ability to volley and her tenacity, helped her to be one of the upper echelons of the sport'. She knew what it took to reach the top. She was President of WISPA from 1991–2002, though technically she was Chairman for the first few years before the title changed to President.[140] Eventually, she left this position in 2002, as she was no longer on tour and WISPA couldn't afford to fly her around the World to fulfil her duties. Initially, Natalie Grainger took over this position. Andrew Shelley moved from England Squash and became CEO from 1994–2010. He ran the office and this took the pressure off the players having to run the Association.

Sarah was fortunate to be in an era where top women squash players could support themselves financially whilst on tour, a far cry from when Heather McKay won a thermos flask for winning the British Open! This has only come about through the players themselves raising sponsorship. In Sarah's case this has included Dunlop, Hi-Tec Rackets and shoes, Qantas, and over the years, Mazda, Festo Pneumatic Control, Green Magic, a power drink, Squashdiscount.com, Squash Design (clothing) and E squash (strings). These sponsorships would earn her more than $US100,000. Also, through the formation of the Women's International Squash Players' Association (WISPA) the international tour was developed. There was increased prize money, contracts were developed and the tournaments themselves, were run more efficiently. This, together with support from the AIS and VIS gave Sarah the financial security to achieve her full potential.

Since her retirement, in 2003 she has moved into court construction with her husband, Cameron Dalley who is a builder. They met through Masters' squash and could see the opportunity to build new courts due to the tiredness of existing squash complexes. The standards of the courts overseas were far superior to those in Australia. She has also been active in the administration of squash. She has served on the Board of Squash Australia from 2007–2009 and has also been the Vice-President of the World Squash Federation since November 2016. She is currently President of Squash and Racquetball Victoria, having been elected in April 2020 after being Vice-President in 2019.

Playing career

- 1981 Won the Australian Under 13 Championship defeating Danielle Drady in the final.
- 1983 won the Australian Under 15 Championship
- 1984 won the Australian Under 17 Championship
- 1984 won the Australian Under 19 Championship
- 1985 Runner-up in the World Junior Championship
- 1985 Captain of the winning Australian Junior Team in the inaugural World Junior Teams Championship
- 1987 Won the World Junior Championships
- 1987 Captain of the Australian Junior Women's Team at the World Championships. England won 2–1
- 1987 Selected for the Australian Senior Women's team for the World Teams' Championships. England won 2–1. Sarah playing at no. 3 Lost to her nemesis Lucy Soutter 3–0
- 1989 Reached semi-finals of the World Championships. Defeated by Martine Le Moignan (the eventual winner).
- 1990 Semi-finalist in the World Championships (Sydney). Defeated by Lisa Opie (no. 2) in 5 close games
- 1992 Selected for the Australian Senior Women's team for the World Championships. Australia won 2–1. This was the first time that they had won since 1983 and there were many more to come!
- 1994–2002 Selected for the Australian Senior Women's team for the World Championships. Australia won 5 World Championships over this period and was runner-up to England only once—in 2000.
- 1995 Runner-up to Michelle Martin in the British Open
- 1996 Selected for the Australian Senior Women's team for the World Championships. Sarah was now number 2 in the team behind Michelle, Liz was no. 3 Australia won 3–0
- 1996–98 won World Open Championship
- 1996–7 Ranked no. 1 in the World

- 1996–98 Runner-up to Michelle Martin in the British Open
- 1997 Australian Open Champion
- 1998 Represented Australia in the Commonwealth Games in Kuala Lumpur—silver medallist in the Individual Championship. Bronze medallist with Carol Owens in the Women's Doubles
- 2001–2003 Australian Open Champion
- 2001–2002 World Open Champion
- 2001–2002 British Open Champion
- 2001–2002 Ranked no. 1 in the World
- 2002 Represented Australia in the Commonwealth Games in Manchester (UK)—gold medallist in the Individual
- 2002 World Cup gold Medallist
- 2005–6 World Master's Over 35 Champion
- 2010 Selected for the Australian Senior Women's team for the World Championships. Australia won 2–1 against England. Playing at no. 3 and with the PARS scoring system Sarah won 3–0. An amazing effort.

Overall, Sarah represented Australia over 80 times, including doubles, World Cup and the test series with England, won 65 WISPA tournaments and 94 finals appearances, was World Champion 5 times and British Open Champion 2 times. She ranks up there with Heather McKay, Michelle Martin, Vicki Cardwell, Rhonda Thorne and Rachael Grinham, as the best players Australia has ever produced. Amazing!

Awards

- 1985 Australian Junior Female Team of the Year
- 1987 Australian Sport Australia Junior Female Athlete of the Year
- 1998 VIS Athlete of the Year
- 2001 Australian Female Athlete of the Year
- 2001 Dawn Fraser Australian Athlete of the Year (she was ahead of Lleyton Hewitt and Ian Thorpe)
- 2002 VIS Athlete of the Year

- 2002 Victorian Sportswoman of the Year
- 2002 Victorian Sportsperson of the Year
- 2004 Member of the Order of Australia (AM)
- 2005 Inducted into Squash Australia Hall of Fame
- 2010 Inducted into Sport Australia Hall of Fame
- 2012 Squash Australia Hall of Fame (Legend)

What hasn't been mentioned above, is the outstanding contribution Sarah has made firstly, in her role as President of WISPA, where she worked tirelessly to develop interest in the game amongst women and girls in underdeveloped countries. Sarah has spent unpaid time in leading promotional tours into these countries and throughout the world. She has been an outstanding ambassador for the sport and for Australia on the world sporting stage as well as an excellent role model for women.[141] She is continuing to contribute to the game in her role as President of S&RV.

Carol Owens

Carol was born in Melbourne and started playing squash at the age of 12. She was fortunate in that her first coach was a good one. None other than Judith FitzGerald. She considered her to be 'a fantastic mentor and technical coach, who was instrumental in all her future success'. Judith also recommended that she should have coaching with Gary Macintosh to work on her tactics and match play. She did this for several years, before taking up a scholarship at the AIS in Brisbane in 1988, where she came under the tutelage of Heather McKay and Geoff Hunt. She stayed at the AIS for two years before returning to Melbourne when the Victorian Institute of Sport was formed and headed by Gary Macintosh. In 1989, she had played in the World Junior Championship in New Zealand, where she had been seeded 6th but finished up in 3rd place—a sign of things to come! She was also a member of the Australian Junior Team, at these Championships, where they lost to England in the final. The team members were Robyn Cooper, Carol, Angela Rolfe and Marianne McDonald. She won the Under 19 Australian Junior Championships, in 1990.

Carol playing Michelle Martin in the 1999 Grand Prix Finals in Hurghada, Egypt.
Michelle won this match 9–4, 9–7, 2–9, 9–4.
(Photo: *Bunbury Herald*, 23-8-21)

She then travelled overseas and started competing as a full time professional on the World Circuit. She made her competitive debut at the Swiss Open, where she finished 17th.[142] Her first final was in 1993 in the Japan Open, where she was runner-up to the Canadian Heather Wallace. Her first major victory came in October in Adelaide in the Brahma Lodge WISPA tournament where she beat Sharon Bradey in 5. She later won the South Australian Open, also a WISPA event where she defeated Leilani Marsh (née Joyce) in 4.

In 1994 she was selected in the Australian team to compete at the World Championships in Guernsey in the UK. The team comprised Michelle Martin, Sarah Fitz-Gerald, Elizabeth Irving, Carol, and Di Davis was the Coach-Manager. They defeated England in the final (see results). Carol gained valuable experience from this trip even though she didn't play in the final. This win was part of a dominance that Australia had attained which lasted for 6–7 of the World Championships, from 1992 until 2004 only losing to England in 2000 which has been outlined earlier. Carol was part of the winning teams in 1996 and 1998, winning her rubber 3–0 playing at No. 2 in

World Women's Champion 2003
(Photo: Courtesy of blog.sport.com, 2003)

1998. She also won a bronze medal in the Commonwealth Games that year, playing with Sarah Fitz-Gerald. Unfortunately, she developed a tachycardia heart condition, which was successfully repaired by ablation surgery and she was able to continue her career.

Carol won her first World title in 2000, however it wasn't easy. She defeated Tania Bailey of England in the Quarter Finals and she had to face Sarah Fitz-Gerald in the semi-finals. She started off brilliantly and raced to a 2–0 lead, when suddenly self-doubt crept into her game. She then lost the next two, however she somehow pulled herself together and won the final game 9–6. Carol was now into the final against New Zealander Leilani Joyce, who had won the British Open the previous year. In another epic battle she came from behind again 7–9, 3–9, 10–8, 9–6, 9–1. She was now World Champion. In 1999 she had decided to take up permanent residency in New Zealand, as she had bought a house there. In 2002, now representing New Zealand, she won a silver medal in the singles and a gold medal in the doubles in the 2001 Commonwealth Games in Manchester.

In March 2003 she won another World Championship, this time playing for New Zealand, defeating Cassie Jackman of England 3–9, 9–2, 9–7, 9–3 in the final. She was now no. 1 in the world. She had been playing the circuit for 10 years and had been in the top 10 since July 1993 and was now 32 years of age.[143] Carol decided to retire while she was on top. In the last year she had travelled to Kuala Lumpur and New York in February, Texas in March, Egypt in June, Britain and New York in October and Qatar and Hong Kong in December. In between these trips, there had been travel to and from New Zealand. It was a time to hang up the racket.

Martin Bronstein's article summed her up brilliantly. 'Squash will sorely miss her presence; she brought a unique style and athleticism to the game. In full flow she made everything look so effortless and no other player could produce such perfect crosscourt lobs and use them so well. Here was a player who had a unique game, one of superb lobs, inch perfect volley drops and tight, tight drives. She had the fitness, she understood tactics and she moved as though on ice and we, in the Press room, will miss her spiky, joke-filled repartee!' If there was a weakness, it was in her own self-doubt. Fortunately, she managed to overcome this sufficiently to win two 2 World Championships representing two countries in the process.

*Unfortunately, in 2000, there had been some dissent between the top players Carol Owens, Liz Irving and Rachael Grinham and Squash Australia, which resulted in these players making themselves unavailable to represent Australia at the World Teams Championships that year. This definitely weakened our team and it is a shame that, too often in sport, administrators and players don't see eye to eye. To be an elite player takes an enormous amount of effort and self-sacrifice. There are rewards of course, however whilst administrators reflect in the glory achieved by the players, their position and requests are often not taken into account when decisions are made. A middle ground needs to be taken. It is not the purpose of this book to go into the politics of sport, just that this point needs to be duly noted.

Playing career

- 1984
  - ~ Runner-up in the Victorian Under 13 Championships
- 1985
  - ~ Winner in the Victorian Under 15 Championships
- 1985
  - ~ Semi-finalist in the Australian Under 15 Championships
- 1986
  - ~ Runner-up in the Victorian Under 15 Championships
  - ~ Runner-up in the Australian Under 15 Championships.
  - ~ Represented Victoria in the Australian Interstate series
- 1987
  - ~ Winner of the Victorian Under 17 Championships
  - ~ Represented Victoria in the Interstate series at the Australian Championships at No.1 in the Under 19 event She was 16 at the time. Captain of the team.
- 1988
  - ~ Won a scholarship to the Australian Institute of Sport in Brisbane.
  - ~ Semi-finalist in Australian Under 17 Championship. Captain of the winning Under 17 team
  - ~ Runner-up in the Queensland Under 19 Championship
  - ~ Runner-up in the Australian Under 19 Championship
  - ~ Captain of the Victorian Under 19 team at The Interstate series in Brisbane
  - ~ Runner-up in the Victorian Under 19 Championship
- 1989
  - ~ Winner of the Victorian Under 19 Championship
  - ~ Selected as to play as no. 2 to play in the Australian Junior Team to play in the World Junior Championships in New Zealand. Lost only one match in the teams' series. Australia finished runners-up to the defending Champions, England. In her singles matches she reached the semi-finals defeating the no. 2 seed Sabine Schone (Germany),

in the semi-finals. She defeated Robyn Cooper (Australia) in the playoff for 3rd.

- 1990
  ~ Winner of the Victorian Under 19 Championship
  ~ Winner of the Australian Under 19 Championship
  ~ Captain of the winning Victorian Under 19 team. Played at no. 1.
  ~ Joined WISPA (Women's International Squash Players' Association). Ranking No 46 (Nov)
- 1991
  ~ Semi-finalist in ACT Open Championships
  ~ Semi-finalist at Victorian Open
- 1992
  ~ Little success on the international Circuit
- 1993
  ~ Winner Japan Open. Starting to make her mark. Second Round defeated Lisa Opie (British Open winner 1991) in 5 hard fought games. In the quarter finals, she defeated Liz Irving (Australian Team representative 1989, 1990, 1992) in 5. In the semi-finals she lost to Michelle Martin (Australian Team representative 1990, 1992) in 4.
  ~ In the Hong Kong Open she defeated Sarah Fitz-Gerald (Australian representative 1992) in 4, 9–7, 9–7, 5–9, 9–7.
- 1994
  ~ Member of Australian winning team at the World Team Championships held in Guernsey
- 1996
  ~ Member of Australian winning team at the World Teams Championship held in Malaysia
- 1998
  ~ Member of Australian Winning team at the World Teams Championships held in Germany She played in the no. 2 position and won her rubber 3–0

- 1998
  ~ Won bronze in the Women's Doubles with Sarah Fitz-Gerald at the Commonwealth Games held in Kuala Lumpur
- 1999
  ~ Runner-up ion the Grand Prix Finals to Michelle Martin in Hurghada, Egypt.
- 2000
  ~ World Champion defeated Leilani Joyce 9–6, 9–5, 7–9, 5–9, 9–6
  ~ Gold medal in the Singles
- 2001
  ~ New Zealand Champion*
  ~ Runner-up in the British Open to Sarah Fitz-Gerald losing 9–10, 0–9, 2–9 *
  ~ Bronze in the World Women's Singles played in Melbourne*
- 2002
  ~ Silver in the Commonwealth Games played in Manchester*
  ~ Gold in the Women's Doubles (Leilani Joyce) played in Manchester*
  ~ Bronze in the World Championships Singles played in Doha*
  ~ Ranked no. 1 in the World (November)
- 2003
  ~ World Champion defeated Cassie Jackman of England 3–9, 9–2, 9–7, 9–3*
  * Played for New Zealand

In addition, Carol Won 21 WISPA titles during her career

Awards

- 1988 Won Certificate of Outstanding Achievement at Australian Sports Awards.
- 2010 Inducted into the New Zealand Hall of Fame

Since retiring, Carol has 'enjoyed great success at Eden Epsom Tennis and Squash Club in Auckland New Zealand'.[144] These were the courts where Paul Wright had coached her to success. 'Coaching the Judy Fitz way, I really enjoy teaching technically. I'm proud to have produced players that have amassed 27 National Junior titles. Six players have represented New Zealand and two players have completed full squash-degree scholarships at Drexel University. I worked full time for Head rackets for six years and Eager for Leisure selling swim products for six years. Squash Coaching started for me full-time at the end of 2017'.

She has now been in New Zealand for 27 years and she will always credit her beginnings and love for the game to Judith FitzGerald, Gary Macintosh and her coach, in New Zealand, Paul Wright. Although her life took her to New Zealand, she will always feel a strong connection to Australia.

Rachael Grinham

Rachael was the next in line to assume the mantle of British Open Champion in 2003, 2004, 2007 and 2009, and World Champion in 2007 after Michelle and Sarah had finished their playing careers. She is the last one to have achieved the No.1 World ranking in 2004–2005. How did Australia keep on producing these Champions? Well, home environment had a lot to do with it!

Rachael was born in Toowoomba, Queensland to squash playing parents Davina and John. You could say her playing career began at the age of 2 when she, and later her sister Natalie, were locked into a squash court at Willows Squash Centre, as cheap babysitting arrangements, and they would chase balls for hours, whilst their parents played. They certainly were introduced to the game early![145]

In terms of competition, she entered her first junior competition at the age of 7 and finished runner-up to Janine Hickey, who later became a top 30 player in the World. Janine was aged 11 at the time. Rachael's first major Junior victory was when she was only 9 years of age at the Queensland Under 11 Junior Age Championships. At 10 she won the Australian Under 13 Junior Age Championship in 1987. This achievement was repeated in 1988. In 1989 she won the Australian Under 15 Championship when she was 12! Rachael lost a bit of interest after that and it wasn't until 1993 at the age of 16 when she won the World Junior Championship in Malaysia, that she decided to make a career out of squash as she had no intention of going to university. Rachael was runner-up in the World Junior Championship in 1995 and led the Australian Junior Women's team to two World Championships in 1993 and 1995.

Her parents and Noel Ziebell from Toowoomba had been the greatest influence up to this point, as well as her sister Natalie, as they were great rivals. The AIS Squash Unit, with Heather McKay and Geoff Hunt, also played a part, however Rachael was very much her own person and she was to determine her own path.

Since joining the WISPA World tour during 1994, her array of strokes and strong temperament initially took her steadily towards the top 20, a barrier she breached in 1997.[146] This rise hadn't been without its down sides, as she had to overcome anterior compartment syndrome during 1996 and 97. Once this was resolved, however, she was on her way! She won her first tournament in 1998, when she was 21 years old, beating Tracey Shenton in the Open Toulouse Central in France.1998 saw her represent Australia at the first Commonwealth Games squash competition in in Kuala Lumpur. She partnered with Robyn Cooper to win a silver medal in the Women's Doubles. She was now 21 and was starting to make her mark. Little did she know what was to come! She left Australia and based herself in Amsterdam, which proved to be a turning point.

In 1999 she won the Swiss Open, the Germering Open and the Indian Open and ended the year ranked No18. In 2000, she climbed 6 places to no. 12, defeating World No1 Nicol David in the final of the Milo National Open. Nicol was 5 years younger than Rachael at this tournament and was still developing into the dominant player that she was to become. She defeated Salma Shabana, sister of the then current World no. 1 male player Amr Shabana, in the final of the Indian Open. She climbed a further 4 places in 2001 to World no. 8. A family final occurred at a WISPA World tour event in Malaysia in February 2001 when she beat sister Natalie in the final. Later that year she beat Nicol David for the DMC title.[147]

Rachael now decided on another change, as her game wasn't improving to the level that was required to reach her potential. This time the move was to Egypt! She found Europe to be too expensive and, when the opportunity came to share an apartment with a friend in Cairo and spend time training in Egypt, she grabbed it with both hands. She only expected it to be a temporary arrangement, but it ended up turning into a permanent base for 8 years. She was paid to play in their competitions, had excellent training partners and was also free to play in numerous tournaments all over Europe. In addition, she was being coached by a good friend, a recently retired Egyptian Women's Professional player with a World top ranking of 18, Maha Zein. Her game took off, as a result.

Initially, 2002 didn't go so well, however as she settled in, results started to come. She defeated Tania Bailey to win the Singapore Open. A month later she won the prestigious Credit Suisse Privilege Ladies Open, one of the finest squash tournaments in the World. She defeated Natalie Grainger of the USA in the final. With her sister Natalie she won a bronze medal at the Commonwealth Games in the doubles and won a bronze medal in the singles. She climbed to no. 6 in the world by the end of 2002. In addition, she was part of the Australian team that won the World Women's Teams event. Now things really started to happen! At the beginning of 2003, she won the Vassar College Class of 32 defeating Vicky Botwright of the UK. She was runner-up in Egypt to World no. 1, Australian Carol Owens. Then she won the British Open, where she defeated the top seed Carol Owens in the semi-finals, a major upset, before defeating Cassie Jackman of the UK 9–3, 7–9, 9–2, 9–5 in the final. She was now British Open Champion! At the end of 2003 she was ranked no. 3 in the World.

2004 proved to be one of the best years of Rachael's career. The base in Cairo had done wonders for her game and her tenaciousness and speed around the court resulted in her achieving the no. 1 World ranking. En route she won the Kuwait Open, the richest squash event in the world, by beating the top seed, Cassie Jackman. Later, she defeated the then world no. 1 Cassie again for the Texas Open. This particular match was the result that took her to the no. 1 world ranking for the first time. Three months later she won the Hurghada International in Egypt defeating local favourite Omneya, Abdel Kawy. She was runner-up to Vanessa Atkinson in the Brunei International and defeated Cassie again to win the Bahrein Classic Title. To cap the year off, she defended her British Open title defeating Natalie Grainger 6–9, 9–5, 9–0, 9–3. At the World Doubles Championships, she won the World Women's Doubles title with her sister Natalie and the Mixed doubles, partnered by David Palmer. She ended the year ranked no. 1 in the World. However, nothing comes easily, as Rachael was about to find out!

2005 saw her lose her no. 1 ranking, finishing the year at no. 2. This was the result of her losing the British Open crown, by being defeated by rising superstar, Nicol David, in the semi-finals and her loss at the World Championships to Nicol as well. She still won numerous titles including the Qatar Challenge, the Hurghada International final, a 5 game thriller, and the PMI Women's Open title defeating her old rival, Vanessa Atkinson of the Netherlands, in the final. Finally, she was runner-up to Nicol David in the final of the World Championships 8–10, 9–2, 9–6, 9–7 played in Hong Kong.

Rachael certainly had her challengers in 2006, as Nicol David of Malaysia was on the rise and Vanessa Atkinson, was still hanging on! Subsequently she was pushed down to no. 3 in the rankings.

Rachael and Natalie battling it out in the 2007 World Championship final, which Rachael won 9–4, 10–8, 9–2 (Photo: *Squash Australia Annual Report 2007*, p25)

There were other prizes to be won, however, and the Commonwealth Games in Melbourne was one of them. She won silver in the singles (being runner-up to Natalie) and then teamed up with her sister Natalie, to win gold in the Women's Doubles. She also picked up a bronze with David Palmer in the Mixed Doubles. This was a far cry from the rewards that the Grinham girls received at their local squash centre which they used to ride to on their bikes. Noel Ziebell, the court owner, is to be commended for encouraging the sisters by providing free court hire, rackets, lollipops and money for video games. From little things big things grow.

At the World Doubles Squash Championships Rachael won the Mixed Doubles with Joseph Kneipp. In singles, she had met her match in Nicol David and she lost 4 tournaments to her the final of the Qatar Challenge, the semis of the CIMB Malaysian Open, the final of the Hotel Equatorial Penang Open and the semi-final of the British Open. She did manage to salvage a win for the year when she won the Weymuller US Open defeating Natalie Grainger. Unfortunately, Nicol was still in her way and she lost to her in the semis of the CPS Hong Kong Open and the World Open. Was there any more to come?

Rachael holding the World Championship trophy. Natalie was the Runner-up.
(Photo: Courtesy of PSA World Tour, 2007)

In 2007, Rachael won five titles: the Hurghada International and the Alexandria Sporting Club Open in Egypt, the Vassar College of 32 Open in the United States, the British Open, where she defeated Nicol David in a cliff hanger 7–9, 4–9, 9–3, 10–8, 9–1 in one hour & twenty-seven minutes! This was followed by the World Open in Spain, where she defeated her sister Natalie 9–4, 10–8, 9–2, in the final. Rachael was now 30 and there were many younger players coming through which was making her life more difficult. But she wasn't finished yet.

2008 She continued to play; however, it wasn't until 2009 before she won another major Championship, the British Open, defeating Madeline Perry of Northern Ireland 11–6, 11–5, 12–10, making it four in total. Note that in this Championship the scoring system had changed to a point a rally which removed some of the endurance factors of the game and favoured the shot maker.

Rachael was ranked in the top 5 in the World in 2010 even though she had time out with injury. She was also a member of the winning Australian team at the World Teams' Championships held in New Zealand. This team comprised Kasey Brown, Sarah Fitz-Gerald Rachael and Donna Urquhart with Michelle Martin as Coach/Manager. She has still continued to represent Australia post 2010. From a training perspective, Rachael spent 70% of her time on court with 30% in off court training activities. She only lifted light weights, preferred running stairs to running around an oval or skipping. She also included swimming in her fitness regime for aerobic fitness together with a strict stretching routine. She owes her longevity in the sport, to her light frame and a sports specific training regime, together with good technique and a sound tactical nous.

Unlike other players that have been mentioned earlier, Rachael has not been inducted into Squash Australia's Hall of Fame. Nor has her sister Natalie. This oversight is probably because they have spent so much of their playing career living overseas to enhance their performance and in Rachael's case, she is still playing competitively. This omission should be duly corrected as they have been very worthy members of the Australian Women's Squash players' sporting achievements on the international stage. Let's hope that this happens sooner rather than later.

Playing career

- 1986 Queensland Under 11 Junior Age Champion
- 1987–88 Australian Under 13 Champion
- 1989 Australian Under 15 Champion
- 1993 World Junior Champion
- 1993 and 1995 led the Australian Junior Women's team to two World Championships
- 1995 Runner-up in the World Junior Championships
- 1998 Represented Australia in Australian Team at the Commonwealth Games in Kuala Lumpur winning a silver medal with Robyn Cooper in the Women's Doubles
- 1998 Won her first WISPA Tournament the Open Toulouse Open in France
- 1999 Won the Swiss Open, Germering Open and the Indian Open
- 2000 Defended her Indian Open and defeated Nicol David in the Milo National Open
- 2002 Member of the Australian winning Team at the World Championships in Odense
- 2002 Represented Australia at the Commonwealth Games in Manchester winning a bronze medal in the singles and a bronze, with her sister Natalie, in the Women's Doubles
- 2002 Won the Singapore Open and the Credit Suisse Privilege Ladies Open
- 2003–4 British Open Champion
- 2004 Winner of the World Doubles Open Championship, with her sister Natalie, and the World Mixed Doubles, with David Palmer
- 2004 Achieved World no. 1 ranking. (Held this from August 2004, until November, 2005)
- 2004 Member of the Winning Australian team at the World Championships in Amsterdam
- 2004 Won the Kuwait Open, the Texas Open, the Hurghada Open and the Bahrein Classic Open

- 2005 Australian Open Champion
- 2005 Won the Qatar Challenge and defended her Hurghada title
- 2005 Runner-up in the World Championship to Nicol David
- 2006 Runner-up to Natalie in the Singles at the Commonwealth Games in Melbourne. Won gold with Natalie in the Women's Doubles and bronze with David Palmer in the Mixed Doubles
- 2006 Won the World Doubles Mixed Championship with Joseph Kneipp
- 2007 British Open Champion defeating Nicol David in 5
- 2007 World Open Champion defeating Natalie in the final
- 2007 Won the Hurghada International, the Alexandria Sporting Club Championship (in Egypt) and the Vassar Class of 1932 in the US
- 2009 British Open Champion
- 2010 Member of winning Australian team at the World Championships in New Zealand

Please note I have not listed all the tournaments won by Rachael here, as they were too numerous and have been mentioned elsewhere. The above were the most prestigious. In addition, I would be remiss, if I didn't list Rachael's achievements post 2010, which is outside the dates I set for this book, the last time Australia won the World Women's Team's event or the World Women's Singles event).

- 2014 gold medal in Commonwealth Games (Glasgow) Mixed Doubles with David Palmer
- 2018 bronze medal in Commonwealth Games Women's Doubles (Gold Coast) with Donna Urquhart
- 1998–2018 Competed in every Commonwealth Games (with the exclusion of Delhi) and medalled every time.
- 2022 Joint Australian flag bearer with Eddie Ockenden (Hockey) for the Commonwealth Games (Birmingham, UK).

To date Rachael is the most decorated Commonwealth Games Female Squash Player of all time.

Natalie Grinham

The younger sister of Rachael, she was also born in Toowoomba and her upbringing was much the same as Rachael. Squash was the centre of their lives. It didn't take her long to win her first Australian Junior Championship. She won the Under 13 in 1990 and by 1995 she had turned professional at 17 years of age. She won the Australian Under 19 in 1997. Natalie also won the MC Hazell Award in 1997 as the best and fairest player of the tournament. She moved to the Netherlands in 1999. At this stage she was very much in Rachael's shadow, however she was selected to represent Australia for the World Championships in the winning teams in 2000, 2002*, and 2004*. She also represented Australia in 2002 in the Commonwealth Games, in Manchester of England, where she won a bronze medal playing with her sister, Rachael. This was a good year as she also won the Australian Women's Open Championship and was runner-up to Vanessa Atkinson of the Netherlands in the World Open Squash Championships 9–1, 9–1, 9–5. There was more to come! In 2005, she was runner-up to Nicol David in the British Open, losing 9–4, 9–1, 9–4 and her highlight year would have to be 2006, where she won gold medals in three events at the Commonwealth Games held in Melbourne, the only player in ANY sport to do so. She defeated Nicol David in the semi-finals and went on to defeat Rachael 2–9, 9–6, 9–1, 9–6 in the

final They combined to win in the Women's Doubles and then she partnered Joseph Kniepp to win the Mixed Doubles.[148] An outstanding performance.

Natalie hadn't finished yet! In 2006 she also reached the final of the World

Natalie and her three gold medals won at the Commonwealth Games, in Melbourne in 2006. (Photo: Courtesy of Rachel Grinham)

Natalie playing in the World Championship Final in Ireland against Nicol David in 2006.
She was defeated in a marathon five game match.
(Photo: Courtesy of Getty Images)

Championships played in Northern Ireland, going down in a marathon to Nicol David 1–9, 9–7, 3–9, 9–5, 9–2. This match was rated as one of the greatest in the World Women's Open history.[149] In 2007, she was runner-up in the World Open again, this time to her sister, Rachael, losing 9–4, 10–8, 9–2. By this time, she was ranked no. 2 in the World—a fine achievement. She reached another World Open final, in 2009, losing 3–11, 11–6, 11–3, 11–8 to Nicol David under the PARS scoring system.

Natalie married a Dutch Squash player Tommy Berden in 1999 and has lived in the Netherlands since. She became a Dutch citizen in February 2008. She last represented Australia at the Commonwealth Games in 2006 and according to the World Squash Federation rules, she had to wait three years before becoming eligible to represent a different country. She then represented the Netherlands for several years from 2009. Natalie gave birth to her first son, Kieran in May, 2010 and made a quick recovery winning the Women's Atwater Cup in Canada. She retired from competitive squash in 2014. She had played in an era where her sister Rachael and Nicol David had been the dominant players. At 5ft 1in she had certainly punched above her weight!

Playing career

- 1990 Australian Under 13 Champion
- 1997 Australian Under 19 Champion
- 2000 Represented Australia in the World Teams Championship in England. England won 2–1
- 2002 Represented Australia in the World Teams Championship in Denmark. Australia won 2–1
- 2002 Represented Australia in the Commonwealth Games in Manchester winning a bronze medal with her sister Rachael, in the Women's Doubles
- 2004 Represented Australia in the World Teams Championship in the Netherlands. Australia won 2–1
- 2004 Australian Open Champion
- 2004 Runner-up to Vanessa Atkinson in the World Open Championship final
- 2005 Runner-up to Nicol David in the British Open final
- 2006 Represented Australia in the Commonwealth Games in Melbourne. Won three gold medals in the Singles, Doubles (with Rachael) and Mixed (with Joseph Kniepp)
- 2006 Runner-up to Nicol David in the World Championship played in Northern Ireland
- 2007 Runner-up in the World Championship to her sister, Rachael
- 2007 Ranked no. 2 in the World
- 2009 Runner-up to Nicol David in the World Championships in the Netherlands
- 2010 Won the Women's Atwater Cup in Canada

10 Unsung Heroes

Beverley Gould (1936–2019)

Beverley was born in New Zealand in 1936. Before she came to Sydney, Beverley had been heavily involved in Sports Administration. She had

Bev Gould

served on various committees in Softball, Table Tennis and Basketball and she had 'enjoyed spectacular success in raising funds for the building of the celebrated Walter Nash Sports Stadium', named after one of their Prime Ministers. Whilst her husband hoped that the move would lessen her involvement in Squash, she became more involved than ever! (Squash Review) She believed that 'I'm not a woman in business, but a person capable of doing the job'! She quickly became involved in administration and 'took great pleasure in seeing the juniors running around with bright happy faces, unconcerned with the standard of their play, but just happy to be involved'. Her pleasure came from coaching, refereeing and administration.[150] She served in the following positions:

- 1978 Formed the NSW Junior Association
- 1978–82 President of the NSW Women's Squash Rackets Association
- 1979–82 Manager Thornleigh Squash Centre
- 1984 Executive Member SRAA
- 1983–86 Secretary NSW Women's SRA
- Delegate on the Australian Women's Association for NSW and W.A.
- Manager of Thornleigh Squash Centre
- Delegate to represent Australian Women's Association at the Men's SRA of NSW
- Developed the inaugural Saturday morning Junior Mixed Teams' Competitions. This initially consisted of 7 districts, 187 teams and 820 players and soon grew

In her role as the first Manager of Thornleigh Squash Centre, when it opened in 1979, she was responsible for making it a viable proposition. In the first year, Thornleigh lost just $1500. Beverley was not happy! The second year it broke even and in the third year it made a good profit. This was due to Beverley's business acumen and attention to detail.

As Secretary of the NSW Women's SRA, she was responsible for receiving monies and entries from Clubs for the various pennant competitions entries each season. If Beverley felt that Clubs should have submitted more teams, or if they dared to submit fewer teams than the previous season, Beverley would soon be on the phone. Eventually, those extra teams came in! Nobody said no to Beverley![151]

Bev at work at the World Championships in Sydney, 1990,
ably assisted by Nola Kadwell
(Photo: Courtesy of Carol Murray)

Beverley also found time to become:

- Accredited as a Referee at National level
- Accredited as a Coach at National level*
- Play in the second top grade in Sydney

* This was where I first met Beverley, when she attended the inaugural NCAS Level 2 course in Canberra in 1987. She always enthusiastic and beautifully turned out!

Beverly's main interest was in Junior development, and she organised overseas trips for NSW Juniors to play New Zealand Juniors. These started with 2 week tours and stopping at 4–6 Junior events around the North Island. This was the precursor to the Trans-Tasman series.

Beverley's greatest achievement was starting the Australian Junior Championships Individual and Teams event in 1982! Prior to this, there was ONLY the Under 19 Championship available and this event now saw the beginning of Under 13, 15, 17 AND 19 events.

Beverley cajoled money, prizes and trophies from everyone she knew, with Mal Hazell of Consolidated Sporting Goods being the major sponsor for many years. Her particular passion, was the Girls' Under 15 event in which her two daughters began playing.

It was through the development of these Championships that Beverley ensured a pathway for Australian Juniors on the World Stage. It was from here that players of the calibre of Rodney Eyles (Australian Open Champion and World Champion 1997), David Palmer (British Open Champion 2001–2003), Anthony Ricketts (Australian Open Champion 2000 and British Open Champion 2005), the Martin family—Rodney, Brett and Michelle (all Australian Champions and Michelle and Rodney World Champions) and Stewart Boswell (Australian Champion 2002, 2006, 2007 and 2009 and currently the National Coach) emerged. Rhonda Thorne, Vicki Cardwell, Sarah Fitz-Gerald and the Grinham girls (Rachael and Natalie) all got their start becoming Australian and British Champions and World Champions in the process. An excellent breeding ground.

In her personal life, Beverley was a well-dressed loving mother of four children and she single-handedly raised a grandson. Beverley was a true lady who was passionate about her sport. Beverley passed away in January, 2019.

It was recommended that the Australian Under 15 Girls trophy be officially named the *Beverley Gould trophy* and-or the Australian Junior Teams trophy be named the *Beverley Gould Australian Teams Trophy*.

Dawn Moggach (OAM)

Dawn has been a tireless supporter of squash for more than 55 years from refereeing to administration, team manager, selector, tournament director, board member and president. Her list of contributions is endless. For this huge contribution she was awarded the OAM in June 2017.[152] She's what you call a stayer. She's seen it all and nothing would surprise her.

'Although I have only interacted with Dawn in more recent years, I understand that her contributions span over a very long period and it is good

Dawn. Still involved in the sport that she loves
(Photo: Courtesy of *Hornsby Advocate*16-6-2017)

to see her formally being recognised for these contributions to our great sport'
Jordan Till (Squash Australia Events Manager).

'Dawn is an inspiration, especially for Women in Sport. Her commitment shows how passion and effort can make a difference', Kay Kendall (Squash Australia General Manager Commercial, Events and Membership)

Squash Australia

- 2007 National Junior Selector *
- 1994 National Women's Selector *
- 2001 Referee Australian Junior Championships since 2001*
- 2002 and 2006 Tournament Director Australian Junior Selection Series
- 2004–2006 and 2008 Referee Australian Teams Championships
- Member President's Council*
- 2014–2015 Chair, National Selection Committee

New South Wales Ltd

- 2009 Director*
- 1985–2005 Junior Selector
- 1982–1999 Manager Junior Teams
- 1995 Life Member

- 1986–1999 Pennant Administrator, Northern District (Sydney)
- 1995–2001 Pennant Administrator, Sydney (All Districts—700 teams)
- 1995–2001 Delegate Australian Squash Referees Association
- 1985 National Referee*
- 1981–86 Vice-President NSW Squash Rackets Association
- 1984–87 Vice-President Squash Rackets Association of NSW (on amalgamation)
- 1984–87 Vice-President Junior NSW Squash Rackets Association
- 1981–82 Vice-President NSW Squash Referees Committee
- 1982–93 Secretary NSW Squash Referees Committee
- 1991 Life Member NSW Squash Referees Committee
- 1972–1983Club Secretary and Life Member, Manly Warringah Squash Club
- 2003 Life Member, NSW High Schools Sports Union*

Awards

- 2013 Distinguished Long Service Award, NSW Sports Federation
- 2011 Australian Junior Championship Service Award, Squash Australia
- 2000 Australian Sports Medal
- 2017 Order of Australia (OAM)

Dawn's been a member of the squash community over many years, who has shared her talents and perceptions over a wide variety of areas. A pity we can't clone somebody like this!

*Unless stated Dawn held these positions continuously (see above) until her retirement.

Well done 'Dawnie' as the kids affectionately call you!

Chris Sinclair

Chris is known in Squash circles for her expertise in Refereeing. She is the only female to have achieved the level of World Squash Referee (WSF) which she attained in 1987. She is also recognised for her work as a World Squash

Federation (WSF) Senior Assessor and Mentor and for the work she performed as the Championship Referee for the 2006 and 2018 Commonwealth Games in Australia. She was the only Australian official in any sport to referee an individual Commonwealth Games final in 1998. She was responsible for developing the expertise of referees to Australian and International standards in preparation for these Games.

Chris has been a leader in the sport since the 1980s, becoming an international Referee in 1987. Chris went on from there to officiate on the (PSA) World Tour, thirty WSF World Championships, the Australian Open and at all the Commonwealth Games since the introduction of Squash in Kuala Lumpur in 1998. She has refereed some of the greatest squash players in the history of the sport, namely, Jahangir and Jansher Khan, Rodney and Brett Martin, Michelle Martin, Sarah Fitz-Gerald, Nick Matthew and Nicol David—to name a few. Chris retired as a World Referee in 2015.

Chris served on the WSF Rules and Referee Committee for many years and was on the Committee for writing new rules. Chris was the Convenor for the Oceania Squash Federation Rules and Referee Committee for 16 years, and the Squash Australia Refereeing Committee for over 30 years. Chris was the Tribunal Chairman for Squash NSW for 10 years and is currently a Director of the Squash Australia Board.

Earlier in her career, she ran Sydney Junior Pennant for many years, administered the Senior Pennant in Sydney's north when there 250 Women's teams and 350 Men's Teams. In addition to this, Chris and two of her colleagues, Beverley Gould and Ted Barlow started the Australian Junior Championships in 1982.

Chris has organised and presented at many international Refereeing Conferences and presented at World Coaching Conferences. Chris has also produced many aids for refereeing squash, including instructional videos, the *Guide to Understanding the Rules of Squash* book, and presentations on all aspects of rules and refereeing.

Chris in her usual position in the chair!
(Photo: Courtesy of Steve Cubbins,
Hong Kong, 2009)

In 2000, Chris was awarded the Australian Sports Medal and in 2001 was awarded the Australian Sports Commission Officials' Development Award, which was judged against all sports. The runners-up were netball and rugby union. In 2010 Squash Australia awarded Chris the Distinguished Service Award and in 2018 she was awarded the NSW Official of the Year for her outstanding achievements and dedication to the sport, both nationally and internationally. This award is judged against all sports in NSW so was quite an achievement. In 2020 she was made a Life Member of Squash NSW.[153]

What many players wouldn't know is that Chris represented NSW in Athletics, Swimming, Diving and Netball in her younger days and was also a national netball umpire. She started playing squash in Melbourne, then moved to Townsville before finishing her playing days in A Grade in Sydney having played the second top grade.

Chris has been an outstanding contributor to the sport in Australia and internationally and as a role model has maintained the highest ethics, behaviour and fair treatment to all throughout her work in squash. Chris believes that her greatest achievements have been in assisting young Australian referees to reach international level, and she derives great pleasure in watching them referee the best players in the World.

It is in her character to be a giving person and she has given over 20 years volunteering for Community Aid and Meals on Wheels. She has also managed to fit in 3 University degrees and she is currently completing a PhD. She does part-time lecturing at various Universities in Sydney and is a Researcher, Historian and Archivist. What one would call a life well-lived. Of course, it's not over yet and it will be interesting to see what lies for ahead for her.

A great Australian, who has contributed to many people's lives and to different areas of the Community!

Rita Paulos

Well, how do you put the enthusiasm, energy and skills maintained over 40 years into a page in a book? Rita epitomises the energy that is required, to get people motivated into playing squash. Anyone, who has met Rita, will recognise that she has a heart of gold and would do anything for anyone. I first met Rita, when I was ACT Coaching Director, at the Interstate series in 1982 and again when she came to Canberra to attend the NCAS Level 2 Course that I had organised in 1987. Of course, she graduated with flying colours. She was a font of knowledge and she was willing to share this with anyone that was prepared to listen. She was, and still is, inquisitive as to the best way to do things.

Rita, like many of us, was a former tennis player, who went to the squash courts (on a wet day) to try a game of squash, in 1957. She took to the game, like a duck to water (pardon the pun) and the rest is history. She started playing at Coorparoo courts and was helped by Doug Robinson, who showed her the basics. She was selected as

Rita at her bubbly best!
(Photo: Courtesy of Rita Paulos)

reserve in the Queensland State team in 1960, played in Brisbane. However, it was some time before she could pursue her passion. She married in 1961 and three children arrived—Peter in 1963, Floyd in 1966 and Jason in 1969. Not to be deterred she was back playing as soon as she could and it was not long before she was a Queensland representative. She played in the Interstate series in 1971, 72 and 73. She was the first Queensland player to turn professional in 1973. It was then she turned her talents to coaching as she could only play in fixtures, but could no longer play in State Championships, State teams etc. until the sport became Open in 1980. She played A Grade competition in Queensland from 1960—1988, and won the Over 50s World Masters in 1990 and the Over 50s Australian Masters in 1994. What we would call a stayer! Her real strength, lay in coaching and working with the Juniors. From 1974 until 1995, she worked tirelessly, at all levels. These activities included:

- Formulation of grass root development with affiliated clubs being formed with a 50-50 grant from the Government. Jan Honeycombe was of considerable help here as she helped the clubs keep records, with names and numbers, which assisted further in that the programmes were able to obtain further grants from the Government
- Coaching clinics in Country Centres including Rockhampton, Gladstone, Bundaberg, Roma, Dalby, Toowoomba and other regions. Her energy was boundless.
- Regions were formed e.g., North Queensland–Townsville, Cairns and Mackay; South Queensland–Gold Coast, Toowoomba, Beaudesert, Roma, and Dalby; Metropolitan–Kangaroo Point, Acacia Ridge, Holland Park and Wavell Heights; Central–Rockhampton, Gladstone, Bundaberg, Maryborough, Emerald and Claremont. These Regions fed into Coaches (Level1) and from there the players went into Club Competitions to Regional Championships, State Championships and then the Australian Junior Championships.

Rita had been appointed Regional part-time Coaching Director in 1984 and, in formulating the above system, it was then her role to visit the various regions and help identify elite juniors who were then fed into the program. They would attend coaching camps in School holidays and they were on their way. It was during this time from 1982–86 that saw the emergence of players of the calibre of Ross Thorne (Australian Champion 1983) Tristan Nancarrow (Australian Champion 1984), Chris Robertson, who was coached by Rita and Rodney Eyles, who was also coached by Rita in the interstate series. Chris became World Junior Champion in 1984, whilst Rodney won the World Individual Championship in 1997. Also from Queensland, Rodney Martin won the World Championship in 1991 and his brother Brett won the Australian Championship in 1994 and 1996. The Women weren't to be outdone either as Rhonda Thorne won the Australian Championship and the World Championship in 1981. This time also saw the emergence of Liz Irving, coached by Rita in the early days, who was Runner-up in the British Open in 1988 and a member of the Australian World Championship Team 1989,90, 92*, 94*, 96*, and 98*. Michelle Martin was Winner of the British Open 1993, 94, 95, 96, 97, 98, World Open 1993, 94 and 96 and Australian Open 1993, 94, 95, 96 and 98 and 99 and Danielle Drady member of the winning World Championship team in 1989 and 90. The program was working.

As well as the above-mentioned players, Rita coached Michelle Toon in 1981, who achieved international ranking and the following players gained scholarships to the AIS: Chris Ward, Marc Hickey, Janine Hickey and Dean Mason. Fifteen other players under her tutelage achieved State rankings. Her nickname was either 'Rita, the Margarine Eater' or 'Rippa Rita', accompanied by a high five. Who else but Rita would sign their emails 'RIP'!

* Australia won

Coaching

Rita became State Coaching Director in 1985 and in this capacity she:

- Compiled: The Level 0 Coaching course for teachers
  ~ A Referee Book *The Most Common Playing Infringements*
  ~ A set of comic rules

- Produced: SWOT Drills Minor Games Manual and Video
  ~ Streets Portable mini court video
  ~ Teaching Squash Step by Step for Secondary Schools and videos
  ~ Skills Circuit cards for Grades 1–10
  ~ Co-creator of the revised Level 1 syllabus
  ~ Developed A website www.squashgame.info

Honorary positions

- State selector (1 year)
- Secretary Brisbane Junior Sub-Committee (5 years)
  ~ Formed in 1986, this was a committee of parents and people interested in Juniors. A Junior Newsletter was developed, with photographs, results etc and this was distributed to the Clubs.

Qualifications

  ~ NCAS Level 2 Coach (6 years)
  ~ Member of the National Technical Committee (4 years
  ~ Qualified Referee
  ~ Attained Certificate in Assessment and Work Place Training

Rita with her great grandchildren—Adaline and Violet
(Photo: Courtesy of Rita Paulos)

Awards

- 2000 Awarded Australian Sports Medal [154]

Her success was due to her boundless enthusiasm, energy, her ability to motivate others and the fact that she worked from the grass roots up. Latchkey kids were encouraged and court owners gave out free equipment, let the kids play for free (with the lights off) and as a result, there was a ground swell of young enthusiastic players coming into the courts en masse. The coaches at the coal face were former players with a love of the game and this was passed on to the young players. Rita has left a great legacy and no doubt you will still see her popping in around the courts to see how her former charges are going. Her blood's worth bottling. Just remember she always signs her emails RIP.'

A full life!

Robyn Prentice

Robyn, is the current President of Masters Squash, in Queensland and she first took up this position in 2018. She has had a long involvement in the game. She started playing in 1961 when she was 17 years of age, after obtaining a voucher from the local petrol station to come and try squash for free. This was through her work at a social club in Toowoomba and she was soon spotted by one of the local fixture players who invited her to play in her team. Despite knocking herself out when she collided with the side wall the first night she played (there are no side walls in tennis), her passion for the sport was ignited and she loved all aspects of the game. She attributed her success, to many of hours of hard work and some sessions with Ian Paton, who assisted her in converting her tennis swing into an effective squash swing. As she was a former A Grade tennis player, she quickly adapted to the game and realised that she had found a new challenge! She applied herself to the aspects of physical fitness, including skipping, ghosting in the backyard and running. She was also fortunate to receive some coaching from the Egyptian, Dardir who was visiting Australia in the '60s. Most of her understanding of the game came from reading

Robyn in her Representative colours in 2006.
(Photo: Courtesy of Robyn Prentice)

and watching matches. During the '60s she was also raising a family and working as a volunteer for Toowoomba Squash. In this capacity she kept squash alive in the Toowoomba region and south-east Queensland not only as a competitive player, but also in her capacity as a Coach, Coach Educator, Publicity Officer, Secretary, Treasurer and then Southern Region Co-ordinator from 1984–88. In 1993, Toowoomba City Council, arranged for a Sporting Oval to be named after her.

Over her playing career, she has seen the highs and lows of Squash in Australia. She represented Queensland from 1971–88, turned professional in 1980, and became a coach working with the indefatigable, Rita Paulos, who knows every trick in the game. She still continued playing competitively and, in 1984 when she ventured into Masters Squash, she was runner-up in the Queensland Over 30 Championships. She was also an Australian representative in the Masters from 1984–88 playing in the Trans-Tasman series. In 1987 she was runner-up to Heather McKay, in the World Over 45s Championships held in Sydney and even managed to get a game off her. No mean feat! ' She played her last representative game for Queensland, in 1988. After that, her involvement was with coaching, and in 1989 Robyn moved to Canada to take a position as Head Squash Coach at the Royal Glenora Club in Edmonton. Here, she won the Canadian Masters and became heavily involved in Master's Squash. She took this concept back to Toowoomba and has been involved in Master's Squash ever since. Masters tournaments provided the opportunity for former champions to continue their enjoyment of the game to show that squash is a game for all age groups. Winners have included:

- Margaret Zachariah World Over 35 Champion 1983
- Heather McKay World Champion Over 45 (1987, 1990), Over 50 (1993,1995)
- Robyn Prentice World Champion Over 40 (1987) Runner-up Over 45 (1990)
- Jenny Irving World Champion Over 50 (1987)
- Vicki Cardwell World Champion Over 35 (1990) Over 45 (2001) Over 55 (2010)
- Di Davis World Champion Over 40 (1990)
- Rita Paulos Over 50 (1990)
- Margaret Doueal World Champion Over 55 (1993)
- Roma Casey World Champion Over 65 (1995)
- Michelle Martin World Champion Over 45 (2012)
- Sarah Fitz-Gerald World Champion Over 35 (2006) Over 45 (2014)
- Sue Hillier Over 50 (2014, 2016, 2017). Over 55 (2018)

There have been many other players who have achieved success at the Masters level, including former Australian Junior Champion, Amanda Hopps World Over 35 Champion in 2008 and Over 40 Champion in 2014. Sarah Nelson also won the Over 40s Championship in 2008 and there have been several other players to have been successful, thanks to the formation of the Australian Masters Championships in 1983.[155] My apologies if I have missed you.

Awards

- 1985 Australia Day Sports Award
- 1985 Darling Downs Sports Star of the Year Award
- 2000 Sports Medal

Robyn's enthusiasm for the game is infectious and she provides a great role model for everyone to stay active, right throughout their lives. Without people, like Robyn, being involved and so giving of their time, many of the Master's events

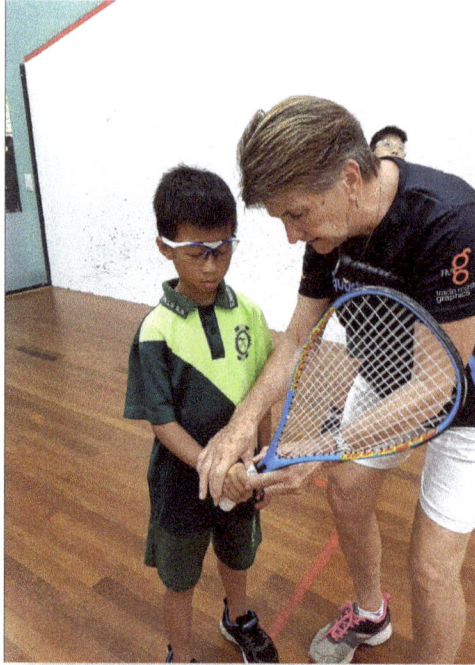

Start them young with the correct technique! Robyn coaching Eric Chiang.
(Photo: Courtesy of Robyn Prentice)

over the past 30 years, would not have taken place. She remains heavily involved in the Queensland Masters Squash Association, as the current President and we owe everyone involved, including Robyn, of course, a big thank you.

Since returning to Australia, in 1999, Robyn has turned full circle in her coaching life and has been Head Coach for Q Southern region, since 2017. She developed the Squash4Life Junior Development Academy in 2013 and continues to coach juniors and adults to aspire to be the best that they can be. Robyn attributes some of the great memories of her coaching life, to helping guide Juniors under her care to achieve their goals.

She has done it all, from managing Squash Centres, representing Queensland in the Interstate series from 1971 and for 13 of the next 17 years, with her last representation being when she was 43. She represented Australia in the Masters Teams event from 1984–88. She was World Master's Champion 40+ in 1987, Runner-up to Heather in the World's

Masters' Championship in 1990, managing to take a game off her, and in 2019, she won the Australian Master's Championship for Over 70s. Add to that numerous coaching roles and you can see that Robyn has a great love of the game and is a stayer.[156]

Margaret Campbell

Margaret became involved in Refereeing in 1974 when she answered a questionnaire on the rules of the game.[157] She rose quickly to a position as Secretary of the Brisbane SRRA. This Association grew and eventually became the QSRRA. Margaret was Secretary and Treasurer of this until 1990 and then became Secretary of the ASRRA and Treasurer of the QSRRA. She refereed at the 1979 and 1991 at World Men's Titles in Australia and the World Women's in Perth, Sydney and Auckland.

She has been Tournament Referee many times, notably at the World Junior Men's and the Australian Junior Championships. In addition, Margaret refereed at every Australian Open from 1979 until 1991, except for 1990 due to illness.

Referees are often not appreciated; however where would the players be without them? Margaret's quiet demeanour and knowledge of the game enabled

her to referee with astuteness and reliability, qualities which were appreciated by the players under her watchful eye.

She was awarded the Life Membership Certificate in 1991

Jeffrey Wollstein (former NCD) awarding Margaret Campbell with her Life Membership Certificate (Photo: *Squash and Fitness News* May, 1992) by the Queensland Squash Rackets Referees Association in recognition of her dedication and devotion to squash in Queensland, Australia and indeed further afield.

Marie Donnelly

Marie became involved in squash back in the 1950s when squash was a very minor sport in Queensland. She began playing in 1950 and her last match was in 1987 in New Zealand. She played A grade from 1950 until 1965. In the early 1960s Marie and her husband, Jim became the lessees of Stone's Corner Squash Centre. It was a small centre of 4 courts in the centre of the Inner Brisbane suburb, Stone's Corner. Her two young sons, Michael and John, started their squash career at this centre, and, in their late teens Michael won the 1976 Australian Men's Championships and both boys were representatives of Queensland Squash teams with Michael also going on to represent Australia in the Men's team.

Her involvement was extensive in squash, from club to national level throughout those thirty years and she was recognised with Life membership of Stone's Corner and Brisbane Women's and Queensland Squash Associations.

Queensland—Winners of the Interstate series 1973
L to R: Marie Donnelly, Rita Paulos, Marion Jackman, Jenny Irving and Lyle Hubinger
(Photo: Courtesy of Rita Paulos)

Marie worked from selling raffle tickets, to organising functions for squash events and most importantly was the frontline in organising and running squash tournaments from local to national level. She was totally dedicated in encouraging and improving squash for everyone, but particularly at Junior level. Brisbane Women's and Queensland Squash named an Intrastate Junior Competition in her honour as the Marie Donnelly Cup.

Marie moved from Stone's Corner Squash Centre to a new centre in Stafford in early 1972 and undertook the task of hosting, with Queensland Squash, the first Women's World Championships in 1976. This was an outstanding success with teams coming from all over the World. In 1981, from the Australian Squash Court Owners, she received an award in recognition of her 'Outstanding Contribution to the Advancement of the Squash Industry'. She was also one of four people involved in organising Squash into the first Australia Games held in 1984.

Besides all the work she undertook in the area of administration in squash, she will always be remembered for the encouragement and assistance she readily provided to all levels of young players. Her vision was to help them improve their skills and her voluntary contribution to the sport in Queensland was magnificent and everlasting in all aspects.

Administration

- 1959–83 Member of Queensland Squash Association
- 1962–80 Club selector for three clubs
- 1963–75 Vice-President of the Brisbane Women's Squash Association
- 1964–78 Queensland selector
- 1965–85 Australian selector
- Manageress of many Queensland teams to the Interstate series over many years
- 1982–3 Executive member of Australian Squash when the headquarters moved to Brisbane
- 1983 Manager of the Australian Women's Squash team in Perth in 1983. This team won the World Title
- 1984 Vice President of Australian Squash

Heather Rhead

Heather was a member of the Australian Junior team that toured New Zealand in 1963. This team was an invitational team designed to promote the game in New Zealand. They toured for two weeks giving exhibitions, coaching sessions etc, throughout the North and South Island. It was a great success.

She was also a Queensland representative from 1961–1965. Some of her team members who achieved at National and international level were Jenny McDevitt—Australian Junior Champion from 1964–1965 and Marion Jackman who became Australian Champion in 1974 as well as representing Australia in 1965, 1967, 1971, 1972 and 1975. Bev Meagher was Australian Junior Champion in 1959 and 1960. Heather was runner-up to Marion in the Queensland Championships in 1964.

Administration

- 1976–80 Member of the SRAQ
- 1977–80 Member Referees Association
- 1981 Executive Member of ASRA (Australian Squash Rackets Association)
- 1982–85 Secretary ASRA
- 1976 Member of the Organising Committee for the first Women's World Championships held in Brisbane
- 1976 Co-compere with Peter Meares for television of the World Championship Final between Heather McKay and Marion Jackman for television

Awards

- 1966 Life Member of Brisbane Women's Squash Rackets Association (BSWRA)
- 2000 Awarded the Australian Sports medal

Australian Invitational Junior Team 1963
Left to Right: Marion Jackman, Heather Rhead, Di Bruce and Bev Meagher
(Photo: Courtesy of Bev Meagher)

Tournaments

- 1964 Won the Brisbane Women's Squash Championships

- 1971 Won the Swedish Championships

Heather was always one of those people who was willing to 'lend a hand'.

Jan Honeycombe

Where would squash be if it wasn't for its volunteers? Jan was one of these. She served in many administrative roles from 1965–84 and in 1984, Jan oversaw the inclusion of Squash into the Australian Institute of Sport. This programme was designed to develop world class squash players. It also provided the stimulus at a state level to grow the number of junior competitors within the nation.

The AWSRA members, who joined the now amalgamated body ASRA in 1981, brought a wealth of expertise in all aspects of women's squash. They were responsible for a smooth transition into a robust national organisation, that was responsible for all squash players in Australia. Most of the women had competed at either the state or national level, which added another dimension to the knowledge base of the executive of the combined association. Another suggestion that was agreed to in principle, was that of equal prize money. [158]

It is the behind-the-scenes people like Jan, that make such an enormous contribution, and provide a base on which the players can perform. Thanks, Jan.

Administration

- 1965–75 President of the Brisbane Women's SRA for 10 years

- 1969–80 Secretary and Administration Officer for Queensland

- 1976 State Organiser for the inaugural World Women's Championships held in Brisbane at the Stafford Squash Centre.

- 1977 Appointed Manageress of the Australian team which toured New Zealand. This team comprised, Margaret Zachariah, Ann Smith, Vicki Cardwell (Vic) and Rhonda Thorne (Qld).

- 1978 Appointed Manageress of the Australian Women's Team to tour the US and Great Britain. 159 This team comprised Margaret Zachariah (1977 Australian Champion), Vicki Hoffmann, (1978 Australian Champion) Anne Smith (Australian representative 1974–77), and Rhonda Shapland (Australian Junior Champion 1973–76). This tour was more diversified with teams from Canada, Ireland and New Zealand competing. Australia defeated Great Britain 2–1 in the final.

- 1981 Men's and Women's squash was amalgamated in Australia, and Jan joined the ASRA Executive

- 1981 Represented Australia in a most effective and efficient manner at the Men's and Women's World governing bodies (ISRF and WSRF respectively) which were held in Sweden and Canada. Australia was a significant contributor at these gatherings, particularly, in the development of strategies to advance squash at the global level.[160]

- 1981–2 Executive member on the ASRA from 1981–82
- 1983–85 Vice-President of ASRA

Playing career

- 1972–74 represented Queensland in the Interstate series.

Patricia (Jean) Walker OAM (1930—2016)

Jean Walker was one of those sparkling personalities that stood out in a crowd. She was always positive and looked on the bright side of every situation. It was at her courts, run by her and her husband Keith, that our most famous female squash player Heather McKay was discovered. Whilst holidaying in Sydney in 1959 Heather, her sister and a friend had rocked up to the Manly District Park Tennis and Squash Centre, after being at the beach and decided to have a go at squash. Jean said 'You're not going on to the courts like that!' (they were pretty scruffy). She insisted on them buying new pairs of socks and they hired shoes, rackets and balls and that was Heather's first introduction to the game.

Jean was a people-person evidenced by her ability to make everyone feel welcome and as a result she attracted people to their courts in droves. Jean and Keith did it tough, in the beginning, and fully deserved their retirement on the Gold Coast in later years. I still remember the night and day lounge Keith and Jean slept on whilst they were building up the business. They only had 2 squash courts, but over time this became the meeting place for all the top Sydney players, both men and women. They included Ken Hiscoe, Owen Parmenter, Cam Nancarrow, Heather McKay, Yvonne West, Barbara Baxter and other Interstate players. International players also made the trek to these very basic courts . They were nothing like the courts of today. Absolutely no frills! It was the AIS of the sixties! This continued for over thirty years. We used to congregate there on Sunday afternoons and had a whale of a time. We learned from each other and put pressure on each other. At the same time, it was a lot of fun—a bit like the basketballers scrimmaging or musicians having a jam session. It was here that I learned to play a boast! Keith was ever the one to keep things simple and his statement of 'line the ball up with your belly button' is still terminology I use in my coaching today—and, *it works*!

On a side note, it was Keith Walker, John Garrett and Fred Barlow, all professionals, who brought Hashim Khan to Australia to play exhibitions in 1959. No amateur players were allowed to play against the professionals so the doubles game, 2 against one—the one being Hashim—was born. The only time when 2 players beat Hashim was when Keith Walker and Vin Toohey beat him 10–8 in the fifth.

From my own point of view, watching Hashim play at Parramatta one wet night, gave me the enthusiasm to pursue the sport. He was playing a State No.1 player Peter Papst, and there was some dispute about how much he was being paid. No agreement was reached, so Hashim proceeded to demolish Peter 9–0, 9–0, 9–0, hitting 27 nicks in the process. He had walked around the court prior to the match, checked out the widest nicks, the warp in the floor and proceeded to carve him up in 8 minutes. 'No more money, no more play.' Of course, the funds were found and Hashim proceeded to amaze everyone further with his wonderful skill. What an inspiration! I'm sure that without the injection of these top players-coaches, including Dardir, the Egyptian coach, over the next few years, the success in Australian squash would not have occurred.

I also remember meeting Jean during Heather and my first Interstate Team trip in 1960. Heather had pipped me for the No.4 spot, however, my court owner at Parramatta, John Luscombe, had shouted me my return air fare and accommodation to the Australian Championships in Queensland and we were the new kids on the block. Anyway, we were all standing by the side of the road, getting ready to cross (we were both 19 at the time) and in all my naivety, I stated 'This is a b.... hard game. I reckon you'd be over the hill by the time you're 30!' Jean was 30 at the time and went on to be involved in squash as a player and later as an administrator for the next 20+ years. Little did I know.

Another side to Jean's character, was that she was a risk taker. If she thought there was a chance of achieving something, she'd have a go. This was epitomized in the Australian Championships of 1960, described earlier in which Heather had to play through the qualifying rounds to get into the main draw. She eventually reached the final and had to play a Queenslander, who was far more experienced and was expected to win. Anyway, it was game-on and Jean, in her inimitable style, decided to run a book on it and we know how Queenslanders love to gamble. She cleaned up big time because Heather won the final 3–1. The next week in the Interstate series Heather, who had been promoted to the No.1 position as she was the Australian Champion, had improved so much that she beat all the No.1s in straight games. She was on her way.

From my experience, another couple of features of Jean's character, was her ability to be the life of the party and appear to drink a lot, but in reality, she sat on the one drink all night and had it topped up with water. A bit of a scam that. Also, she was smart enough, when playing for NSW, to save herself until last because by then the match would already be decided. She had Heather, No. 1 in Australia, Barbara Baxter, No. 3 in Australia and Pat McClenaughan, Australian Junior Champion, so success was assured. Canny!

Now to move on to her administrative career, where she really left her mark.

Administration

- 1961–64 President of the NSW Women's SRA

- 1965–1978 President of the Australian Women's Association

- 1971 Manager of the Australian Women's team (1971) that took squash to the world—visiting Singapore, Pakistan, Denmark, Germany, Great Britain USA and Canada

- Manager of the Australian Women's Team at the World Championships (1976)

- 1978 Was the main instigator in the formation of the Women's International Squash Rackets Federation (WISRF)

Playing career

- Represented NSW in the Interstate series from 1960–65

- Was a member of the Australian Women's team that visited New Zealand in 1964

Awards

- 1978 Awarded Life Membership of (AWSRA)

- 1983 Awarded OAM—Order of Australia for her contribution to squash

In her 14 years as President of the AWSRA, she gave a considerable amount of her time to the formation of regular competition between squash-playing countries. In the period from 1965 to 1970 squash began to boom. Women's teams from New Zealand and Great Britain toured Australia and Australian teams visited New Zealand and Great Britain on an irregular basis. Prior to 1965 there had been no formalised international competition. There had only been the one official international match against Great Britain in 1963–4 which Australia won 3–2. This defeat spurred the Great Britain team to visit Australia in 1965, where they were soundly beaten again! In 1966–7, an Australian team was formed comprising Heather McKay, Marion Hawcroft Barbara Baxter and Marlene Tierney, whilst Robyn Kennedy was sent for experience. This team toured the UK for 7 weeks and defeated the UK 2–1 in a Three Test series. It was against this background that Jean endeavoured to formalise regular international competition.

This took a while, but at her instigation in 1971, she was successful in taking squash to the world and she managed the first Australian touring team which visited Singapore, Pakistan, Denmark, Germany, Great Britain, USA and Canada. It was the objective of this tour to encourage and develop women's squash in these countries. Jean, also took the opportunity to do the groundwork to establish the first World Women's Championship, which was eventually held in Brisbane in 1976. There was great interest in this as the men

Carol Murray (left) presenting Jean with her award
(Photo: Courtesy of Carol Murray)

had already conducted 8 World Championships. The Australian team on the tour played to a very high standard and featured the incredible Heather McKay, Marion Jackman and Jenny Irving. Mavis Baker was making her debut in representing Australia. A very formidable and experienced team indeed. This was clearly seen as they achieved a clean sweep in the Test series against the UK 3–0. Heather won her 10th consecutive British Open Championship. This equalled the record set by Janet Shardlow. Heather defeated Jenny Irving 9–0, 9–3, 9–1 in an all-Australian final in 25 minutes. Australia had 3 of the 4 players in the semi-finals, with Fran Marshall being the sole British player remaining. She had been defeated by Jenny 9–7, 9–5, 9–6, whilst Heather had been pushed by Marion 9–7, 9–0, 9–4. A very good result indeed. Marion was unfortunate to lose the first game after having a 7–2 lead, but such is the tenacity of Heather. This had been a very successful tour, with the Australian women being completely dominant.[161]

It wouldn't take long for the next Test series to eventuate. It was on to Australia in 1972. This was only the second time an official team had visited Australia. The other time had been in 1965. Jean, in her President's Message, in the programme, stated that 'We are hopeful that this visit will prove so successful, that a team from Great Britain would visit every four years, with a similar arrangement for an Australian Team to visit Great Britain'. Let's see what happened.

Australia whitewashed Great Britain 3–0 winning all matches 3–0. We had come a long way!

The next team to tour was in 1975, managed by Carol Hunter. They toured Sweden, Canada and the US as well as competing in Great Britain. (This very successful tour has been reported earlier). The time was ripe for the first World Women's Championships to be played in Australia and Jean was concentrating her efforts towards staging this and they did eventuate! They were held in Brisbane and the countries that competed were Australia, New Zealand, England, Wales, Ireland, Canada and South Africa* (*they didn't compete in the Team's Event). Jean was also Manager of the Australian Women's Team and they won the international series defeating England 2–1 in the final. Australia's dominance continued.

Carol recalled 'that the presentation to Jean Walker, during the Women's World Championships in Sydney was to honour her dedication, services and leadership towards Women's squash at all levels—NSW, Australia and the international game as well. She had worked tirelessly for decades to create opportunities for Individual and Team competitions in Women's squash, not only within Australia, but also at the international level. By liaising with many Women's Associations and key administrators around the world, she was the perfect ambassador for promoting the Women's Game and instigating events. The World Individual Championship and various World Seniors Titles were held together in Sydney and it was a huge platform for Women's Squash and brought many women players together from around the globe.'[162]

It was agreed that to witness this wonderful event taking place was the culmination of years of effort. Much of this was a direct result of Jean Walker's years of dedication and determination to foster and provide opportunities for Women's squash. With her influence being felt from grass roots level in Australia to the international scene in Women's squash, many players benefitted and this seemed a fitting time for Jean to be honoured.

It was not long after in 1978, that the inaugural meeting of the Women's International Squash Rackets Federation (WISRF) was held in London, with Australia becoming a full member. Jean was the main impetus behind this. As a result, she was awarded the Order of Australia (OAM) in 1983, for her huge contribution to squash as an administrator, player and for her encouragement of junior players.[163]

The die had been cast and the second World Women's Championship was held in England in 1979, this time including a Teams' event and in 1981 the third was held in Canada. In this short period of time, the Women's World Championships were held 5 times and the competition had expanded from 6 to 14 countries.

In her later years, Jean would see the game grow from a very small group of elite players and a couple of thousand competition players to well over 10,000 players competing regularly in competition.

Bob Finch (former President of Squash Australia), wrote in her Eulogy on 26/1/2016, which was circulated by Squash Australia, that 'Jean was highly respected and admired by all who came to know her be they from squash, tennis, or life. She was a remarkable woman who loved life and people and her vision to expand the game of Women's squash internationally had born fruit with the game now played in over 60 countries compared to the 10 of the '60s.'[164]

Well done, Jean. We need a few more like you!

Carol Murray (née Hunter)

Carol was introduced to the game of squash, when she was 13 years of age, by Julie Napier, daughter of Vin who was President of ASRA from 1960–67. A former swimmer and tennis player, Carol made the relatively easy transition from tennis to squash, culminating in winning the Australian

Junior Championship in 1967. She had been runner-up the previous year. She also won the NSW Junior Championship that year. Carol was a NSW Junior representative from 1964–67 and a Senior representative from 1973–74.

Carol had been fortunate to travel to New Zealand in 1968 with the Australian Touring Junior team. These were goodwill tours and provided valuable experience for our Kiwi friends across the ditch and were a continuation of the visits commenced in 1960 and continued in 1963.This team played three Test matches against the New Zealand National Team which they won comfortably. The prime purpose was to increase interest in Trans-Tasman Test matches in New Zealand. There was good Press coverage and it created tremendous interest as the women's game was then growing in popularity. At this stage, as the sport was still amateur, players were billeted with squash families, which was a great way to get to know everyone.

The team members were: Kay Mansfield (Manager), Sandra Walsham, Mavis Baker and Carol. [165]

The opportunity arose for Carol to become Manageress of the Australian Women's team in 1975. This was a 7-week tour from 28-1-75 until 16-3-75 and visited Sweden, the UK and finally Canada. The team was extremely successful sweeping all before it. Carol managed this team very effectively and wrote a very comprehensive report at the conclusion of the tour. The flexibility of her management style was evident in her statement 'if the girls were tired at any stage, we cut back their practice sessions'. This worked extremely well. Also, she was aware of the individual differences in the players' approach to keeping fit as 'there was no set pattern for practice as each girl had a different method of keeping fit'. She allowed them to choose whether they had a hard or light practice session, depending on their perceived needs. This approach obviously assisted in the success of the tour and the wellbeing of the players. At the conclusion of this tour, Australia had won the series every time since its inception. In the British Open in 1975, Heather McKay, who was now a professional and a non-team member, and Marion Jackman, Sue Newman and

Margaret Zachariah made it an all-Australian semi-final for the first time ever. Heather defeated Marion in the final 9–3, 9–1, 9–5.

The full Australian Team was: Marion Jackman, Sue King, Margaret Zachariah, Lyle Hubinger and Chris van Nierop. The team was now a mixture of players from all over Australia and not dominated by any one state, in particular. They had also proven that they could stand on their own feet and were no longer dependent on Heather McKay to win vital rubbers.[166]

Carol, had shown her administrative ability previously, as she had been Secretary of the Australian Women's Squash Rackets Association (AWSRA), from 1967–76. Jean Walker had been President during this time and it was a period of great change. Carol took over from Jean as President (AWSRA) from 1976–80, until the amalgamation of the Men's and Women's Associations in 1981, when it moved to Brisbane.

There was still more to be done! Carol was called upon when the World Championships were to be held in Sydney in 1990. This event was run by the NSWSRA and was a labour of love for all concerned. The early games up to the quarter and semi-finals were held at Thornleigh in Sydney and the finals were played at Homebush on an all-glass court. This tournament was now fully international with 121 players competing from 18 Countries. A Teams' event followed and for the first time in Australia, matches were televised in Prime time and Mazda became the official sponsor. Everyone was pleased, when it at least broke even, thanks to the efforts of all concerned. The tournament had come of age, however, this didn't translate into success for the home team, as Susan Devoy of NZ defeated Martine Le Moignan of England 9–4, 9–4, 9–4 in the Women's Final and England defeated Australia 2–1 in the Teams' Final.

Carol then became Vice President of the ASRA in 1992 and also became Vice-President of the Oceania Squash Federation. Squash was accepted as a demonstration sport in the Commonwealth Games held in Malaysia, in 1998 and has been included in every Commonwealth Games since. The ASRA was hopeful that this would be a stepping-stone for inclusion into the Olympic Games, even as a demonstration sport! Unfortunately, (at the time of writing) this has not been the case.

Playing career

- 1964–67 NSW Junior representative

- 1966 Runner-up in the Australian Junior Championship

- 1967 Won the NSW Junior Championship

- 1967 Won the Australia Junior Championship

- 1968 Toured with Australian Junior touring side to New Zealand

- 1973–74 NSW Senior representative

Administration

- 1967–76 Secretary of the AWSRA

- 1975 Manageress of the Australian Women's team, which toured UK, Sweden and Canada. They swept everything before them and was a highly successful team

- 1976–80 President of the AWSRA

- 1990 One of the Co-ordinators of the World Championships held in Sydney

- 1992 Vice-President of the ASRA

- 1992 Vice-President of Oceania Squash Federation*

Carol wasn't as heavily involved with squash, after this and she returned to her private life. She had married Stuart in 1970 (they met playing squash) and they had 2 girls, Rowena and Celia, who now, of course, have grown up. They have three grandchildren, Lewis and May, who live in England with Rowena, and Celia has a daughter, Clementine. Carol and Stuart make regular trips to visit them. Carol and Stuart live in a lovely apartment, (near Barangaroo on Sydney Harbour) play golf regularly and enjoy travel and gardening. They enjoy good health, a very pleasant lifestyle and Carol still has regular contact with her many squash buddies.

Author's Comments

These are only some of the many unsung heroes that have been involved in Australian Squash. There are the parents that run Junior Club tournaments, serve on Committees and encourage their kids to play. There are those who just love squash and serve in a multiplicity of roles from running tournaments to taking teams away, organising fund raisers, refereeing matches etc. For the purposes of this book, I have had to concentrate on those who have contributed at National/International level and also served the sport over many years. My apologies, if you don't see your name here. I hope that you are being recognised by your State Association and if not, through the rewards that come by just being a volunteer. Many thanks to all those unsung heroes!

11 Australian Squash Families

Australian families have made a huge contribution to our success in sport on the World stage. Squash is one of the sports that has a strong family culture with parents and children often playing throughout their lives. Several Australian squash families have been blessed with having high achieving parents or siblings and I will outline the main ones here. They have dominated the World stage over several decades and have created a culture of expecting to achieve. Other champions have emerged from everyday families and with their parental support have also gone on to great heights. Many have been outlined earlier in this book. One of the things I have noticed, is that when I played in the Australian Junior Championships in 1960 (I'm showing my age here!)—there were four competitors in it! Nowadays, as evidenced by the Australian Junior Championships held at Carrara on the Gold Coast in 2020, there were hundreds of kids playing. They were, in many cases, forming friendships that they will have for life. In this chapter, I will outline the stories of some of the families that help develop this camaraderie from the early days of the 1940s until the present day. Hopefully, this can inspire the future families to encourage their young ones to take up the sport.

The Meagher Family

As mentioned previously, Betty Meagher was the pioneer of the Australian Women's Game and she formed the AWSRA and the VWSRA in 1952. She won the Australian Women's Amateur Championship in 1946 and 49–50 and had the vision and curiosity to want to see how the game was played overseas. She travelled overseas in 1950 and on her return the opportunity arose for her to purchase the Flinders Lane Squash Courts, in Melbourne. It was her intention to make it the centre of women's squash activities and she decided to combine her career of accountancy with that of squash court management along with her husband, Alan, and this venture succeeded. It was through this environment that her children learnt to play squash.

Bev first held a racket at the age of three and did not start playing competitive squash until she was 11[167]. She entered her first Australian Championship at the age of 12 and went on to win the Australian Junior Championship in 1959–60 aged 15 and 16. She also won the Victorian Junior title 3 times. She was virtually brought up on squash courts working in reception at the Elwood Squash Centre,

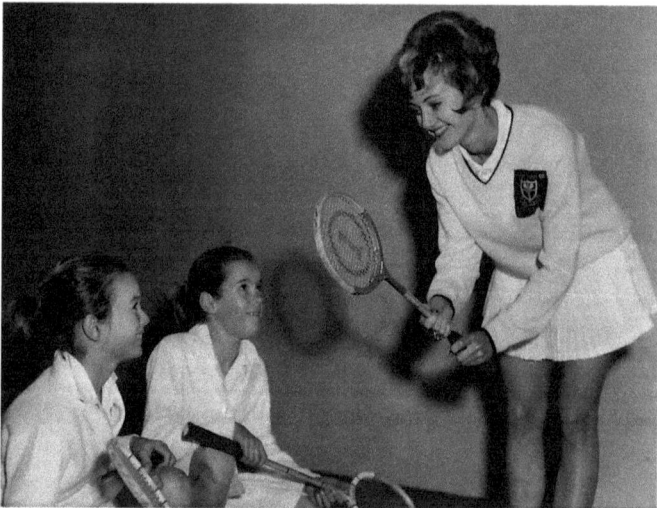

Bev (15) coaching her sisters—twins Robyn (l) and Lindy (r)—aged 8
(Photo: Courtesy of Bev Garfield)

*The continuing generations**
Back row (L to R): Olivia (Bev's daughter) Sarah Fitz-Gerald
Front row: (L to R) Bev with granddaughter (Charlotte) and Judith FitzGerald.
(Photo: Courtesy of Bev Garfield)
*The Meaghers and FitzGeralds have kept in regular contact throughout
all of their lives—70 years!

answering the phone, taking bookings and looking after the customers. She also honed her skills against her Mum, who was still playing A grade.[168] Highlights were her trip to New Zealand in 1960 as part of an Australian Touring team. This team was chosen according to availability as it was early days. The team comprised Victorian players, Lois Wright No.1, Bev Meagher No.2, Joan Morey No.3 and Fay Grant no.4. It was a tour mainly to promote the sport in NZ.[169]

In 1963, Bev travelled to New Zealand again, this time accompanied by Heather Rhead (Q) Marion Jackman (Q) and Di Bruce (Vic). This was again an invitational team, based on availability and several exhibition matches were played to encourage the young juniors. Bev won the North and South Island Junior Championship on this occasion. Jenny Irving and Dot Deacon (Q) were the captain/chaperones. In 1965, Bev became the first female coach in Australia to turn professional. She was also delighted to coach the Under 19 Victorian Team at the AIS, in 1988.[170]

An outgoing personality Bev is always up for a laugh.

Bev's twin daughters, Robyn and Lindy, both started to play as soon as they could hold rackets however, whilst they became handy players, they didn't go on to compete at the highest level. [171]

The FitzGerald Family

Judith FitzGerald (née Tissot) 1930–2020 was a pioneer of the Women's game in the 1950s and with Betty Meagher, they provided the platform from which Australian Women's squash rose. This has been detailed earlier so to avoid too much repetition, I will only give a brief summary here. Suffice it to say, that Judith started to play squash in 1947 when Betty was Champion and she then went on to win 4 Australian Championships in 1952 and 1956–58, making the transition from State level tennis. Judith was also one of the few women that travelled overseas to play both tennis and squash. She played at Wimbledon from 1953–54 and reached the fourth round of the British Open Squash Championships in 1955. Judith was inducted into S&RV Hall of Fame in 2002 and was awarded the Distinguished Service Award by Squash Australia in 2007.

Judith's daughter Sarah was one of six siblings (there were three boys and three girls in the family) and she was the youngest, born in 1968. The sisters played tennis and the boys played football (amongst other sports). 'The family needed a squash player' however, she was the only one who seriously pursued a career in squash.[172] Nonetheless, from the photograph following, one can see that it was a very active and competitive household and with an Australian Champion as a Mum, Sarah had a very good role model.

Sarah learning the basics from her Mum, Judy. Photo: Source Sarah Fitz-Gerald)

L to R: Sarah, Damien, Louise and Anthony—a sporting family. The other two siblings,
Kylie and Mark did play sport but weren't as competitive.
(Photo: Source Sarah Fitz-Gerald)

The Hunt Family

The Hunt family produced three children that represented their state (Victoria) for many years. Tricia, the youngest of the family, started playing when she was 11 and represented Victoria in the Interstate series for 8 years from 1966-73. She was also Captain of the team for 6 of those years. She won the Victorian Junior Championship in 1967 and was runner-up in the Australian Junior Championship in the same year. She retired in 1973 after having her first son. She became President of the VWSRA in 1973. In 1975, after discussions with the President of the SRAV, Sid Myers, it was decided to combine the two Associations. A Committee was formed to consider a merger. The two Associations amalgamated in 1976 and became the VSRA with a new Constitution and renewed enthusiasm. Tricia continued to play squash in State Women's and Masters' pennants, until her retirement in 2006. Instead of squash, she now plays golf regularly with groups of old 'squashies' including her brother, Bill. She is also pursing her passion in art, by painting and drawing most days.

At the Australian Championships in 1967
L to R: Tricia, Bill, Connie, Geoff and Vic
(Photo: Courtesy of Tricia Hunt)

Geoff had started out playing tennis, before he made the switch to squash. He also enjoyed fishing on Port Phillip Bay and at Mallacoota, which may have helped him to develop the patience that was required in squash. Vic from an early age, would have Geoff and Trish hitting the ball up and down the side wall on both sides, for hours on end. This was the style which was trademark Hunt and stood him in good stead, for the 400 shot rallies he had with Jonah Barrington, in later years.

His brother Bill was four and a half years older and initially could beat Geoff, but not for long. In 1963, he was runner-up to Geoff in the Victorian Championships, where he was expected to win. Geoff was 16 at the time and two years later Geoff won the Australian Amateur Championship defeating Ken Hiscoe in the final. The two brothers did study the game and after Comp matches, they talked well into the night, discussing various tactics—much to their mother's disgust. Bill was a member of the Victorian team 1962–64 and 1966–70 and his highest Australian ranking was 5 and highest Victorian ranking was 2. He was selected to play for Australia in a tour to South Africa, but declined. Bill was Coach of several Men's Junior Australian Teams which

L to R: Vic talking squash to his attentive charges Tricia, Bill and Geoff
(Photo: Ian Trengrove, *Geoff Hunt on Squash,* Cassell, London,1974, p17)

won the World Junior Championships in 1980, 1984 and 1988. Bill also coached Victorian Interstate Senior and Junior teams consecutively from 1974–83.

Of the three children, Geoff was the most successful He won 4 World Opens from 1975–80. He was awarded the MBE in 1972 and the AM in 1982 for his services to squash and became Head of the AIS Squash Unit with Heather McKay in Brisbane in 1985.

Their father Vic, was an A grade squash player, who didn't take up the game until he was in his 40s. He did go on to win the World Over 75 Master's Championship, in 1995. He kept himself extremely fit, still bench pressing in his 80's! Vic was still going to the gym daily from the age of 93, with his portable oxygen bottle, as by then he suffered from pulmonary fibrosis. He lived until the ripe old age of 96.[173] In Geoff's words 'He was a sound analyst of the game, and I was extremely fortunate in my family circumstances. Few others have had the opportunities that were presented to me to learn the game thoroughly'[174]

However, in Tricia's words, 'Mum was the glue that kept it all together'.

They all played pennants on different nights of the week and she was the taxi. I'm sure there are many parents out there that can identify with that role! 'She used to sit in the car to wait for Geoff to finish. This was because in those days, the top-grade men's pennant was mostly played in private Men's Clubs and women were banned.' In her memoirs, she wrote, that she 'regularly had to wash and hang out 120 socks per week!'[175]

They were quite a family, and Vic, Bill, Geoff and Tricia were all awarded the Australian Sports medal in 2000, in recognition of their services to squash. Perhaps Mum (Connie) should have got one, too?

The Irving Family

Jenny first started playing squash in 1957 and her achievements have been outlined earlier. It was to this environment that her daughter Liz, was born in 1965. They were both very athletic and natural games players. Jenny's squash was the centre of her life and it wasn't long before that interest was transferred to Liz, however, Jenny insisted that it was Liz's choice.

There can't be too many families out there where BOTH the mother and the daughter have been Runner-up in *both* the Australian and British Open Championships and represented Australia for a combined total of 24 years—12 each. They also achieved a World ranking of No 2. Once again, skills had been passed on from Mother to daughter!

Jenny Irving passing on some tips to Liz (aged 13)
(Photo: Wayne Smith, *Courier Mail,* February, 1978)

The Cardwell Family

Vicki, as recorded earlier, has always been involved in sport and trained to be a physical education teacher from 1973–76 in Adelaide. Squash was the sport she selected, after she had excelled at a number of sports at school, including softball, tennis, netball and athletics. She reached the pinnacle of her chosen sport in 1983, when she won the World, British and Australian Open titles and achieved the No.1 World ranking.

Vicki met husband, Ian, in July 1981 at the Victorian Open and after a long-distance courtship (pun intended) they married in January 1982. In January 1983, Vicki announced that she would retire from the international tour, after the World Open in November that year. Ian and Vicki started their family, with Josh being born in 1985 and Sarah in 1991. Both children were encouraged by their squash playing parents to play squash and eventually they went on the PSA tour. Josh reached a career high ranking of 148 and Sarah a career high world ranking of 41 in 2017.

Sarah won the Australian Junior Championship Under 15 in 2006, Under 17 in 2008 and Under 19 in 2010. She first represented Australia in 2009 in the World Junior Teams event, played in Chennai, India, then she continued doing what she values most, representing Australia in the World Women's Teams events. Firstly, in France (2012), and then in Canada (2014) and China (2018). She also represented Australia in the Commonwealth Games in Glasgow (2014) and Gold Coast (2018)

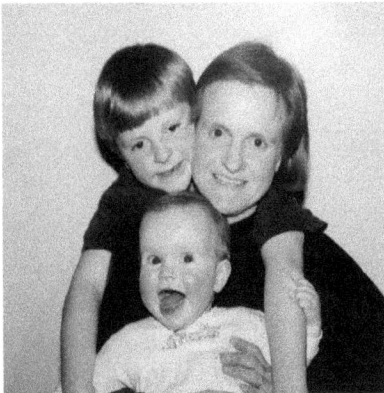

and in the World Doubles Manchester (2018) and Gold Coast (2019). Sarah has continued to pursue a career in squash, while completing a Degree in Business Studies at the Swinburne University of Technology.

Josh, Vicki and Sarah—family
(Photo: Sarah Cardwell)

Vicki and Sarah at the Australian Open in Canberra
(Photo: The Cardwell family)

Joshua has enjoyed success in the USA, as coach of the first Avon Old Farms team, in any discipline, to win a National Championship, winning division 1 of the National High School Squash Championships, the largest squash tournament in the world in terms of overall number of participants in 2014. Joshua continues to coach, encourage and develop squash players and now pursues his career as Coach Cardwell at The Hill School in Pennsylvania, USA.

Sarah in action at the Australian Open in 2012
(Photo: Squash mad.com)

The Martin Family

As outlined earlier, Michelle was born into a very sporting family. She was the fourth of six children and her older brothers, Brett and Rodney, also went on to become top professional players.

Michelle's brother, Rodney was World Champion in 1991, Australian Champion 1990, 1992 and 1993, and Brett was Australian Champion in 1994 and 1996 and at one stage was ranked no. 2 in the World. All three of them represented Australia in winning teams throughout the 1980s and 90s. Michelle was World Champion three times, represented 6 times, Rodney 3 times and Brett 5 times. An amazing family. Their uncle, Lionel Robberds, was an Olympic rowing cox and Commonwealth gold medallist. Good genes there.

Michelle's story has been told earlier in the book, suffice it to say with so much rivalry and camaraderie from her brothers and other siblings, the competitive spirit and will to survive was instilled fairly early.

Back to front: Robert (holding Grant) Dawn (holding Tanya), Brett and Wayne, Rodney and Michelle (aged 8)
(Photo: Courtesy of Michelle Martin)

Brett and Rodney with Michelle after she'd won her first British Open, in 1993.
(Photo: Courtesy of Michelle Martin)

Her Mum, Dawn and father, Robert, certainly had their hands full and top marks for producing such a successful family.

The Grinham Family

Rachael and Natalie Grinham were born in Toowoomba, Queensland to squash playing parents Davina and John. You could say their playing career began when they would chase balls for hours on a court whilst their parents played next door. They certainly were introduced to the game early. [176]

In terms of competition, Rachael entered her first junior competition at the age of 7 and finished runner-up to Janine Hickey who later became a top 30 player in the World. Janine was aged 11 at the time. Rachael's first major Junior victory was when she was only 9 years of age at the Queensland Under 11 Junior Age Championships. At 10 she won the Australian Under 13 Junior Age Championship, in 1987. This achievement was repeated, in 1988. In 1989, she won the Australian Under 15 Championship, when she was 12! Rachael lost a bit of interest after that, and it wasn't until 1993 when she won the World Junior Championship aged 16 in Malaysia, that she decided to make a career

Mum, Davina, was one proud lady at the Commonwealth Games in 2006
(Photo: Courtesy of Rachael Grinham)

out of squash, as she had no intention of going to university. Rachael was runner-up in the World Junior Championship in 1995, and led the Australian Junior Women's team to two World Championships in 1993 and 1995.

The highlights for Rachael would be—British Open Champion 2003–4, 2007 and 2009, Australian Open Champion 2005, World Champion 2007. She was also ranked no.1 in the World in 2004–5. In addition, she represented Australia in winning World Championship teams in 2002, 2004 and 2010 and the Commonwealth Games in 1998, 2002, 2004 and 2006. She is the most decorated Commonwealth Games medallist across all sports.

Natalie has also been very successful and eventually emerged from Rachael's shadow. She won the Australian Open in 2004 and was runner-up in the British Open in 2005 to Nicol David. In the World Championships she was runner-up three times. In 2006 to Nicol David, 2007 to Rachael and 2009 Nicol. She achieved the no. 2 ranking in the World in 2007–8. Natalie also represented Australia in the World Teams event in 2002*, 2004* and 2006 (*winning team) and the Commonwealth Games in 2002 and 2006. Her special highlight was to win three gold medals, in front of a home crowd in Melbourne, winning the Singles defeating Rachael in the final, the Women's doubles with Rachael and the Mixed Doubles with Joseph Kniepp. Outstanding.

Other Family Connections

There are many other family success stories which have contributed to Australia's amazing record at the international level, both Men and Women and I will name a few more, however the main emphasis of the book has to been to record the achievements of the women, over a very long period.

Heather McKay, of course, came from a very large family (11) and no doubt the rivalry amongst her siblings would have contributed to her success, due to the competition and the need for self-reliance. Many other international players mentioned earlier, had parents with sporting backgrounds. Cam Nancarrow, World Amateur Men's Champion 1973 and Australian representative 1967–76, was married to Mavis Baker, an Australian representative in 1971–72. Their son, Tristan won the Australian Championship in 1984 and represented Australia in 1993.

Di Davis was an Australian representative in 1983–5 and Coach/Manager of many successful Australian teams—both Junior and Senior through until 1998. Her son Byron, represented Australia at the World Junior Championships in 1992 and won a silver medal in the Doubles in the Commonwealth Games in 1997, playing with Rodney Eyles. He was Coach/Manager of the Australian Men's World Championship teams in 2003, 2005, 2007 and 2009. Byron became Head Coach at the AIS upon Geoff Hunt's retirement and was Assistant Coach at the Commonwealth Games in 2006 and Head Coach in 2010. An amazing contribution from one family.

The above is just a small indication of the contribution that many families have made, to the Australian success story in Squash. The longevity of the families as players and then coaches (in some cases) has led to the skills being passed forward. We now need to regroup and re-establish the methods that led to our remarkable success prior to, and including, 2010.

12 Professionalism and Prize Money

In 1976 a meeting took place in Brisbane between international players and administrators from several major squash nations. They were there as part of the World Open, the first non-national Open Championship held for women. What was agreed was that a separate women's organisation was needed at the International level. An attempt was made to begin an independent body in 1978. It didn't take hold. It then became part of the ISRF under the Chairmanship of the former great champion, Janet Shardlow. It was the WISRF. The founding members of this embryonic association included Fran Marshall and Angela Smith of the UK, Sue Newman, Barbara Wall, Marion Hawcroft and Lyle Hubinger from Australia and Irene Hewitt from Ireland. They paved the way for the WISRF and the subsequent formation of the separate players' association, WISPA. Its role was not to take on the mantle of a governing body, but to organise and control Women's World Championships and to act as an informal link between women in member countries. As the game had gone Open, it became clear that there was a need to co-ordinate women's calendars, produce rankings lists and generally look after the interests of senior players.

At the World Open in Perth Western Australia in 1983, the players' gathering decided that the women should follow the men and institute a players' association and so the World Squash Players' Association (WSPA) was formed. This wasn't its final format. In February 1984, the first general meeting of WSPA was held in New Zealand. The 'I' (for International) hadn't been added at that stage. The 23 founding members elected Robyn Blackwood of New Zealand as Chairwoman and Rae Anderson as Secretary-Treasurer. These 23 players were juggled into a merit order and the first ranking list was produced. Susan Devoy of New Zealand was No. 1—a place she would hold for many years to come.

Over the next couple of years, formalities were put in place: aims stated as 'the advancement and betterment of the women's and rankings listed were to be published quarterly'.

A system of event grading for ranking purposes was agreed. The minimum prize fund being only $500. As an indication of how this grew in 1998, Grade C was $500–$5,999, B was $6,000–$9,999 and A was the highest level, $10,000.

Note: As a point of interest, Heather McKay won $2,000 for her World Championship victory in 1976. Prior to that, the most she had won in a tournament was $300! Vicki Cardwell won $1,500 for her World Open victory in 1983, and Rachael Grinham won less than $5,000 for winning the Australian Open in 2005. Times had certainly moved on and made it much easier for women players to become full-time professionals.

The Tour grew rapidly during this time and in 1988 was poised to break the $200,000 barrier. There were a similar number of events, and, by 1998 prize money had increased to $600,000—a threefold increase. It was about this time that the then Chairman, Melanie Warren-Hawkes initiated a new ranking system, that added weighting to results in respect of rounds reached and prize fund levels, which built on the introduction of the first ranking programme. By the 90s the 'I' had been introduced and membership was now exceeding 100, including players from every continent, and events taking place on all of them, except South America, which joined the Tour in 1996. In November1991 at the age of 23, the players decided that Sarah Fitz-Gerald would make an excellent Chairman for the body even though the title had changed to President. By1994, Heather Hills became a full-time administrator of WISPA. The tour has grown significantly since then and as the graphs below will show. The future looks bright and really extends beyond the scope of this book (2010). However, I thought it would be interesting to outline the fact that the game IS growing and is not in decline, as many in Australia believe. It is in transition and we need to grab the opportunities with both hands if we are to compete successfully at the international level into the future.

Other developments have been WISPA becoming the World Squash Association in 2012. In November 2014 the Women's Squash Association and the Professional Squash Association (PSA) merged and the PSA became the governing body for both Associations from 1st January, 2015.[177]

During this evolution the world squash scene has changed dramatically in terms of prize money and in the number of countries where tournaments are held. Graphs illustrating this are shown below.

Graph 1[178]

Number of Female Tournaments by Prize Money Categories.... Since 1998

This graph illustrates the decrease-increase in the number of tournaments internationally in the respective prize money categories. There has been a sharp decrease in the number of tournaments offering $0–$5000, and whilst the other categories have fluctuated, there has been a steady increase in the $100,000—$200,000 category over the period 2012–13—2018–19. This greatly enhances the ability of a successful player to support themselves on the World stage.

Graph 2 [179]

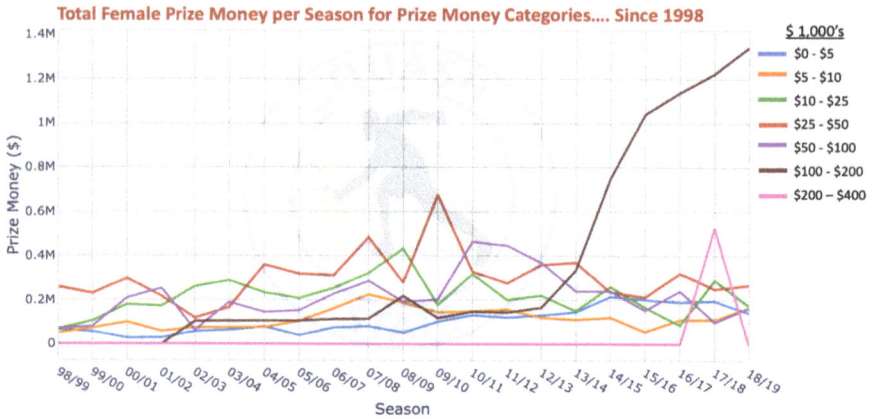

Total Female Prize Money per Season for Prize Money Categories.... Since 1998

This graph shows the total prize money available from 1988–9 to 2018–19 and this has risen from approximately $300,000 to over $2m. The tour has certainly become far more lucrative.

Graph 3 [180]

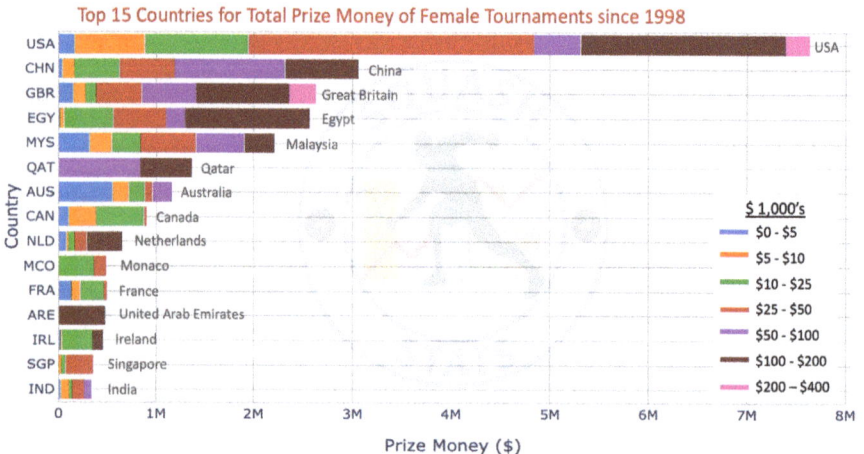

Top 15 Countries for Total Prize Money of Female Tournaments since 1998

This graph is quite interesting as it shows the shift in emphasis as to where the main tournaments are played. The UK is no longer the centre for the game of squash, as it was in the '60s. For players aspiring to make a living on the World circuit, the USA provides the most opportunities. Australia comes in 7th and hence the absence of our players overseas for a large part of the year.

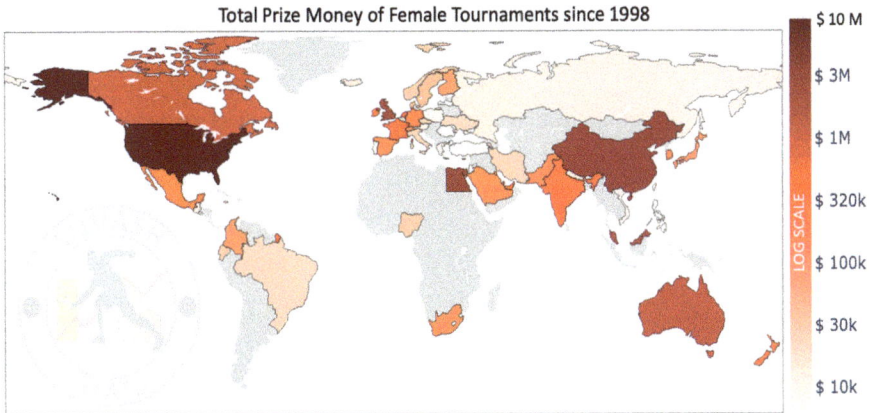

Total Prize Money of Female Tournaments since 1998

Graph 4 [181]

This diagram illustrates the distribution (by value) of the tournaments internationally.

As an aside, there is now equal prize money for Men and Women in the World Championships and in the top five countries: USA, China, Great Britain, Egypt, and Malaysia. In terms of highest annual prize money, there is an equal split between male and female tournaments. [182]

The addition of squash to the LA28 Olympic Games came only five months after another defining changing moment for the PSA earlier in the year.The investment made into Squash Media & Marketing (SMM) by Squash SM&E Holdings, the sport, media & entertainment group of Mark Walter. This injection of funds will enable the PSA to deliver on their ambitious strategy and multi-year business plan. They plan to optimise the structure of the PSA tour empowering a more stable and longer term calendar of World events for men and women. The number of Challenger and Satellite tournaments will increase. These changes should come into effect at the start of the 2024-2025 season.

Also the PSA aims to double the total player compensation on the PSA tour over the next five years from close to $9,000,000 in 2022-23 to $18,000,000 by 2027-28. Furthermore they are looking to increase the number of sanctioned events from 823 to 1500 and steadily grow the membership base from 1500 to 1800 players during this same period.' [183]

The sport has come a long way.

13 The Olympics

The question was asked at the beginning of the book—'Why isn't Squash in the Olympics'? It is not for want of trying. Well now, it's finally there! On 16th October, 2023 the US squash CEO announced that Squash had been included as an Olympic sport for Los Angeles in 2028. [184]It's been a long journey.

Squash has been pushing the IOC since 1986, when squash first became a recognised sport by IOC, to gain a place on the Games programme. Squash made its first bid to be in the Olympic Games in Barcelona, in 1992.[185] Under the leadership of Presidents Tunku Imran and Susie Simcock, the campaign continued for Atlanta in 1996. If Australia had nominated squash (being the host nation) it would have possibly won 5 gold medals. Unfortunately, this was not to be and Taekwondo was chosen instead. The campaigns continued in Athens 2004 and Beijing 2008. During all this time there was no formal procedure for gaining admission to the Games and the process of lobbying was frustrating and occult in nature.[186]

In 2012, there were up to 12 sports vying for limited opportunities for inclusion and a more disciplined method of selection was required. This came about with the appointment of Jacques Rogge as the IOC President. Under his leadership a formal bid process was instituted for selection for the 2012 Games in London. Five non-Olympic sports comprising squash, roller sports, golf, karate and rugby sevens had been studied by the Olympic Programme Commission as part of a two-year analysis. From these five sports the IOC members selected Squash and Karate as the two sports that could potentially be chosen to join the Olympic Program for 2012. After a close and tense series of votes, squash and karate were voted ahead of rugby sevens, golf and roller sports as the delegates' choice. However, under Rule 46 of the Olympic Charter, a vote was required in order to grant a non-Olympic sport Olympic Sport recognition. Neither Squash nor Karate secured the two-thirds majority required and consequently, the London Games were confirmed with a reduced number of sports.[187]

With the experience of 2005, the IOC created an even more formalised process for selection of the programme for 2016. Following a change to the Olympic Charter, the two-thirds majority rule needed for Olympic recognition had been changed to a simple majority. Hopes were high! The 5 sports from the 2005 list were joined by baseball and softball to undergo detailed evaluation. By now, it was apparent that substantial time, effort and finance had to be put behind the bids. A Task Force was established in January 2009 and with representation from WSF, PSA and WISPA, George Mieras was appointed as Olympic Bid Co-ordinator with a budget that was personally approved by the new WSF President, N. Ramachandran. The first vital action was to appoint Scott Garrett as Bid Manager.[188]

The seven points that were put forward are listed below:[189]

- Squash is relevant today as the world's healthiest and most exciting sport. Squash is a popular, accessible sport, played the world over

- The game is well organised to take advantage of inclusion in the Olympic Games

- An Olympic medal will be the sport's highest honour

- Squash's top athletes will definitely compete

- Squash can take the Olympic Games into new markets

- The impact of squash on the Olympic Games will be high, the cost low

Unfortunately, the sport lost out to golf and rugby 7s. It was just after the Global Financial Crisis and it appeared that the IOC needed to strengthen their financial situation.[190] A fully strategised bid for selection for the 2020 Games was also unsuccessful. The IOC had made a commitment to remove a sport to make way for a new sport and so took out wrestling. They then added the new sport from a shortlist including squash. It was wrestling! At this time the host Japan was not permitted to request any additional sports of their choice, however, they wanted baseball and karate, which are two highly popular sports in Japan, to be added. So, in an arrangement with the IOC, baseball, which was now joined with softball, and karate were accepted alongside the new IOC choices of surfing, skate boarding and speed climbing. This desire to include youth-oriented activities to enhance the urban street cred of the IOC was clear. The IOC own the Olympics and it is their choice to make.[191]

Currently, the IOC has no interest in adding an established sport, such as squash, which is structured, athletic, worldwide, innovative and has a flourishing professional tour played in approximately 50 countries.[192] The motto 'faster, stronger, higher' has morphed into 'drive for youth'. Squash was also unsuccessful in its bid for Paris in 2024 where the IOC prevailed upon the hosts to nominate breakdancing as a host selection. However, the WSF is seriously considering whether it would make another bid for Los Angeles in 2028, it would be time consuming, costly and unlikely to succeed. Even though Squash is now played in 185 countries on 50,000 courts worldwide, this still may not be sufficient to get the sport over the line.

However, fortunately they did make a bid which was successful due to the collaborative effort of the World Squash Federation (WSF), the US Squash Association and the Professional Squash Association (PSA) together with a game-changing investment from Squash SM&E Holdings, a sports, media and entertainment group led by Mark Walter.[193] The fact that squash can be played at an existing venue, has also seemingly swayed LA chiefs.[194]

The inclusion of squash in the LA28 Olympic Games is expected to inject new capital into the sport on a worldwide basis, specifically at the Federation level as the National Governments and their Olympic Committees will look to provide their athletes with the best possible conditions to prepare for the biggest multi-sport event in the world. The decision is a significant and exciting milestone in squash's history as Squash is included in the Olympics for the first time. It is very likely that this will have a positive effect on the professional game in the next five years, through enhanced interest from potential promoters, sponsors, brand partners, media outlets, host cities, tourism boards, investors, fans and other key stakeholders.[195] The future is looking bright!

14 Future Directions

The purpose of this book has been to record the History of Women's Squash in Australia from the 1930s to 2010 and to learn about the circumstances that led to the Golden Age. This was an extremely successful period and it would do well for Squash to reflect on this history and to ascertain factors that led to this phenomenal run, in order to consider the future directions for the sport. As Marshall McLuhan said 'We look at the future through a rear view mirror. We march backwards into the future'. That is learn from the actions of the past that led to such success or failure.

By now you will have learned that the growth and success of the women's game commenced through the persistence of a few women, initially Mrs Joan Long Inness and Mrs Ross Grey Smith who wanted to play the game, even though squash courts in the 1930s were strictly a male domain. Also, the formation in 1952 of the AWSRA and VWSRA at Betty Meagher's initiative resulted in more women being encouraged to play. Heather McKay's achievements 1962–1979, led to considerable success on the world stage and the subsequent development of international matches, World Championships and the growth of the game. This was backed up by the sound administration of Jean Walker who ensured that these events took place. From 10 countries playing squash in the 60s it rose to 60 in 2016.[196]

The environment in Australia, throughout the 1960s until 2010, was vibrant with excellent court facilities, court owners encouraging young players to play, families also encouraging their kids to join in, good coaching was available, (locally and at various Institutes of Sport throughout the country)and Australia had a 'culture' of expecting to win.

In the 1960s–1970s, these were Kevin Kennedy, Vin Napier, Fred Barlow, Keith Walker, Kevin Parker (NSW), Brian Boys (Vic), Aub Amos (Q) and later Dardir. Also overseas, Nazrullah Khan helped many an Aussie player at the Lansdowne Club in London. There were a only a few female coaches in the beginning—Betty Meagher (Vic) and Yvonne Barlow (Swan–NSW), in the 1950s and Judy FitzGerald (1960–1980). In the 1980s–1990s, Rita Paulos, Barbara de Bruine, Di Davis, Robyn Prentice and Karen Cagliarini together with Roger Flynn (Victoria) and Ken Watson (WA) have been instrumental in developing top players, whilst Heather McKay and Geoff Hunt brought them up to International level at the AIS. The environment of good coaches, supportive court owners, and excellent practice partners paved the way for the development of a winning culture which has been detailed earlier in the book.

In general, in the 1950s and 60s, Australian sport was excelling, with the performances of Hoad and Rosewall in the Davis Cup and later John Newcombe and Tony Roche. The swimmers, Dawn Fraser, Lorraine Crapp, Jon Hendricks, John Devitt and Gary Chapman, Betty Cuthbert; Herb Elliott, Ron Clark and Shirley Strickland in Athletics and many other sports, too numerous to mention here, were also outstanding on the World stage. It is also worth mentioning that during the '60s–'80s, there weren't the distractions of social media and devices, the diversity of individual fitness choices or the mobility of the community that now prevail. People therefore focussed on their chosen activity and endeavoured to excel. Sarah Fitz-Gerald agrees with this stating 'kids today have a hell of a lot more sports to choose from.' [197]

It is also important to mention the stability and expertise of the squash administration: Ted Barlow was Secretary-Manager of NSW Squash 1965–91, Bev Gould initiated Australian Junior Age Championships in 1982, Vic Belsham was President of ASRA from 1976–84, Bob Finch was President of ASRA from 1976–92, Chris Sinclair, an international referee has been involved in administration in NSW since the early 1980s and Paul Vear has been an historian, squash court owner, innovator, and administrator for over 30 years. This stability has enabled Squash to evolve and become a force on the World stage establishing networks. The formation of WSPA in 1984 enabled the sport to flourish and for the players to become full-time professionals. The infrastructure at the time of writing in 2021 is now far more worldwide than it was up until 2010. The game has exploded in Egypt, is flourishing in the US and growing quickly in Europe, Asia and South America. 'There are squash courts from Ushuaia, the southernmost court in Chile to Svalbard Island, inside the Arctic Circle.'[198]

Today, from an Australian perspective, our results on the international scene are disappointing. There are no male or female players in the top 20 on the PSA World rankings. Why is it so? What can we learn from the past?

Firstly, one of the limitations that squash faces in Australia today, is the reduction in the number of available courts. In the 1970s and '80s it seemed that there was a squash court in every suburb and everyone was playing it. According to Squash Australia, in the '80s and '90s there were over one million participants. In 2016, squash participants had dropped to only 100,000 people nationally. What happened? When Rory Gibson interviewed former CEO Richard Vaughan he replied, 'the facilities were always in great locations—in the CBD or the middle of established suburbs. Land prices have increased faster than just about anywhere else in the world since the 1980s and as numbers of participants were falling it made economic sense to sell off your centre.'[199]

Is the shortage of courts anything new? Not really. The same issues were faced in the '30s. What is the solution? Squash Australia needs to lobby governments to build indoor community facilities that have a multiplicity of indoor sports, for example, table tennis, badminton, basketball, volleyball, tennis, swimming and squash. Courts with moveable walls can be used for boxing, concerts and theatre-in-the-round. Sporting organisations could house their administration there, not unlike those at the Melbourne Sport and Aquatic Centre. Also shopping mall owners need to be approached. Squash and Fitness Centres and the above-mentioned sports can be housed in shopping malls. Families could go there for the day. Work out, shop, go to the movies etc. This would address the problem of participation, but not necessarily the quality of performance.

Secondly, from my perspective, the above is all well and good, however, you still have to have skilled personnel at the coalface to introduce people to the sport. If you join a golf club, there are golf pros on site to teach you how to play and members to encourage you to join the club. If your kids want to play soccer, Little Athletics, rugby or tennis there are registration days, uniforms to be purchased and a structure through which the players progress. The squash centres that implement a similar structure thrive. It is the personal touch and the love of the game that will identify some of our future players. It is important to remember that most children have made their choices in sport by the ages of 12–13 and after that, my observations as a teacher and coach are that it's too late. The squash centre becomes a home away from home and has been responsible, in the past, for the development of many of our champions through the Junior ranks, for example, Sue Newman, Barbara Wall, Rhonda Thorne, Robyn Friday, Carin Clonda, Liz Irving, Michelle Martin, Sarah Fitz-Gerald, Carol Owens, Danielle Drady, Rachael and Natalie Grinham.

Thirdly, talented, experienced coaches, who are producing players should be identified and encouraged. They would be in charge of regional hubs where young players within an approximate 50km radius are encouraged to attend and be identified. They could then be placed in junior, development and elite squads which encourage them to progress through the ranks. These should be visited by National Mentor Coaches to help the younger coaches get established. They could also be used to identify raw talent throughout the country. Heather McKay came from Queanbeyan and to take a leaf out of Tennis Australia, some of their best players have also come from the country, for example, Margaret Court from Albury NSW, Yvonne Cawley from Barellan NSW and Ash Barty from Ipswich Qld. They could also scout the indigenous community. The satellite coaching programme, initiated in the late '80s, needs to be reintroduced, together with biennial coaching conferences. The Australian Coach of the Year should be sponsored to attend any international coaching conference that may be being conducted in that particular year and attend the World Championships. They would be required to disseminate information so gained to a coaches' conference and/or via the coaches' newsletters or seminars.

Fourthly, scholarships should be reintroduced for players who are achieving at the national level. These would be graded according to the age level, however it would give players the opportunity to CHOOSE their OWN coach and CHANGE this, as necessary. Former AIS or State Institute (or equivalent) Scholarship holders, should be encouraged to put back in to junior clubs, as part of the terms and conditions of their scholarships. There are many club players and parents who want to encourage their kids to play, however they often don't have the expertise to start their children off with the correct technique and these errors have to be corrected later. In Gymnastics, they put their best coaches at the beginning of a player's career.

Fifthly, State Coaching Director positions should be re-established, as full-time paid positions, to run coaching courses, visit schools and co-ordinate the mentor and satellite coaches' activities. Today, there is so much emphasis on participation to get our numbers up, which wasn't a problem in the past, however without good coaches our future top players aren't going to emerge.

We can also learn from other sports. At a coaching conference I attended in the late 1980s, Bill Sweetenham, then Head Coach of Australian Swimming, stated that 'we need 240,000 swimmers at our grass roots level, to get our 24 medallists at the international level'. Nothing has really changed in this regard, but the pathways have to lead through the hands of recognised coaches.

It's a shame that many of our former top players find coaching positions overseas that are obviously more lucrative than what they can find in Australia. Liz Irving has coached overseas with great success (her story has been told elsewhere) with Nicol David winning 5 World Championships. Rachael Grinham also achieved her potential by playing in Egypt for 8 years, where she received financial support. Similar stories appear in the men's game with Rodney Martin, Brett Martin, Anthony Hill, Rodney Eyles and Chris Robertson all having held, or currently holding, overseas coaching positions. Without offering these former top players secure coaching positions in Australia, their talents will be used overseas to our detriment.

In addition, we need to attract top international players to play in our championships and inspire our youth, by gaining sufficient sponsorship for the tournaments.

The question I'm sure you will be asking is, where does the money come from? Is it possible to have, for example, a 5% levy on the sale of squash balls, rackets and clothing? Can we raise our sponsorship level so that we are not so dependent on the Australian Sports Commission for funding? Players today get many endorsements. Are the clothing, drink, and equipment companies possibilities to obtain endorsements to encourage the youth of our country to reach the highest levels?

Squash Australia's recent initiatives have been addressing the issue of the need for increased participation. So far, there has been an increase, with numbers rising by 20,000 per year since 2016.[200] The initiatives are also dedicated to assisting with new squash facility development. Court owners can now obtain assistance for existing facilities to improve what they have to offer. There is now a Facilities Working Group which has a new affiliation portal which provides information on best practice guides to assist with success and sustainability. Court numbers are on the increase and Sarah Fitz-Gerald and her husband Cameron Dalley are heavily involved building new centres throughout the country. These developments can link into the promotions designed to increase the number of participants and provide data and statistics to get sponsors involved in the future developing markets.

Sarah has also noted 'that a lot of Aussie squash talent based overseas is returning home. These, too, need to be tapped into.' [201] Some of this has occurred already with Karen Cagliarini recently being appointed Victorian State Coaching Director. Unfortunately, this is an unpaid position, which surely must be rectified. The position had not been filled for many years and is a step in the right direction. Karen was a former World no. 36 and won numerous events at junior and senior levels including the 2000 Victorian Open. She has also been involved in coaching and junior development since 1990 and brings a wealth of experience to the position. Sarah Fitz-Gerald is President of S&RV, a three-year appointment. This is an outstanding appointment and I'm sure that she will bring dynamism to the position with her wide experience.

Another development which is also encouraging is the re-emergence of Amanda Hopps onto the squash scene. Amanda was under-13 Australian Junior Champion in 1984, under-15 in 1986 and under-19 in 1988. She is also a former PSA player and reached her highest world ranking of 57 in 2006. Amanda has been recognised as a talented pathway coach and recently participated in the AIS Elevate Women Coach Program. Coming from WA this will be a big boost to their programs. She recently stated that 'Coaches are the backbone of sports development. The reasons we coach are that we have an inbuilt passion for the sport and want to pass on the skills and knowledge to those that are interested.'[202] Yes! This program also links in with the AIS's National Coach Development strategy launched in 2021, which is aimed at making Australia the world leader in modern high performance coaching development before the end of the decade. Amanda will be able to link with another enthusiast Sue Hillier who is the current State Performance Pathway Co-ordinator and former WA Champion. Sue, thinks 'the squash community could do more to celebrate the achievements of its most inspirational players, including female World Champions. We need these role models for the next generation to come through'.

Former World Champion Vicki Cardwell is currently the State Regional Development Officer, in South Australia. A squash tragic, Vicki is passionate about the sport, and states 'I coach because I enjoy the reward of seeing players embracing the challenge of being the best that they can be!' Another very big positive, this time for South Australia.

In Queensland, Lisa Camilleri, another PSA player who competed on the World tour for 17 years and reached a World ranking of 28, is also becoming involved. She is now taking her young family, in a motorhome, on a squash tour around rural and regional Queensland, promoting the game. She is travelling from Mackay to Ingham, Rockhampton, across to Mt Isa, visiting towns along the way. This is a trip which will cover thousands of kilometres. From Mt Isa she is hoping to take her coaching clinic into the Northern Territory. 'Now her passion is to give back to squash, raising the sport's profile and encouraging participation along the way!'

So, things are happening!

The sport globally has also changed significantly since its inception, with the future looking bright. There is a full professional circuit for the top players, with excellent prize money to sustain a very comfortable lifestyle. The sport has World Championships as well as many other lucrative tournaments and is included in the Commonwealth Games and now the Olympics. There is also a strong Masters' circuit enabling lifetime involvement and participation in the sport. We now need to address the issues outlined above in Australia, to ride the wave of the future developments in the sport. It is time to move forward.

Timeline

1913   First squash courts in Melbourne Club. They were converted from Rackets courts. Sir Norman Brookes (Kooyong member) was the mover behind this. He was well known in tennis circles.

1920s   The gymnasium in Sydney used by the Bjelke Petersen School was converted to a squash court. It was used by Lord Mountbatten (during the visit of the Prince of Wales) who was an avid player. This court was for Men only.

1927   Royal Melbourne Tennis Centre (American dimensions)

1932   Royal Sydney Golf Course built two courts. Other courts were also built at Crib Point Naval Base (Vic), Royal Melbourne Tennis Club, South Yarra Club and the Lawn Tennis Association Victoria (now Kooyong). Royal Melbourne set aside a Squash Court and allowed women in as squash players!

1932   Commercial Court built in Canberra House, Little Collins Street, Melbourne. First Australian Men's Championship held.

First Women's Tournament held in Victoria. Won by Ross Grey Smith (who insisted in playing against the men in Bjelke Petersen's Annual Squash Tournament).

1933   NSW Squash Rackets Association formed

1934   Australia Squash Rackets Association was formed in Melbourne. Women's Squash Rackets Association formed in Great Britain (approximately 20 years before Australian Women's Association)

1935   Langridge Courts were built in Sydney (Men only). First Pennant Competition under auspices of ASRA 5 clubs in one grade

1937   First Annual Report of ASRA

1938   Royal Sydney Golf Club commenced a Pennant Competition

1940   SRAV have 18 clubs in 5 grades

1939–45 World War II. Very little competition

1946   Australian Women's Championships recommence. Won by Betty Meagher who subsequently became the trailblazer for several years, winning again in 1949 and 1950.

1950   Betty Meagher travelled overseas and competed in a number of tournaments in the UK She was runner-up in the Hampshire Open Championships. She also competed in the British Women's Open Championship losing in the second round 9–7. 9–6, 9–0

1951–2   Betty Meagher on return from overseas purchased courts in Melbourne, from Gordon Watson, who had travelled by sea to London with Betty and her husband Alan in 1950

1952   Australian Women's Squash Rackets Association formed, together with the Victorian Women's Association. Founded by Betty Meagher, who was President of both.

1952   Judith FitzGerald (Tissot) won the Australian Women's Championships.

1953   WA and SA founded their Associations. First Women's Tour of New Zealand. F. Williams, M. Maher, B. Malcolm, R. Maddern, B. Meagher

1954   Over 1000 Women players and Interstate Team's Events. Invitation to WSRA to send two players, Janet Morgan and Sheila Speight to Australia for exhibitions and to participate in tournaments. They were a level above the Australians and Janet Morgan defeated Sheila Speight in the final of the Australian Championships 9–2, 5–9, 9–2, 9–3. They also visited NZ on a promotional tour.

1954–55   Judith FitzGerald (Tissot) travelled to London independently. She reached the 4th Round of the British and won the East of England, the West of England and the Isle of Wight Championships.

1956–8   Judith FitzGerald (Tissot) won the Australian Women's Championship.

1960   Heather Blundell played in the NSW Country Women's tournament. This was her first tournament. She won the Junior and Open event. A few months later, Heather lost to Yvonne West in the NSW Open event (in the quarter finals) and defeated Barbara Baxter in the final of the NSW Junior Championships. Heather was selected in the NSW team at no. 4 and won the Australian Championship, having to play through the qualifying rounds. She was Australian Champion after 6 months of competitive play.

1960–61   AWSRA decided to send a Women's Team to the UK by sea. The team comprised the State Champions—Jan Shearer (SA), Yvonne West (NSW). They were soundly beaten by the UK team 3–0 in an unofficial match. Jan Shearer did win the British Junior Open.

1961   An invitational Australian team (all Under 21) visited NZ. By now 200 women were playing squash in Victoria and there were over 300 junior female players. Members were Lois Wright (Vic) Bev Garfield (Vic-née Meagher) Joan Morey (Vic) Fay Grant (SA) and Caroline Kent (Vic)

1962   Heather Blundell travelled independently to the UK. She lost her first match in the Scottish Championships to Fran Marshall (the current British Open Champion) in 5. She was never to lose again. A few weeks later, Heather won the British Open final 3–0 against Fran.

1963   An Australian Junior Women's team was invited to tour New Zealand. The team comprised Bev Garfield (Meagher) and Di Bruce (Vic), Heather Rhead and Marion Hawcroft (Qld) and Jenny Irving (Vic) as manageress. Dot Deacon (Linde–Qld) was an unofficial visitor with the team. The two Queensland players were the first to gain overseas selection for their state. They had a successful tour, defeating the NZ Open team. Dot won the Senior event in the Northern Island Championship and Di won the Junior event. Their standard was already much higher than the Kiwis. Heather Blundell won her second British Open and second Australian title

1963–64   All states were now affiliated with the AWSRA. The funds of the Association were in dire straits with them being forced to obtain an overdraft of 100 pounds! The AWSRA were granted permission for one official match against the UK. The girls raised their own funds. They defeated the UK 3–2. This was the first time the British had ever been beaten on their home soil. Heather won her third British Open and her third Australian Open.

1965   UK sent a team to Australia. The Australian team of Heather Blundell (NSW), Marion Hawcroft (Qld) and Jenny Irving (Vic) won the series 3–0, however, all tests were only won by a 2–1 margin. Heather won her fourth British Open and her fourth Australian title

1966–7   An Official Australian team was sent to play the first Test series against Great Britain. Funds were raised by AWSRA and the whole team travelled by air. The tour was of 7 weeks duration.

Australia defeated UK 2–1 after losing the first test. The team was Heather McKay (NSW), Marion Hawcroft (Qld) Barbara Baxter (NSW) and the reserves were Robyn Kennedy (Vic)

Marlene Tierney (SA) Heather McKay won her fifth British Open and her fifth Australian title. She continued to win the Australian titles consecutively until 1973 (when she moved to Canada) and the British until 1977–16 consecutively

1968–70   No teams' events were held

1971   AWSRA fully funded a promotional tour which included Canada, US and Honolulu. Australia d UK 3–0. Team members were Heather McKay (NSW), Marion Jackman (Hawcroft) (Qld), Jenny Irving (Vic), Mavis Baker (NSW) and Jean Walker (NSW) (Capt)

1972   UK sent team to Australia. The Australian team of Heather McKay (NSW) Marion Jackman (Qld), Jenny Irving (Vic), Mavis Baker (NSW) Jean Walker (NSW) (Capt) soundly defeated the UK without dropping a game. In just under 20 years the wheel had gone full circle!

1973–4   No teams' events were held Marion Jackman won the Australian Amateur Championship

1975   Australia sent a fully funded team to UK by air (exhibitions and Test series) with promotional tours to Sweden and Canada. The game was becoming more international. In the UK Australia won the Test series 3–0, only dropping one game out of 9. Australia had 6 of the 8 top seeds for the British Open (which Heather won). She couldn't compete in the Teams Event as she was now a professional. The Australian team comprised Marion Jackman (Qld), Sue Newman (NSW) Lyle Hubinger (Qld), Margaret Zachariah (Vic), Chris van Nierop (WA) and Carol Murray (Manager–NSW).

Sue Newman won the Australian Amateur Championship

1976   Inaugural WORLD Championship held in Brisbane thanks to the tireless efforts of Jean Walker (President AWSRA). Heather McKay defeated Marion Jackman 9–2, 9–2, 9–0 in an all Australian final. An international Teams event was held and the Australian team of Sue Newman (NSW) and Chris van Nierop (WA) defeated the UK 2–1. Jenny Irving was Captain of the team and Jean Walker (NSW) was Manageress

Sue Newman won the Australian Amateur Championship

Heather McKay d Marion Jackman in the inaugural World Open Championship

1977   Margaret Zachariah Won the Australian Amateur Championship

1978   Formation of the Women's International Squash Rackets Federation. Jean Walker was instrumental in its establishment.

Formation of WSPA (Women's Squash Players Association). The founding members of the Association were I. Hewitt (Ireland), Lyle Hubinger, Marion Jackman (Australia), Fran Marshall (Great Britain), Sue Newman, (Australia), Angela Smith (Great Britain), Barbara Wall (Australia). This didn't really get off the ground at this stage, but it was a start.

1978   British Open Championships Sue Newman (Aus) d Vicki Hoffmann (Aus) in another, all-Australian affair. The Australian team of Margaret Zachariah, Vicki Hoffmann, Anne Smith and Rhonda Shapland defeated Great Britain 1–0 in the final of a Round Robin event. Jan Honeycombe was the Manageress of this team.

Vicki Hoffmann won the Australian Amateur Championship

Sue Newman won the British Open Championship defeating Vicki Hoffmann

1979   British Open Championships Barbara Wall (Aus) d Sue Cogswell (GB)

Vicki Hoffmann won the Australian Open Championship and won it again in 1980, 1982–84 and 88–9. If you include the Amateur Championship, she won in 1978, she won a total of 8! *

*These results won't be included in the years following to avoid repetition.

In the World Championships Australia had 6 of the top 8 seeds. Heather McKay d Sue Cogswell (UK). Heather retired soon after this with an incredible record.

In the inaugural World Teams event, the Australian team of Barbara Wall, Vicki Hoffmann and Sue King (Capt), with Reserves, Rhonda Shapland and Anne Smith were defeated by Great Britain 3–0. The British had won the World teams title and our consecutive run had ended. These World Teams Championships were to be held biennially.

1980 Australian Championships Open Vicki Hoffmann d Sue Cogswell

British Open Championship Vicki Hoffmann d Sue Cogswell

In the Test series (held in Perth–Australia) Australia d Great Britain 2–1. The team comprised Vicki Hoffmann, Rhonda Thorne (Shapland) Sue King and Barbara Oldfield. Margaret Zachariah was Captain The British team was Sue Cogswell, Lesley Moore and Barbara Diggens. The Aussies had avenged their earlier defeat, in 1979 and were on top again. This was the last of the Great Britain v Australia Test series.

*Note the World Individual Championships were only held every two years

1981 Amalgamation of the Men's and Women's Australian Associations. Equal prize money for Men and Women was agreed to (in principle).

Rhonda Thorne won the Australian Open defeating Vicki Hoffmann 10–9, 9–6, 9–6

Vicki Hoffmann won the British Open defeating Margaret Zachariah 9–6, 9–4, 9–0 in another All Australian Final.

Third World Championship held in Canada. The competition had expanded from 6 countries to 14 countries. Rhonda Thorne d Vicki Hoffmann 8–10, 9–4, 9–5, 7–9, 9–7 in the final. The playing time of the match was 1 hour and 57 minutes, and still holds the record for longest World Championship match, in another All-Australian Final.

In the Teams' event, the Australian team of Heather McKay, (Manager/Coach) Vicki Hoffmann, Rhonda Thorne, Barbara Oldfield and Rae Anderson defeated the UK 2–1 to become World Champions.

A Junior Women's team was sent overseas to compete in a 3 Test series in the UK. The team comprised Robyn Belford, Robyn Friday), Michelle Toon and Wendy Williams. They were unsuccessful, but gained valuable experience.

1982   Vicki Cardwell won the British Open defeating Lisa Opie (UK)

1983   Australian team of Rhonda Thorne (Capt), Carin Clonda, Jan Miller, and Di Davis won the World Women's Teams' Event, defeating Great Britain in the final 1–0*. Marie Donnelly was Manager and Judith FitzGerald was Coach-Manager. *Note: This was a Round Robin event.

Robyn Friday won the inaugural World Junior Event. There was also a Junior Teams' event and the Australian team was Carol Kennewell, Liz Irving, Robyn Friday and Helen Paradeiser and the girls gained invaluable experience.

Vicki Cardwell won the British Open defeating Lisa Opie Vicki was ineligible to represent Australia in the Teams' event due to a two-year ban that had been imposed, in 1981.

1984   This year saw the emergence of Susan Devoy (New Zealand) on the World stage. She went on to win the British Open eight times (1984–1990 and 1992) playing a British player every time except for Liz Irving in 1988. Australia didn't win the British again until the Michelle Martin in 1993. Susan was also World Champion (1985, 1987, 1990 and 1992**). She was a force to be reckoned with.

**Note: These results will not be repeated in the years below to avoid repetition.

1985   Australia lost three of its top players as Vicki Cardwell had retired to start a family, Rhonda Thorne retired from competitive squash and Liz Irving was out with a back injury It was time to regroup. The Australian team selected to play in Ireland were, Jan Miller (Captain), Carin Clonda, Dianne Davis and Tracey Smith (replacing Liz Irving). There were now 14 countries competing and teams were divided into 4 pools and then played off in semi-finals and finals. Australia were defeated in their pool 3–0 by New Zealand (ably led by Susan Devoy, British and World Open Champion). They were then defeated by England in the semi-finals 3–0, whilst New Zealand were defeated by England 2–1 with Susan Devoy being the only winner for New Zealand.

Jan Miller (South Australia) won the Australian Open

The AIS (Australian Institute of Sport) was being formed at the Gold Coast and Geoff Hunt and Heather McKay were recruited to run the program. This program was developed to enable Australia to regroup and identify talent so that it could be a force to be reckoned with in the future. In fact, it laid the groundwork for amazing success in the Women's game during the '90s and through until 2010. The Australian Women's team won 7 out of 11 Women's Teams' Championships contested (1990–2010) with 4 consecutive wins from 1992–1998, GB/England won 3 and Egypt won 1.

WISPA (Women's International Squash Players Association) was re-activated (originally formed in 78). It was the governing body for the women's professional squash circuit between 1985 and 2011. This organisation provided the means for the Women players to become professional and earn a decent living.

1986   Lisa Opie (GB) won the Australian Open

The Australian Junior Age Championships were a feature run by Beverley Gould and there is no doubt, that the conduct of this event and the annual overseas tour programme of the past decade, together with the Coaching Accreditation Scheme and the Australian Institute of Sport Squash Unit contributed to the improved calibre of Australia's elite players both at the Junior and Open level'

The ASRA entered into a five-year contract with Australian Squash Promotions Limited for the conduct of an Australian event on a transportable see-through glass court.

ASRA conducted a week-long National Coach Education workshop at the AIS, in Canberra, to assist State Coaching Directors in effectively implementing the National Coaching Accreditation Scheme (NCAS)

Internationally, an inaugural Asian Pacific meeting was held and this was the first step to mould all nations in our region into a cohesive force in World Squash Affairs. The game was becoming global, with the emphasis to create a spectator sport with the development of the transportable see-through perspex court, a white glo-ball and world class players, to provide the environment to attract 2000 spectators to watch world class squash. Players of the calibre of Jahingar Khan participated and Ten Network televised the Championships, nationally.

1987   The Australian team of Vicki Cardwell (Captain), Sarah Fitz-Gerald, Michelle Martin and Robyn Lambourne (Friday) travelled to New Zealand for the World Championships. Again, there were 14 teams competing. Australia managed to defeat New Zealand in a thrilling semi-final where Vicki defeated Susan Devoy in 5. Unfortunately, in the final Lisa Opie of England proved strong and defeated Vicki in 4 and whilst Robyn Lambourne defeated Martine le Moignan in 5, Sarah (in the early stages of her career) was defeated 3–0 by Lucy Soutter. England won 2–1

Sarah Fitz-Gerald won the World Junior Championship defeating Donna Vardy of England 3–0

Lisa Opie (GB) won the Australian Open d Liz Irving in the final

Referees were contributing on the World scene, which indicated our significance as a World Squash power. David Donelly greatly influenced the ISRF Rules and Refereeing Committee rewriting some of the rules in their entirety and David and Chris Sinclair attained International Referee Accreditation. David Donelly and Harry McMaster officiated at the ICI World Open and Teams Championships in Birmingham and London, and Margaret Campbell, Neil Butler and Chris Sinclair officiated at the Honda World Women's Championships in New Zealand. Bob Finch continued to Chair the ISRF Fixtures Committee and was Australia's representative at the ISRF Annual general meeting in London. Australia was making its presence felt at all levels of the game.

The Australian Open was held at the Sleeman Complex in Brisbane and squash was starting to take the sport to the public.

Barbara Slotemaker de Bruïne (ACT Coaching Director) conducted the inaugural Level 2 Course in Canberra. With the contacts she had made at the University of Canberra doing her Sports Studies degree, she was able to involve first class lecturers, including Geoff

Hunt, Julie Draper (Biomechanics) John Gross (Psychology) and many others. Thirteen coaches from all over Australia attended, including Rita Paulos (Q), Simon Weatherill (Vic) and also Alan Ngan (Hong Kong).

1988   Australia hosted the 21st ISRF seminars and Annual General Meeting held in Brisbane, at the time of the World Expo. New rules of the game were adopted (with effect from 1st May, 1989) with a reduced height of the tin from 19 inches (48cms) to 17inches (43cms), one serve and point-a-rally (PARS) scoring system. Anti-doping rules and regulations were added to the ISRF Constitution. Minor changes to approved racket specifications to manage the advent of new materials used in the manufacture of rackets and strings.

Nigel Champion resigned as National Coaching Director and Barbara Slotemaker de Bruïne was appointed. The NCAS Level 2 manual was being developed and a National Coaching seminar was held at the QEII complex. Quality speakers included Geoff Hunt, Heather McKay, Jeff Wollstein (Physiology), Ian Lynagh (Psychology) David Keating (Administration) and Judy Walker (Nutrition). At the conclusion of seminar, it was recommended that a National Coaching seminar should be an annual event with the emphasis directed towards the more practical aspects of coaching. This was helping to lay the groundwork for Coach Education and subsequent improved methodology in the training of our future players. A second Level 0 coaching manual was also developed targeting the Primary School level with lessons which could be conducted, in the school grounds

The AIS squash unit was granted another 4-year term due to the success of its players. A STEP (Sports Talent Encouragement Plan) was introduced where grants were made to selected athletes ranked 15th or better in the World. Squash beneficiaries during

1988 (amongst the women), were Sarah Fitz-Gerald, Robyn Friday and Michelle Martin—forces to be reckoned with in the future.

ASRA maintained a strong presence and influence at international level including Bob Finch (Chairperson, International Fixture Committee), Margaret Zachariah (ISRF Women's Committee), Carin Clonda (Chairperson WISPA) and David Donelly (ISRF Rules and Referees Committee).

Victorian Squash was revamped to incorporate the players and venue operators and the Victorian Squash Federation was formed. This meant that Squash and Squash and Racquetball centres would come under one body. This would alleviate the financial difficulties being experienced by the VSRA and put squash in Victoria on a more sound financial footing. It was a successful move and enabled the VSF to obtain substantial sponsorship from both the public and private sectors. As a result, a transportable four-walled perspex court was purchased and utilised both in Victoria and Interstate including Melbourne Central, Martin Place, Homebush in Sydney, the World Trade Centre and King Club in Melbourne. This made the public more aware of the sport and court bookings over the next few years increased by between 15% and 30% both in Victoria and Nationally. This meant that our pool of potential champions was also on the increase.

1989   The World Teams' Championships were played in the Netherlands and the English team were on a roll. Our team comprised some of the old (Vicki Cardwell and Liz Irving) and some of the new (Danielle Drady—with Michelle Martin and Sarah Fitz-Gerald waiting in the wings), and they were no match for their more seasoned opponents—Martine Le Moignan, Suzanne Horner and Lisa Opie. Liz Irving l Martine Le Moignan 3–1, and Danielle Drady l Suzanne Horner 3–2, in a close tussle. England won 2–0

On the home front, Squash in Australia, made decisions deemed necessary for the betterment of the sport as a major recreational and competitive sporting activity. For the following two years a major ISPA-WISPA approved Australian Championship, (financially guaranteed by Squash players), would be held. The community at large would be able to see major world-class tournaments in Australia. The decision to host the World Women's Individual and Teams event, in Sydney, in 1990, would see the attention of World Squash, on Australia

Bob Finch was elected Vice President of ISRF at the Annual Meeting. held in Singapore. He was to hold the position for the next seven years (the maximum period allowable), which was an indication of the professionalism of Squash Administration and Management in our country. He was the first Australian elected as an officer of the ISRF and this resulted in close ties with the participating countries, including the Asia-Pacific. This would result in opportunities for tournaments to be held World-wide and would give the profile required for sponsorship and the development of increased prize money for the players.

David Donelly attended the ISRF Rules and Referees Committee meetings, making a great contribution on the international scene.

The new NCD (Barbara Slotemaker de Bruïne) produced the Aussie Sports manual which contained lesson plans for Grades 4–6. Slow motion cinematography was recorded by the Biomechanics lab under the guidance of Bruce Mason of Heather McKay's stroke production at the AIS, in Canberra. Fourteen coaches attended the Level 2 Coaching Course conducted in Sydney, and the number of Level 1 Coaches had grown from 51 in 1985 to 822. There were now more coaches qualified to introduce youngsters to the game of Squash

The National Coaching Committee was active and discussed:

- Honorary Accreditation for Level 2 recommended inclusions for the Level 2 Manual
- Developed a Coaching Newsletter
- Formed the Australian Coaches Association
- Evaluated the Aussie Sports lesson plans and
- Standardised Level 1 examinations and assessment procedures

The inaugural meeting of the Squash Sports Science Advisory Committee was held. Attendees included Ian Lynagh (Psychologist), Ian Gillam (Sports Scientist) and Bruce Abernathy (Bio mechanist). They decided to:

- Review all sports science information that may have relevance to Squash
- Act as an advisory body to the NCD in all matters pertaining to the science of squash and where necessary re-write articles for the proposed Coaches Newsletter
- Advise the National Coaching Committee on Sports Science requirements for the Level 3 Coaching Course

A National Coaches' Workshop was held in Queensland which was attended by 25 coaches. Topics included skill development, fitness training, nutrition, tactics, mental preparation, techniques for assessing players and general issues such as the formation of a Squash Coaches' body and a proposed Coaches' Newsletter.

On the Refereeing front, Chris Sinclair, David Donelly and Graham Corderoy were among 24 referees world-wide that attained ISRF international status. Chris Dittmar chaired the ISRF Players' Association, David Donelly chaired the Rules and Referees Committee, Margaret Zachariah was on the Women's Committee and Barbara Slotemaker de Bruïne contributed to the ISRF by serving on the Committee. We were heavily involved on the international scene in all areas.

1990   This was a significant year with the Mazda World Women's Squash Championships being held at Homebush, in Sydney, on the four-walled perspex court. The Australian team of Robyn Lambourne, Danielle Drady, Liz Irving and Michelle Martin were about to test their wings Vicki Cardwell was the Coach and Margaret Zachariah was the Team Manager and Sarah Fitz-Gerald played in the Individual. They had experience and youth on their side. However, it was not to be. Michelle Martin d Suzanne Horner 3–2. Lisa Opie d Danielle Drady 3–1 and Martine Le Moignan d Liz Irving 3–2. it was close, but it wasn't to be. England 2–1

In the Individual Championship final, Susan Devoy (NZ) defeated Martine Le Moignan (England to collect her third World Championship

The Championships had been a great success with the largest—ever entry (128) for a World Women's Squash Championship. The dreams and vision of early pioneer Betty Meagher and more recently those of Jean Walker, had been realised. The sponsorship by Mazda, television courtesy of the ABC, the use of a four-walled perspex court with a specially illuminated white ball easily seen on tv screens, was a far cry from the Lansdowne Club in Mayfair, London, with sweating walls and small spectator facilities, which had been the former home of the British Open. Also, results were co-ordinated by a computer system developed by the ComSquash Group and this assisted in the management of the triple-plate draw and 18 country World Teams event. This was a new era!

For the second time in three years Squash Australia was honoured to host the Annual General meeting of the World Squash Federation (WSF) and its multitude of sub-committees This reflected the growing credibility and the professionalism of Squash management in this country.

One element in the modernisation of the National body was to adopt the business name of Squash Australia (instead of ASRA) and the development of a new logo and identity. Also, the Victorian Squash Federation's aim was to upgrade the Australian Open Championship and make it one of the most prestigious events on the international calendar. This was achieved with the help of a $50,000 donation from Squash Australia (SA) and it was to be held in the King Club in Melbourne, which could seat 750 spectators. They appointed an extremely talented Tournament Director, Greg Hutchings and the Men's event attracted six of the World's top seven players (including Jahingar Khan) whilst the Women's event attracted nine of the World's top eleven. Rodney Martin won the Men's Final defeating Chris Dittmar in the final. Rodney had defeated Jahingar in the semi-finals Susan Devoy defeated Michelle Martin in the Women's final in 4. These Championships gained almost half an hour television news-sports coverage and this together with the sponsorship of the Heart health Foundation and Victorian Health Promotion Foundation ensured that prize money was attractive to participating players. This together with the appointment of a public relations company Ingrid Roepers (IRPR) ensured the success of the Championships. The vision of the Victorian Squash Federation (VSF) and the professionalism of the Executive Director, Paul Vear and his team, had been achieved.

Other factors that would herald in the success of the next two decades were emerging. The Australian Annual Junior Age events, sponsored by the Commonwealth Bank, produced a new batch of future Australian and World class representatives. A significant statistic of the year's events was the number of winners produced by Queensland, which incidentally, had the highest proportional density of qualified coaches to total players, in the country.

The National Coaching Accreditation scheme was working! The female players that emerged in this time were Natalie Grinham (U13 Girls' Champion) and Carol Owens, who won the Under 19 Championship defeating Robyn Cooper in 5 in the final. All of these players went on to represent Australia.

This year saw the end an era at the AIS Squash Unit, with five of the most successful players finishing their scholarships. The World scene was now sufficiently developed that a competent squash player could earn on a living on the professional circuit and funds were also made available to players for overseas travel. no. more need for raffles! Heather McKay also reduced her coaching commitments and the AIS unit was fortunate to gain the services of Ken Hiscoe the player responsible for the emergence of Australia as an international force in the '60s.

1991   The Australian Heart Health Open was again held in Melbourne and Michelle Martin defeated Liz Irving in 4 gruelling games. The seven best women in the World had competed for the title.

Women's Committees were being formed at the National level to cover the areas of encouraging girls to play and to improve communications and development of a wider network with women involved in all areas of Squash and sport generally.

Coach Education was continuing and coaches needed to keep coaching or lose their accreditation. The Aussie Sports Manual and video was completed and distributed to schools and Level 0 organisers. These could also be used by the Level 1 coaches as there were many games and activities in the appendices, suitable to all age levels. The Level 2 Manual was to be ready for production in May 1992.

The Elite Coaches seminar was held in Adelaide and there was opportunity for cross fertilisation of ideas from Tennis, with the attendance of their NCD, Dennis Collette. Bruce Elliott (Biomechanist) discussed the advantages of the long v the short grip, Jeff Wollstein spoke of the long-term development of the elite athlete and Geoff Hunt and Gary Macintosh spoke of the requirements of their respective Institutes. This kept the coaches from all over Australia in the loop of the latest ideas and requirements for their pupils to progress and was an essential ingredient in their coach development. Networks were established and it was resolved to hold another Coaching seminar in Sydney in 1992. The AIS Satellite Coaching Programme continued to grow, with 20 coaches receiving funding of $1000 to assist in the identification of talent.

State Institutes of Sport started to develop with the Victorian Institute (under Gary Macintosh) developing many future top women players including Sarah Fitz-Gerald and, Carol Owens.

The British Open saw the first All British final since 1961, with Lisa Opie defeating Sue Wright

1992   Australian Women annex the World Women's Teams title after a break of 10 years (1983). The team of Robyn Lambourne, Liz Irving, Michelle Martin and Sarah Fiz-Gerald, under the guidance of Team Coach-Manager Di Davis defeated New Zealand 2–1. Liz Irving defeated Phillipa Beames 3–0, Susan Devoy defeated Michelle Martin 3–0 and it was up to Robyn Lambourne to secure the final rubber against Donna Newton, which she did 3–1. Di had been in the Australian team that last won in 1983 and she was delighted with the win.

In the Individual World Championships Susan Devoy d Michelle Martin

The Heart Health Australian Open was again held in Melbourne, this time in the 1300 seat John Batman Theatre located in the superbly appointed World Congress Centre. The top eight women in the World competed in this tournament. Again, the victor was Susan Devoy (NZ) who defeated Cassie Jackman of England in the final in 4. Our players, Robyn Lambourne and Michelle Martin were defeated by Cassie Jackman and Susan Devoy in the semi-finals.

The Australian Open was selected as one of the seven world events to be included in an International Super tv series culminating in the World final in Germany in 1993. A one hour highlights package of the Open was produced and screened to more than 200 million viewers in   countries. Squash was definitely going global and reaching the community and wider population.

As a result of the initiative of forming a Women's Committee in 1990, Squash Australia received a special commendation in the Prime Ministerial Women and Sport Awards for the Girls pilot Squash Program that was trialled in Victoria. Vicki Cardwell had administered the very successful program, whilst Di Davis carried out the coaching. This programme was also conducted in NSW under the guidance of Michelle Martin whilst Margaret Foley was coach of the South Australian programme.

Squash Australia took a global approach to increasing awareness of women's issues in squash—including junior participation, women in administration, decision-making roles, coaching coverage of Women's Squash in the National Squash Newsletter and promotional material etc. The topic of gender equity was extended to the international level when (SA) invited Sue Baker-Finch from the Sport Australia Women in Sport unit to make a presentation at the AGM of the ISRF held in Vancouver.

The Australian Squash Rackets Referees Association made the decision to restructure the body and create a Rules and Refereeing Committee under the umbrella of SA instead of the existing arrangement. A position of National Director of Refereeing was envisaged. Margaret Campbell was the interim occupant of the position. David Donelly, Neil Butler, Chris Sinclair and Margaret Campbell travelled to Vancouver to referee at the Women's World Individual and Teams' Championships. Here, a three official system operated throughout the main event, which proved to be very effective. A Refereeing Manual was also produced this year to explain the rules changes becoming effective in May, 1993.

The Oceania Squash Federation was formed during May, in Auckland. Former World Squash president, Murray Day was elected President, with Carol Murray (former Australian Vice-President) elected Vice-President. Col Clapper a former Australian Vice-President became the Honorary Executive. It was envisaged that this fledgling group of Oceania nations would provide the springboard for further development of Squash in our region. The inaugural Oceania Junior Championship was held with teams from Australia, New Caledonia, New Zealand, Papua New Guinea and Vanuatu competing in a week-long tournament.

Australia continued to be represented at the ISRF AGM with Ron Griffiths (SA Vice-President) attending. At this meeting the ISRF changed its name to the World Squash Federation (WSF). Bob Finch was re-elected as Vice-President of the WSF and continued as Chairman of the World Championship Committee. David Donelly was instrumental in the development of the new rules of the game and Margaret Zachariah continued to serve on the Women's Committee. In addition, Lynette O'Reilly served on the Development Committee and Jeff Wollstein (the new NCD) was a significant contributor to the Coaching Committee. Australia was well represented at the international level in several areas.

Barbara Slotemaker de Bruïne conducted the inaugural Level 2 Coaching Course in New Zealand and then resigned from the

NCD position (due to family commitments) in February. The number of accredited Level 1 coaches had increased to 984 and the number of Level 2 Coaches (In Australia) stood at 20. The Level 2 manual was completed and it was envisaged that it would be printed and distributed during 1993. Membership of the Professional Squash Coaches Association of Australia (PSCAA) reached 196 with 165 full members and 31 Associates (uninsured). Coaches Insurance consisting of Professional Indemnity and Public Liability was finalised with IEA during the year. Jeff Wollstein took over this position, and with strong support from Roger Flynn (VIS) continued to implement the NCAS.

With the help of an Australian Sports Commission grant, the inaugural State Coaching Directors' workshop was conducted in Melbourne. It was professionally organised and facilitated by Roger Flynn. Apart from the Northern Territory, all states were represented. Its purpose was a revamp of PSCAA, standardisation implementation of the NCAS and planning coaching-development programmes.

Coaching-Coach development was still a very high priority on Squash Australia's agenda and in November the AIS facilitated the 5th National Coaches Conference. A record number of coaches (50) participated. There was greater emphasis on the practical aspects with on-court workshops being conducted by Geoff Hunt, Heather McKay, Len Atkins, Roger Flynn and Dean Landy. Lectures were also conducted in Sports Medicine, Talent Development (with an in-depth analysis of Talent Development plans used by Tennis Australia) and Gender Equity in Sports Coaching.

The Satellite Coaching program continued with 20 more coaches being appointed by Geoff Hunt. The scheme was becoming more competitive each year with the standard and success of each regional program progressively increasing. A larger number (25) scholarship holders were selected into the AIS Squash Program. They were to be coached by Geoff Hunt and Ken Hiscoe. Jeff Wollstein (formerly the Exercise Physiologist and Assistant coach) reduced his workload when he became the full time NCD.

The ground had been laid for Australia to succeed at the international level for many years to come through grass roots development, education of coaches and opportunities to compete at the international level. The players that came through included Michelle Martin, Danielle Drady, Liz Irving. Sarah Fitz-Gerald as well as Rodney Martin and Brett Martin, Chris Robertson, Anthony Hill and Rodney Eyles.

On the administrative side, Bob Finch retired as President of Squash Australia after serving for the sport for 17 years. His drive and vision, together with that of Vic Belsham (and many others) resulted in the success of the Sport at international level.

Note: Most of the information from 1986–1992, was obtained from The Belsham Years, 1976–92, which has been an invaluable resource, hence I have not quoted individual pages.

1993   Saw the emergence of Michelle Martin to the top of the World Stage. She won the British Open defeating Suzanne Horner of England She also won the World Open defeating Liz Irving in an All-Australian final. This was to be the start of a marvellous career.

There was no World Team's event this year as they were only held biennially. The Individual event was now held annually.

Michelle Martin won the Australian Open from 1993–96 and again in 1998–9. A total of 7 overall ***

*** These results won't be included further on to avoid repetition

1994   Michelle defeated Liz in the final of the British Open. Again, she won the World Championship defeating Cassie Jackman of England.

In the Team's event the Australian Team of Michelle Martin, Liz Irving and Sarah Fitz-Gerald defeated the English team of Suzanne Horner, Sue Wright and Cassie Jackman 3–0, with none of the girls losing a game. They had come a long way and were indeed top of the world.

1995   Michelle again won the British Open Championship against her compatriot, Liz Irving. In the World Open (another all Australian final) she defeated up and coming Sarah Fitz-Gerald. Michelle had completed her hat trick of both titles. An amazing achievement!

1996   Michelle defeated Sarah in the British Open final 3–1. Their rivalry continued, however, this time Sarah defeated Cassie Jackman in the World Championship final 3–0. A new star had been born.

In the World Teams' event the Australian team of Michelle Martin, Sarah Fitz-Gerald and Liz Irving defeated the English team of Cassie Jackman, Linda Charman and Fiona Geaves 2–1. Michelle had a tough match against her old foe, Cassie Jackman, being defeated 3–2. Sarah rose to the challenge and defeated Linda 3–0. Liz finished the job defeating Fiona 3–0 and Australia's reign continued.

1997   Michelle was not to be denied and came back with a vengeance to defeat Sarah 3–1 in the British Open final. In the World Open Sarah defeated Michelle in a marathon 3–2. They were certainly pushing each other.

Sarah Fitz-Gerald won The Australian Open

1998   Change was afoot and Squash had been admitted into the Commonwealth Games held in Kuala Lumpur. Matches to be played included Singles, Doubles and Mixed Doubles. Australia had a strong team including Sarah Fitz-Gerald, Michelle Martin, Carol Owens, Rachel Grinham and Robyn Cooper. The Men's team was David Palmer, Paul Price, Craig Rowland and Byron Davis. The coaches were Geoff Hunt ably supported by Di Davis. Phil Trenorden was the Manager.

Michelle was thrilled to win the gold medal defeating Sarah (the top seed), in the final of the Individuals, 9-0, 9-6, 9–5. She teamed up with Craig Rowland to win gold again in the Mixed Doubles. Rachel Grinham and Robyn Cooper defeated Carol Owens and Sarah Fitz-Gerald, in the play off for silver, in Women's Doubles match. This was a new development and one welcomed by the players. Rodney Eyles and Byron Davis won silver in the Men's Doubles.

The British Open was still held and Michelle again asserted her dominance in this event, defeating Sarah 3–0. In the World Championships held in Stuttgart, the tables were turned and Sarah defeated Michelle in another cliff-hanger 3–2. In the World Teams' event, Australia was not to be denied and defeated England in the final 3–0. Michelle defeated Sue Wright 3–2. Carol Owens defeated Jane Martin 3–0 and Sarah defeated Suzanne Horner in the dead rubber 2–0. Australia was still on top.

1999   This year saw the changing of the guard*. In the British Open final Leilani Joyce from New Zealand emerged to claim the crown defeating Cassie Campion (Jackman) in the final 3–1 and Cassie Jackman defeated Michelle in the World Championship final 3–0.

*Note: Sarah was out with a meniscus tear (which required surgery) and Michelle retired soon after this to become a Mum.

2000   Leilani Joyce was again victorious, in the British Open, this time defeating Sue Wright 3–0

In the World Championship final played in Scotland, a new star had emerged in Carol Owens (Australia). She defeated Leilani in a real battle 3–2.

In the World teams' event, Australia had to regroup after the retirement of Michelle, and the unavailability of Carol Owens (who had moved to New Zealand), Liz Irving (injury) and Rachel Grinham (unavailable). This time the team of Sarah Fitz-Gerald, Natalie Grinham (a newcomer) and Robyn Cooper, couldn't manage a win. They lost 2–1 to England. Sarah defeated Linda Charman 3–0. However, Natalie had a lesson and was defeated by Tania Bailey 3–0, whilst Robyn put up more of a battle but was defeated 3–1 by Stephanie Brind.

Leilani Joyce (NZ) won the Australian Open

2001   Sarah Fitz-Gerald defeated Carol Owens (now playing for NZ) 3–0n the British Open. In the World Open Championship, Sarah Fitz-Gerald defeated Leilani Joyce (NZ) 3–0. She was now undisputed No1 in the World*. She had a stellar year as she also won the Australian Open. * Note the World Individuals were now being held annually.

2002   Sarah Fitz-Gerald again won the British Open, this time defeating Tania Bailey 3–0. In the World Individuals, Sarah defeated Natalie Pohrer (Grainger) 3–1. She also won the Australian Open.

In the World Teams' Championship held in Denmark, the Australian Team of Sarah Fitz-Gerald, Natalie Grinham, Rachael Grinham and Robyn Cooper (Reserve) defeated England 2–1. Sarah defeated Linda Charman 3–1. Natalie defeated Stephanie Brind 3–1 and Rachael lost the dead rubber 0–2. Australia was still the dominant nation.

This was a busy year as the Commonwealth Games was also a feature and it was held in Manchester, England. Sarah Fitz-Gerald, Rachel Grinham, Michelle Martin and Robyn Cooper were the Women's Team representatives and Di Davis was the Coach. The Men's Team comprised Byron Davis, Rodney Eyles, David Palmer, Paul Price and Craig Rowland. Geoff Hunt was the Coach. There was mixed success. Sarah Fitz-Gerald won the gold medal in the Women's Singles and Rachael Grinham won the bronze, David Palmer won the bronze in the Men's Singles tied with Stewart Boswell. Stewart Boswell and Anthony Rickets won silver in the Men's Doubles and David Palmer and Paul Price won the bronze. Natalie and Rachael Grinham won the bronze in the Women's Doubles and Robyn Cooper and Joseph Kniepp won a bronze in the Mixed Doubles.

2003   This year saw the emergence of Rachael Grinham. She won the British Open defeating Cassie Campion 3–1. However, Carol Owens (NZ) won the World Championships defeating Cassie 3–1and Carol became the new World no. 1.

Sarah Fitz-Gerald won the Australian Open

2004   Rachael Grinham won the British Open again defeating Natalie Grainger of England 3–1 and Vanessa Atkinson (Netherlands) defeated Natalie Grinham in the final of the World Open 3–0. In the World Teams Championships Australia defeated England 2–0. Rachel defeated Cassie Jackman 3–2 and Natalie defeated Linda Elriani (Charman) 3–0. The dead rubber between Amelia Pittock and Fiona Geaves wasn't played. Rachel Grinham was ranked no. 1 in the World at the end of this year

Natalie Grinham won the Australian Open

2005   This year saw the changing of the guard with a new champion. This time from Malaysia—Nicol David. She was to be the next dominant force until 2014! She won the British Open defeating Natalie Grinham 3–0. Also, the World Open defeating Rachel Grinham 3–1

Rachael managed to salvage some pride winning the Australian Open

2006   Nicol David defeated Rachel Grinham 3–0 in the British Open final. In the World Open, which was played in Ireland, Nicol had a real battle with Natalie but again won 3–2. Her reign was about to begin, or was it?

In the World Teams' Championship England defeated Egypt and it was the changing of the guard!

Kasey Brown (Australia) won the Australian Open

2007   This time Rachael Grinham prevailed and defeated Nicol David 3–2 in the British Open in what must have been a match and a half! Rachel also pulled off an amazing double by winning the World Open, this time defeating her sister, Natalie 3–0

Shelley Kitchen (NZ) won the Australian Open

2008   Nicol David again won the British Open defeating Jenny Duncalf of England 3–0. In the World Championships played in England; Nicol defeated Vicky Botwright of England 3–1 under the new PARS scoring system.

A. Au (Hong Kong) won the Australian Open

In the World Teams Championship played in Cairo, Egypt defeated England and it appeared as if our reign had come to an end? no, not quite!

2009   Rachael Grinham defeated Madeline Perry of England to win her third British Open 3–0. In the World Championships, Nicol David defeated Natalie Grinham (now playing for the Netherlands) 3–1

The Australian Open was once again won by an outsider—this time J. King (NZ)

2010   This year was to be our swan song. There was no competition in the British Open and Nicol David defeated Omneya Abdel Kawy (Egypt) 3–0 to win the World Championship (her fifth). In the World Teams' Championships where there were now 5 regions (Africa, America, Asia, Europe and Oceania—16 countries) competing in the different pools, Australia defeated England 2–1 in the final. Sarah Fitz-Gerald (playing at no. 3) came out of retirement to play, and defeated Sarah Kippax 3–0 . Rachael Grinham (No1) lost to Jenny Duncalf 3–0 and Kasey Brown No. 2 sealed the win, defeating Laura Massaro 3–1. Our reign was over and we haven't won another World Individual or Teams Championship since!

Madeline Perry (Ireland) won the Australian Open, just to rub salt into the wound.

The Golden Age was over!

Appendix-Results

Australian Amateur Women's Squash Champions					
Year	Winner	State	Year	Winner	State
1932	Bettine Grey-Smith	Vic	1959	Pat Parmenter	NSW
1933	Bettine Grey-Smith	Vic	1960	Heather Blundell	NSW
1934	Pamela Walker	NSW	1961	Heather Blundell	NSW
1935	Joan Long Innes	NSW	1962	Heather Blundell	NSW
1936	Dorothy Stevenson	Vic	1963	Heather Blundell	NSW
1937	Bettine Grey-Smith	Vic	1964	Heather Blundell	NSW
1938	Mary Armytage	Vic	1965	Heather Blundell	NSW
1939-45	No Competition–WWII		1966	Heather McKay (née Blundell)	NSW
1946	Betty Meagher	Vic	1967	Heather McKay	NSW
1947	Val Watts	Vic	1968	Heather McKay	NSW
1948	Val Watts	Vic	1969	Heather McKay	NSW
1949	Betty Meagher	Vic	1970	Heather McKay	NSW
1950	Betty Meagher	Vic	1971	Heather McKay	NSW
1951	Val Watts	Vic	1972	Heather McKay	NSW
1952	Judith Tissot	Vic	1973	Heather McKay	NSW
1953	Joan Watson	Vic	1974	Marion Jackman	QLD
1954	Janet Morgan	England	1975	Sue Newman	NSW
1955	Marea Maher	Vic	1976	Sue Newman	NSW
1956	Judith Tissot	Vic	1977	Margaret Zachariah	Vic
1957	Judith Tissot	Vic	1978	Vicki Hoffmann	SA
1958	Judith Fitz-Gerald (née Tissot)	Vic			

	Australian Open Women's Squash Champions					
Year	Winner	State/Country	Year	Winner	State	
1979	Vicki Hoffmann	SA	2001	Sarah Fitz-Gerald	Vic	
1980	Vicki Hoffmann	SA	2002	Sarah Fitz-Gerald	Vic	
1981	Rhonda Thorne	QLD	2003	Sarah Fitz-Gerald	Vic	
1982	Vicki Cardwell (née Hoffmann)	SA	2004	Natalie Grinham	QLD	
1983	Vicki Cardwell	SA	2005	Rachael Grinham	QLD	
1984	Vicki Cardwell	SA	2006	Kasey Brown	NSW	
1985	Jan Miller	SA	2007	Shelley Kitchen	New Zealand	
1986	Lisa Opie	England	2008	Annie Au	Hong Kong	
1987	Lisa Opie	England	2009	Joelle King	New Zealand	
1988	Vicki Cardwell (née Hoffmann)	SA	2010	Madeline Perry	Northern Ireland	
1989	Vicki Cardwell	SA	2011	Nicol David	Malaysia	
1990	Susan Devoy	New Zealand	2012	Nicol David	Malaysia	
1991	Michelle Martin	QLD	2013	Not Held		
1992	Susan Devoy	New Zealand	2014	Not Held		
1993	Michelle Martin	NSW	2015	Joelle King	New Zealand	
1994	Michelle Martin	NSW	2016	Dipika Pallikal Karthik	India	
1995	Michelle Martin	NSW	2017	Rachael Grinham	QLD	
1996	Michelle Martin	NSW	2018	Low Wee Wern	Malaysia	
1997	Sarah Fitz-Gerald	Vic	2019	Sivasangari Subramaniam	Malaysia	
1998	Michelle Martin	NSW	2020	No competition—COVID19		
1999	Michelle Martin	NSW	2021	Rachael Grinham	QLD	
2000	Leilani Joyce	New Zealand				

	British Open Champions 1922–2010		

Year	Champion	Runner-up	Score
1922	Joyce Cave	Nancy Cave	11–15, 15–10, 15–9
1923	Silvia Huntsman	Nancy Cave	6–15, 15–9, 17–15
1924	Nancy Cave	Joyce Cave	15–8, 15–13
1925	Joyce Cave	Nancy Cave	15–3, 6–15, 16–13
1926	Cecily Fenwick	Nancy Cave	15–12, 15–11
1927	Cecily Fenwick	Nancy Cave	4–9, 9–6, 9–2, 9–5
1928	Joyce Cave	Cecily Fenwick	4–9, 9–5, 10–9, 9–6
1929	Nancy Cave	Joyce Cave	9–6, 3–9, 9–2, 3–9, 9–6
1930	Nancy Cave	Cecily Fenwick	10–8, 9–1, 7–9, 9–5
1931	Cecily Fenwick	Nancy Cave	9–7, 10–8, 9–10, 9–1
1932	Susan Noel	Joyce Cave	9–5, 9–7, 9–1
1933	Susan Noel	Sheila Keith-Jones	9–4, 9–0, 9–2
1934	Susan Noel	Margot Lumb	9–7, 9–0, 9–6
1935	Margot Lumb	Anne Lytton-Milbanke	9–4, 9–0, 9–1
1936	Margot Lumb	Anne Lytton-Milbanke	9–5, 9–5, 9–4
1937	Margot Lumb	Sheila McKechnie	9–3, 9–2, 9–0
1938	Margot Lumb	Sheila McKechnie	9–3, 9–2, 9–1
1939	Margot Lumb	Susan Noel	9–6, 9–1, 9–7
1940			
1941			
1942			
1943	No competition (World War II)		
1944			
1945			
1946			

Year		Champion		Runner-up	Score
1947		Joan Curry		Alice Teague	9–3, 10–9, 9–5
1948		Joan Curry		Janet Morgan	9–5, 9–0, 9–10, 6–9, 10–8
1949		Joan Curry		Janet Morgan	2–9, 9–3, 10–8, 9–0
1950		Janet Morgan		Joan Curry	9–4, 9–3, 9–0
1951		Janet Morgan		Joan Curry	9–1, 2–9, 9–3, 9–4
1952		Janet Morgan		Joan Curry	9–3, 9–1, 9–5
1953		Janet Morgan		Marjorie Townsend	9–4, 9–2, 9–4
1954		Janet Morgan		Sheila Speight	9–3, 9–1, 9–7
1955		Janet Morgan		Ruth Turner	9–5, 9–3, 9–6
1956		Janet Morgan		Sheila Speight	9–6, 9–4, 9–2
1957		Janet Morgan		Sheila Speight	4–9, 9–5, 9–1, 9–6
1958		Janet Morgan		Sheila Macintosh née Speight)	9–7, 6–9, 9–6, 9–7
1959		Janet Morgan		Sheila Macintosh	9–4, 9–1, 9–5
1960		Sheila Macintosh		Fran Marshall	4–9, 8–9, 9–5, 9–3, 9–6
1961		Fran Marshall		Ruth Turner	9–3, 9–5, 9–1
1962		Heather Blundell		Fran Marshall	9–6, 9–5, 9–4
1963		Heather Blundell		Fran Marshall	9–4, 9–2, 9–6
1964		Heather Blundell		Fran Marshall	9–2, 9–2, 9–1
1965		Heather Blundell		Anna Craven-Smith	9–0, 9–1, 9–2
1966		Heather McKay (née Blundell)		Anna Craven-Smith	9–0, 9–0, 10–8
1967		Heather McKay		Anna Craven-Smith	9–1, 10–8, 9–6
1968		Heather McKay		Bev Johnson	9–0, 9–0, 9–0
1969		Heather McKay		Fran Marshall	9–2, 9–0, 9–0
1970		Heather McKay		Marcia Roche	9–1, 9–1, 9–0
1971		Heather McKay		Jenny Irving	9–0, 9–3, 9–1
1972		Heather McKay		Kathy Malan	9–1, 9–1, 9–2

Year	Champion	Runner-up	Score
1973	Heather McKay	Cecile Fleming	9–1, 9–0, 9–1
1974	Heather McKay	Sue Cogswell	9–2, 9–1, 9–2
1975	Heather McKay	Marion Jackman	9–3, 9–1, 9–5
1976	Heather McKay	Sue Newman	9–2, 9–4, 9–2
1977	Heather McKay	Barbara Wall	9–3, 9–1, 9–2
1978	Sue Newman	Vicki Hoffmannn	9–4, 9–7, 9–2
1979	Barbara Wall	Sue Cogswell	8–10, 6–9, 9–4, 9–4, 9–3
1980	Vicki Hoffmannn	Sue Cogswell	9–5, 9–5, 9–3
1981	Vicki Hoffmannn	Margaret Zachariah	9–6, 9–4, 9–0
1982	Vicki Cardwell (née Hoffmannn)	Lisa Opie	9–4, 5–9, 9–4, 9–4
1983	Vicki Cardwell	Lisa Opie	9–10, 9–6, 9–4, 9–5
1984	Susan Devoy	Lisa Opie	5–9, 9–0, 9–7, 9–1
1985	Susan Devoy	Martine Le Moignan	9–6, 5–9, 9–6, 9–5
1986	Susan Devoy	Lisa Opie	9–4, 9–2, 9–3
1987	Susan Devoy	Lucy Soutter	2–9, 4–9, 9–4, 9–2, 9–1
1988	Susan Devoy	Liz Irving	9–7, 9–5, 9–1
1989	Susan Devoy	Martine Le Moignan	8–10, 10–8, 9–3, 9–6
1990	Susan Devoy	Suzanne Horner	9–2, 1–9, 9–3, 9–3
1991	Lisa Opie	Sue Wright	6–9, 9–3, 9–3, 9–4
1992	Susan Devoy	Martine Le Moignan	9–3, 9–5, 9–3
1993	Michelle Martin	Suzanne Horner	9–7, 9–0, 9–4
1994	Michelle Martin	Liz Irving	9–1, 9–5, 9–3
1995	Michelle Martin	Liz Irving	9–4, 9–7, 9–5
1996	Michelle Martin	Sarah Fitz-Gerald	1–9, 9–5, 9–1, 9–7
1997	Michelle Martin	Sarah Fitz-Gerald	9–5, 9–10, 9–5, 9–5
1998	Michelle Martin	Sarah Fitz-Gerald	9–4, 9–2, 9–1
1999	Leilani Joyce	Cassie Campion	5–9, 9–6, 9–3, 10–8

Year	Champion		Runner-up		Score
2000		Leilani Joyce		Sue Wright	9–7, 9–4, 9–2
2001		Sarah Fitz-Gerald		Carol Owens	10–9, 9–0, 9–2
2002		Sarah Fitz-Gerald		Tania Bailey	9–3, 9–0, 9–0
2003		Rachael Grinham		Cassie Campion	9–3, 7–9, 9–2, 9–5
2004		Rachael Grinham		Natalie Grainger	6–9, 9–5, 9–0, 9–3
2005		Nicol David		Natalie Grinham	9–6, 9–7, 9–6
2006		Nicol David		Rachael Grinham	9–4, 9–1, 9–4
2007		Rachael Grinham		Nicol David	7–9, 4–9, 9–3, 10–8, 9–1
2008		Nicol David		Jenny Duncalf	9–1, 10–8, 9–0
2009		Rachael Grinham		Madeline Perry	11–6, 11–5, 12–10
2010			No competition		
2011					
2012		Nicol David		Nour El Sherbini	11–6, 11–6, 11–6
2013		Laura Massaro		Nicol David	11–4, 3–11, 12–10, 11–8
2014		Nicol David		Laura Massaro	8–11, 11–5, 11–7, 11–8
2015		Camille Serme		Laura Massaro	11–3, 11–5, 8–11, 11–8
2016		Nour El Sherbini		Nouran Gohar	11–7, 9–11, 7–11, 11–6, 11–8
2017		Laura Massaro		Sarah-Jane Perry	11–8, 11–8, 6–11, 11–6
2018		Nour El Sherbini		Raneem El Weleily	11–6, 11–9, 14–12
2019		Nouran Gohar		Camille Serme	11–3, 11–8, 11–3
2020		Postponed due toCOVID-19 pandemic in the United Kingdom			
2021		Nour El Sherbini		Nouran Gohar	9–11, 13–11, 5–11, 11–7, 11–2

Wikipedia–

https://en.wikipedia.org/wiki/British_Open_Squash_Championships#Women's_championship

* Note that Heather McKay won 16 consecutive British Opens and two World Championships and was undefeated from 1962 until the end of her career in 1979. In her 16 wins, in the British Open, she lost a total of 100 points in the finals—an average of 6.25 per match. If you take out the two best performers' results (Fran Marshall 34 points and Anna Craven-Smith 26 points—a total of 60) then the average comes down to a staggering 4 points over the remaining 10 matches! A reign that is still unmatched by any player.

Rank		Player Name	Number of Titles	Runner-up	Final Appearances
1		Heather McKay	16	0	16
2		Janet Morgan	10	2	12
3		Susan Devoy	8	0	8
4		Michelle Martin	6	0	6
5		Nicol David	5	2	7
6		Margot Lumb	5	1	6
7		Vicki Cardwell	4	1	5
7		Rachael Grinham	4	1	5
8		Nancy Cave	3	6	9
9		Cecily Fenwick	3	3	6
9		Joyce Cave	3	3	6
9		Joan Curry	3	3	6
10		Susan Noel	3	1	4
10		Nour El Sherbini	3	1	4
11		Sarah Fitz-Gerald	2	3	5
12		Laura Massaro	2	2	4
13		Leilani Joyce	2	0	2
14		Sheila Macintosh	1	5	6
14		Fran Marshall	1	5	6
15		Lisa Opie	1	4	5

		Silvia Huntsman	1	1	2
		Barbara Wall	1	1	2
16		Sue Newman	1	1	2
		Nouran Gohar	1	1	2
		Camille Serme	1	1	2

Wikipedia–

https://en.wikipedia.org/wiki/British_Open_Squash_Championships#List_of_
British_Open_Women's_champions_by_number_of_victories

World Women's Individual Championship				
Year	Location	Champion	Runner-up	Score
1976	Brisbane	Heather McKay	Marion Jackman	9–2, 9–2, 9–0
1979	Sheffield	Heather McKay	Sue Cogswell	6–9, 9–3, 9–1, 9–4
1980	No competition			
1981	Toronto	Rhonda Thorne	Vicki Cardwell	8–10, 9–4, 9–5, 7–9, 9–7
1982	No competition			
1983	Perth	Vicki Cardwell	Rhonda Thorne	9–1, 9–3, 9–4
1984	No competition			
1985	Dublin	Susan Devoy	Lisa Opie	9–4, 9–5, 10–8
1986	No competition			
1987	Auckland	Susan Devoy	Lisa Opie	9–3, 10–8, 9–2
1988	No competition			
1989	Warmond	Martine Le Moignan	Susan Devoy	4–9, 9–4, 10–8, 10–8
1990	Sydney	Susan Devoy	Martine Le Moignan	9–4, 9–4, 9–4
1991	No competition			
1992	Vancouver	Susan Devoy	Michelle Martin	9–4, 9–6, 9–4
1993	Johannesburg	Michelle Martin	Liz Irving	9–2, 9–2, 9–1
1994	Saint Peter Port	Michelle Martin	Cassie Jackman	9–1, 9–0, 9–6
1995	Hong Kong	Michelle Martin	Sarah Fitz-Gerald	8–10, 9–2, 9–6, 9–3
1996	Petaling Jaya	Sarah Fitz-Gerald	Cassie Jackman	9–0, 9–3, 9–4
1997	Sydney	Sarah Fitz-Gerald	Michelle Martin	9–5, 5–9, 6–9, 9–2, 9–3
1998	Stuttgart	Sarah Fitz-Gerald	Michelle Martin	10–8, 9–7, 2–9, 3–9, 10–9
1999	Seattle	Cassie Campion	Michelle Martin	9–6, 9–7, 9–7
2000	Edinburgh	Carol Owens	Leilani Joyce	7–9, 3–9, 10–8, 9–6, 9–1
2001	Melbourne	Sarah Fitz-Gerald	Leilani Joyce	9–0, 9–3, 9–2
2002	Doha	Sarah Fitz-Gerald	Natalie Pohrer	10–8, 9–3, 7–9, 9–7

Year	Location	Champion	Runner-up	Score
2003	Hong Kong	Carol Owens	Cassie Jackman	3–9, 9–2, 9–7, 9–3
2004	Kuala Lumpur	Vanessa Atkinson	Natalie Grinham	9–1, 9–1, 9–5
2005	Hong Kong	Nicol David	Rachael Grinham	8–10, 9–2, 9–6, 9–7
2006	Belfast	Nicol David	Natalie Grinham	1–9, 9–7, 3–9, 9–5, 9–2
2007	Madrid	Rachael Grinham	Natalie Grinham	9–4, 10–8, 9–2
2008	Manchester	Nicol David	Vicky Botwright	5–11, 11–1, 11–6, 11–9
2009	Amsterdam	Nicol David	Natalie Grinham	3–11, 11–6, 11–3, 11–8
2010	Sharm El Sheikh	Nicol David	Omneya Abdel Kawy	11–5, 11–8, 11–6
2011	Rotterdam	Nicol David	Jenny Duncalf	11–2, 11–5, 11–0
2012	Cayman Islands	Nicol David	Laura Massaro	11–6, 11–8, 11–6
2013	Penang	Laura Massaro	Nour El Sherbini	11–7, 6–11, 11–9, 5–11, 11–9
2014	Cairo	Nicol David	Raneem El Weleily	5–11, 11–8, 7–11, 14–12, 11–5
2015	Kuala Lumpur	Nour El Sherbini	Laura Massaro	6–11, 4–11, 11–3, 11–5, 11–8
2016	El Gouna	Nour El Sherbini	Raneem El Weleily	11–8, 11–9, 11–9
2017	Manchester	Raneem El Weleily	Nour El Sherbini	3–11, 12–10, 11–7, 11–5
2018–19	Chicago	Nour El Sherbini	Nour El Tayeb	11–6, 11–5, 10–12, 15–13
2019–20	Cairo	Nour El Sherbini	Raneem El Weleily	11–4, 9–11, 11–5, 11–6
2020–21	Chicago	Nour El Sherbini	Nouran Gohar	11–5, 11–8, 8–11, 11–9

Wikipedia–
    https://en.wikipedia.org/wiki/World_Squash_Championships

The Test Series

The International Test Series commenced in 1960 with an unofficial match between Australia and Great Britain. The other results are tabled below.

Year		Winner	Result		Host
1960-61		Great Britain	3-0*		England
1964		Australia	3-2#		England
1965		Australia	3-0		Australia
1967		Australia	2-1		England
1971		Australia	3-0		England
1972		Australia	3-0		Australia
1975		Australia	3-0		England
1976		Australia	2-1**		Australia
1978		Australia	1-0**		Canada
1980		Australia	2-1**		Australia

*Unofficial match

One international match

** Different format—Round Robin

Note: In 1960–61, this unofficial match was played with 3 players and in 1964, one international match was played (Australia v Great Britain) with 5 players. It was after this, in 65, that a three Test series commenced with a team of 3 players as it was more manageable. The Test series were generally played in different locations in the host country.

Australia was undefeated in all the Teams' matches from 1964–1980 (9). A remarkable achievement.

Australian Women's Teams—Test Series	
1960* Yvonne West Aline Smith Jan Shearer (Capt.)	**1972** Heather McKay Marion Jackman Jenny Irving Mavis Baker Jean Walker (Captain)
1964# Heather Blundell (Capt.) Jenny Irving Pat McClenaughan Barbara Baxter Helen Plaisted	**1975** Marion Jackman Sue Newman Margaret Zachariah Lyle Hubinger (Reserve) Chris van Nierop Carol Murray (Manager)
1965 Heather McKay Marion Hawcroft Jenny Irving	**1976**** Sue Newman Chris van Nierop Margaret Zachariah Jenny Irving (Captain)
1967 Heather McKay Marion Hawcroft Barbara Baxter Marlene Tierney (Reserve) Robyn Kennedy (Reserve)	**1978** Margaret Zachariah Vicki Hoffmann Anne Smith Rhonda Shapland (Reserve) Jan Honeycombe (Manager)
1971 Heather McKay Jenny Irving Marion Jackman (Hawcroft) Mavis Baker Jean Walker (Manager)	**1980** Vicki Hoffmann Rhonda Thorne (Shapland) Margaret Zachariah Sue King (Newman) Barbara Oldfield Brian Boys (Manager)

Women's World Teams' Championships				
Year	Winner	Result	Runner-up	Host
1979	Great Britain	3-0	Australia	England
1981	Australia	2-1	England	Canada
1983	Australia	2-1	England	Australia
1985	England	2-1	New Zealand	Ireland
1987	England	2-1	Australia	New Zealand
1989	England	3-0*	Australia	Netherlands
1990	England	2-1	Australia	Sydney
1992	Australia	2-1	New Zealand	Canada
1994	Australia	3-0	England	Guernsey
1996	Australia	2-1	England	Malaysia
1998	Australia	3-0	England	Germany
2000	England	2-1	Australia	England
2002	Australia	2-1	England	Denmark
2004	Australia	2-0**	England	Netherlands
2006	England	2-0	Egypt	Egypt
2008	Egypt	2-1	England	England
2010	Australia	2-1	England	New Zealand

* Australia forfeited the third rubber

** Last match wasn't played

Wikipedia–

https://en.wikipedia.org/wiki/WSF_World_Team_Squash_Championships

Australia won 9 of the Teams' matches of the 17 contested and were runners up 5 times. If you add the period from 1964—1980, they won 18 of 26 international Matches contested—69.2%.

In the current era, Egypt is starting to show similar dominance winning in 2008, 2012, 2016 and 2018 (matches weren't held in 2020 due to Covid), however, they still have a long way to go to match this record!

Australian Women's World Championship Teams

1979	1990
Barbara Wall Vicki Cardwell (Hoffmann) Sue King (Captain) Anne Smith Rhonda Shapland	Robyn Lambourne Michelle Martin Danielle Drady Liz Irving Vicki Cardwell (Coach) Margaret Zachariah (Manager)
1981	**1992**
Rhonda Thorne (Captain) Rae Anderson Vicki Cardwell Barbara Oldfield	Robyn Lambourne Michelle Martin Sarah Fitz-Gerald Liz Irving Di Davis (Coach-Manager)
1983	**1994**
Rhonda Thorne (Captain) Carin Clonda Jan Miller Di Davis	Michelle Martin Sarah Fitz-Gerald Liz Irving Carol Owens Di Davis (Coach-Manager)
1985	**1996**
Jan Miller (Captain) Tracey Smith Carin Clonda Di Davis Margaret Zachariah (Manager)	Michelle Martin Sarah Fitz-Gerald Liz Irving Carol Owens Di Davis (Coach-Manager)
1987	**1998**
Vicki Cardwell (Captain) Sarah Fitz-Gerald Michelle Martin Robyn Lambourne (Friday)	Michelle Martin Sarah Fitz-Gerald Carol Owens Liz Irving Di Davis (Coach-Manager)
1989	**2000**
Vicki Cardwell (Captain-Coach) Danielle Drady Liz Irving Robyn Lambourne	Sarah Fitz-Gerald Natalie Grinham Robyn Cooper Laura Keating Vicki Cardwell (Coach)

Women's World Teams' Championships (cont)	
2002 Sarah Fitz-Gerald Rachael Grinham Natalie Grinham Robyn Cooper Ken Watson (Coach-Manager)	**2008** Kasey Brown Lisa Camilleri Amelia Pittock Donna Urquhart Michelle Martin (Coach-Manager)
2004 Rachael Grinham Natalie Grinham Amelia Pittock Melissa Martin Michelle Martin (Coach-Manager)	**2010** Kasey Brown Sarah Fitz-Gerald Rachael Grinham Donna Urquhart Michelle Martin (Coach–Manager)
2006 Kasey Brown Amelia Pittock Melissa Martin Diane Desira Michelle Martin (Coach Manager)	

Squash Australia, 'Annual Report', 2013

Quiz

How well have you been reading?

1. One of our famous Australian player's middle name is Pamela. Who is it?

2. One of our Australian players made the mistake of stating that she was going to push Heather at the British Open. What was her name? You'll have to search for this!

3. What was the subsequent score?

4. In what year did Australia send the first Women's team overseas?

5. What was the result?

6. How did they travel?

7. In what year was the UK defeated by Australia, for the first time?

8. When did the Test series begin?

9. Who was the first female President of Australian Women's Squash?

10. How many consecutive British Opens did Heather win?

11. What was her nickname?

12. What was her secret weapon?

13. Who was the only unseeded Australian female squash player to reach the final of the British Open?

14. In what year?

15. Which Australian player represented from the 1964 until 1972, and her daughter went on to become no. 2 in the world and a coach of World no. 1 Nicol David.

16. What was the name of the Australian Champion of the '50s, whose daughter subsequently went on to win the British Open in 2001 and 2002.

17. What was the name of the British player, who won 10 British Opens from 1950–1959?

18. Name the only two players who managed to defeat Heather McKay.

19. In what years did this occur?

20. Who was the youngest competitor in the inaugural World Squash Championships in 1976? (a clue—she went on and won the World Championship in 1981)

21. Who had the nickname 'Thunder Thighs'. She was an Australian Champion who did win a British Open Championship.

22. What does 'Position 3' mean? It is not related to squash!

23. Who has the record of winning the most points from Heather in the British Open finals? (You may have to do some sums for this!)

24. To whom do the initials F.F. refer? They belong to a former Australian Amateur Champion and a runner-up in the British Open in 1975.

25. What do the initials stand for?

26. What was the full name of a well-known female administrator and player? Her first name was Patricia.

27. Who signs their emails RIP?

28. What was the maiden name of the No1 seed in the Australian Amateur Championship in 1960

29. What trophy did Heather win for one of her British Amateur Championships?

30. Who has won the most medals at the Commonwealth Games of all female squash players?

31. What female squash player won 3 gold medals at the Commonwealth Games in Melbourne in 2006?

32. Name the three female players who were called the 'Terrific Trio' during their tour overseas in 1987

33. Who was 'Swinger'?

34. Who was 'Boom Boom'?

Acknowledgements

As readers would know, a book is never written without the assistance from many interested parties. Much of the information has been obtained from interviews with the players (from the Australian and British teams), who have kindly given me their time and many of their stories. Other contributors have been individuals, coaches, administrators and connections from the educational sector. This included teaching colleagues in the ACT Education System, lecturers at the University of Canberra (Sports Studies section) and the Australian Institute of Sport. Without their input this book wouldn't have been the same.

Australian Players

Those who have been of considerable help are Bev Garfield (Meagher)—on behalf of her mother Betty Meagher (1919–1986) and Sarah Fitz-Gerald, daughter of Judy FitzGerald (Tissot—1930–2020). They both dug around in their mothers' photo albums of the 1940s and '50s and came up with some gems to be included in the book. Jan Tilly (Shearer)—what a find! Thank you for sharing the photos of the first Australian Women's Team to go overseas in 1960. June McCraw (Speedie) who filled me in on some details of Heather's first Australian Championship in 1960. June was seeded no. 1 and was beaten by this newcomer in the semis. Heather McKay, who willingly shared her enormous collection of newspaper clippings, photos and stories. Jean Walker (1930–2016) who provided valuable material on the 1971 Australian Women's tour and of the background behind the first World Women's Championship, which was held in Brisbane. She had been a prime mover in getting this tournament to be held in Australia, in 1976. Jenny Irving, who unfortunately had lost much of her memorabilia in the floods in Queensland, however, she was still very willing to give me the information she had. With such longevity in the sport (actively playing from 1962–87) and her daughter Liz, going on to achieve similar success, their stories had to be told. Patricia Hunt provided me with information on the Hunt family, which demonstrates how the home environment can nurture a champion. Carol Murray, who provided me with some invaluable information on the touring team of 1975, photos of Jean Walker and information on the 1990 World Championships. Marion Jackman who enlightened me to the fact, that she had actually taken three games off Heather, (in 1968, 72 and 73—a mighty achievement) together with other details of events throughout her long career. Margaret Zachariah, an absolute mine of information on touring teams, and details of various Championships. Sue King, who provided me with accommodation, and filled me in on the 1976 World Championships (providing me with a programme, which helped established the authenticity of this Championship) and details of the initial attempts to start WISPA. Barbara Wall, whose story should be an inspiration to anyone wanting to pursue their dreams. She had to lose weight, train hard and be single-minded in her pursuit of the British Open Championship title. Her persistence paid off! Rhonda Thorne, who in her quiet, organised way, filled me in on the details of her marathon win over Vicki, in the 1981 World Championship. Vicki Cardwell, always a willing contributor and her information on her career and that of her children Josh and Sarah, has added considerably to the content of this book. Robyn Lambourne whose CV was admirable and reflected the grit and determination which is evident in all the players who achieve at the international level. Di Davis, whose longevity in the sport at the Australian and international level both as a coach and as a player, should be an inspiration to anyone wanting to give back to the sport. Jan Miller who was always quick off the mark both in her playing and in her response to my emails! She provided valuable photos of the Australian touring team of 1985. Carin Clonda, who overcame severe medical problems to represent Australia twice. This again reflected the determined attitude of our national representatives. Michelle Martin, another outstanding champion, who was always keen to share her story. Her family photos also added another dimension. Sarah Fitz-Gerald, (mentioned earlier, with regard to her mother's career), also made a huge contribution with her story and the role of her family. She is still contributing as President of S&RV. Danielle Drady also assisted by providing information for her profile. Rachael Grinham, still a 'jack in the box' and bursting with energy, was very keen to share her story, together with that of her sister, Natalie. Robyn Prentice, whose longevity in the sport as a player, coach and now President of the Masters' Association, is an indication of how the sport can get into your blood. This added another dimension to the book.

International Players

International players who have been of exceptional assistance, are Sheila Macintosh (Speight, now 91) and Anna Craven-Smith. Sheila visited Australia with Janet Shardlow (Morgan) in 1954 at the invitation of the Australian Squash Rackets Association. Sheila filled in many of the gaps of the tour of 1954 and some other memory joggers of more recent times. They annihilated the Aussies on this tour; however, it took only 10 years before the roles were reversed. Sheila was a member of the British Team from 1952–1972 either as a player or manager and is in the Guinness Book of Records for representing the UK in squash for 20 years! Sheila was runner-up in the British Open Championship to Janet Morgan (another Heather) from 1954–59, before finally winning it in 1960, when Janet had retired. She was a mine of information and very willing to share her knowledge. She was also inducted into the British Hall of Fame for her services to squash. Also, Anna Bullock (Craven-Smith), who was runner-up to Heather McKay in three British Open finals (1965–67) and was most helpful in finding photos that formed part of the story.

Administrators

Vic Belsham AM (1926–2006) whose booklet *The Belsham Years 1976–1992,* proved to be an invaluable resource. Bob Finch AM (former President of ASRA), who was always willing to check the facts. Chris Sinclair, whose long-term involvement (both as an administrator and as an international referee) provided me with valuable photos and stories and a considerable amount of editing. Paul Vear OAM, an historian in his own right and involved in Squash at all levels for over 40 years. His research gave me access to information, which otherwise would not have been there. Unfortunately, Paul passed away on 20/1/22, and won't be able to read this book to which he had made such a huge contribution. Col Clapper AM (Life Member of Squash Australia) for his advice on Squash and the Olympics. Dawn Moggach OAM another stalwart, with a long-term involvement at the National level in a variety of roles. Ken Watson (former National Coaching Director and Life member of Squash Australia) who checked the records for me in WA and dotted the i's and crossed the t's on the information I had provided. Jan Honeycombe (Q), who was heavily involved in the submission which secured the 1976 World Women's Championship. Sue Hillier (State Performance Pathways Co-ordinator–WA) who helped considerably with information on the WA players and, more importantly, put me in touch with Andrew Shelley MBE (World Squash Library). What a find that was! Information for which I had been searching for over two years, on the 1972 Test series, was delivered within an hour of my request. Also, Andrew's checking of the facts and details on the chapters on WISPA, the Olympics and Future Directions was also invaluable. Finally, the toing and froing as to whether the World Championships, in 1976 were officially the first, were thoroughly investigated. Examination of the evidence, concluded that they were and Wikipedia and the World Squash Federation consequently changed their records! Rightly so. Rita Paulos (State Coaching Director, Queensland Squash) whose enthusiasm and wide network enabled me to hunt down the players and their contact details. Bert Armstong (Squash Historian–Victoria) who chased up early Australian Championship programmes that verified the facts, so that I didn't have to rely on players' memories (we're all getting older!). Arthur Wilks OAM (ACT Education) who helped me get started with some sound advice. Paul Andrews (teacher at Telopea Park High) who provided me with various books on squash to assist in my research. Greg Blood (former librarian, AIS) an early reader of the manuscript. Christine McCaffrie (ACT Education System) also an early reader of the manuscript. Bob Alexander (squash player and neighbour), who provided me with a stack of old Squash Player magazines for my bedtime reading and research. Peter Taylor and Geoff Walsh, both former ACT players who, after the book was published, spotted a couple of errors that had 'slipped through'. Finally, Heather McKay whose 'eagle eye' (no it hasn't diminished!) also after the book was published, spotted some incorrect facts and 'put me straight'. Margaret Zachariah (Victoria) was also very helpful in providing the 'finishing touches'

So, like the marathon runner that staggers to the finish line, to Peter Gamble (Echo Books) for his availability, skill and patience in getting this book published and to Marcus Fielding (Echo Books) for providing the guidelines and editing facility. Also, to Leanne Aust (ACT Company Director and former squash pupil), who read and reread the manuscript to make sure that it was up to speed and Kathie Barnes (long-time friend) who provided advice on the endnotes. Also, I mustn't forget to mention our son, David, who helped solve the 'road blocks' of computers, that somehow 'got in the way'! Even so, while thanking all that have contributed, responsibility for any mistakes is entirely my own.

Finally, I would be remiss, if I didn't mention my husband, Chris, who cooked many a meal, made countless cups of coffee and read many a draft, as I laboured on through this mammoth task. He was a huge help.

Hats off to all of you and my apologies if I have omitted your name. Suffice it to say that your input also contributed to this great story.

Barbara

About the Author

B arbara and I first met in July,1960 at the beginning of my career. It was at the NSW Junior Championships where she was runner-up to me in the final. We played many times during the 60s and were both members of the Australian team in 1964 and 1967. She later became ACT Coaching Director and National Coaching Director in the 1980s. I was Assistant Coach to Geoff Hunt at the AIS at that time and we often discussed the best coaching methods to improve the players. I consider her achievements in the game of squash outstanding, not only as a player but, particularly, as a coach. I thoroughly recommend this book for all those squash players out there and for members of the community, that enjoy reading about Australia's sporting history.

Heather McKay AO MBE
World Champion 1976 and 1979
British Open Champion 1962–1977

I met Barbara in the 1960s when we were players representing NSW and WA respectively in the Australian Individual and Interstate Teams Squash Championships. Barbara immediately attracted attention because of her technical and tactical skills combined with a fierce competitive spirit and scrupulous sportsmanship. It wasn't long before she was selected in the Australian team which competed successfully in Great Britain in 1964.

Our paths didn't cross again until the early 1980s as I had been overseas and Barbara had married and was raising two young children as well as pursuing a successful career in teaching. She had also taken up coaching and was rapidly becoming one of Australia's most respected, competent and successful coaches with many of her pupils winning National Age Championships and gaining scholarships at the AIS.

After being the ACT Coaching Director for a number of years, she became the National Coaching Director (NCD) in the late 1980s with the result that serious consideration was now being given, perhaps for the first time, on not only how to coach squash but also how to train people to become effective coaches. With the rare combination of formal education and practical experience in teaching and extensive knowledge and understanding of squash, Barbara became a key figure in the development over a number of years of a comprehensive national coach education system. This system involved three levels of coach tuition and three corresponding levels of tutor and assessor education. She did this in her role as NCD by conducting a number of coach education courses, both nationally and locally and making presentations at coaching conferences, workshops and seminars.

It is worth noting that the Australian coach education system which Barbara helped design, prepare and implement was adopted in whole or in part by the squash associations of regions and many countries in Asia, Europe, North and South America and in Africa.

Barbara is one of the most knowledgeable, experienced and competent squash people who I have known in over 60 years of involvement in the sport.

She has been an excellent role model for squash throughout the whole of her career, a career in which she has made outstanding contributions to the development of squash.

This book is yet another contribution which should help promote women and girls in squash. It documents some amazing stories of the early pioneers and outstanding champions. I have no hesitation in endorsing this book as a 'must read' for all those budding young squash players out there.

Dr KJ Watson BSc (Hons) PhD ASM
Former NCD 1982–4
Life Member of Squash Australia
Life Member of WA Squash

Barbara has given nearly 60 years of outstanding service to Australian Squash at many levels.

She has represented Australia three times as a player in 1962, 1964 and 1967, however, she has made an even greater contribution in the coaching area. This was both in the coaching of players, but more importantly in the coach education component of the sport where she energised and unified the coaching scene in this country. When appointed National Coaching Director in 1988, it was her vision that led to the stabilisation and unification of squash coaches across the country into a formidable national network.

Barbara worked with the Australian Sports Commission to develop many and varied valuable resources for our coaches such as the Aussie Sports manual, which was designed for use with Primary School Age children. She also produced the Level O Youth workbook for beginning coaches and reignited the National Coaching Accreditation Scheme. At a different level, Barbara arranged for the production of a High-Speed Cinematography project featuring Heather McKay, that formed the basis for biomechanical research that provided an invaluable aid for coaches.

In her role as NCD she developed a system of AIS satellite coaches throughout the country, initiated Biennial National Coaching Conferences, held in different States, to maximise participation. In addition, she served on the National Coaching Committee, the National Historical Committee and formed the Australian Squash Rackets Coaches Association (ASRAC).

In 2010, she was awarded by Squash Australia the Distinguished Service Award for her outstanding service to Squash in this country.

Over the past few years, Barbara has been involved in writing a much-needed book on A History of Women's Squash in Australia. In her usual thorough manner, she has interviewed numerous squash personnel across the country to make sure that she 'gets the facts right'. I thoroughly recommend this book as a source for future players and administrators at all levels. *

Paul Vear OAM

General Manager of S&RV

General Manager of Australian Racquetball

Former Executive Director of the Victorian Squash Federation
    from 1998–2008

Executive Director of the Victorian Racquetball Federation from 1979–2008

* Unfortunately, Paul passed away on 20th January, 2022, and didn't get the chance to read the final product.

I n the words of JFK 'Ask not what your country can do for you—ask what you can do for your country'.

Similarly, all those 'squashies' out there—Masters, former players, coaches, former AIS scholarship holders, present players—who should be asking themselves what they can do to revitalise this exciting sport.

Let's see the Aussies fly the flag again!

Girls, go out and have some fun! Can you name the players?

Endnotes

1   Michael Palmer, *Guinness Book of Squash*, Guinness Superlatives Limited, Enfield, Middlesex, 1984, p7

2   Jeffrey Wollstein, 'First Squash Courts in Australia', unpublished document, 23rd November, 2005, p1

3   Wollstein, p2

4   Paul Vear, 'Squash & Fitness News', May 1992, p27

5   'Other than Golf', The Royal Sydney Golf Club Magazine, https://www.rsgc.com.au/cms/guests-sports/squash-guests/, p237

6   Paul Vear, 'History of the Victorian Amateur Open Squash Championships', unpublished document, p1

7   NSWSRA, 'Squash Rackets Association Formed', Sydney Morning Herald, 21st December,1933,p20, http://nla.gov.au/nla/news-article 17034488

8   W.J. Mudford, 'Squash Rackets Association of NSW 1938–92–A History', https://nsw.squash.org.au/w/about/nsw-squash-history, p2

9   W.J. Mudford, 'The Emergence of Public Courts', p,12 http://www.nsw.squash.org.au/w/about/nsw-squash-history

10   Paul Vear, 'History of the Victorian Amateur/Open Squash Championships', unpublished document, p1

11   Freda Irving, 'Squash is a smash hit with women', The Age, Melbourne, 1958

12   Irving

13   Irving

14   'Other than Golf', The Royal Sydney Golf Club, https://www.rsgc.com.au, p236

15   'Other than golf', p236

16   'Popular Game—Need for more courts', newspaper article, (source and date unknown), p10

17   'Popular Game', p10

18   'Popular Game', p10

19   Paul Vear, 'A walk through the History of the Victorian Squash Championships', unpublished document, p3

20   Vear, p3

21   'Annual Report', Squash Australia, 2013, p52

22   'Past and Future', WSRA handbook,1951 (source Sheila Macintosh), p35

23   Betty Meagher, letter to Judith Tissot, 16th July, 1984

24   Meagher, letter, 1984

25   'Past and Future', WSRA handbook,1950 (source Sheila Macintosh)

26   Meagher, letter, 1984

27   Meagher, letter, 1984

28   'Squash Teams Abroad', article from unknown New Zealand newspaper, 23rd August, 1955

29   'Squash teams Abroad', 23rd August, 1953'

30   JJanet Morgan, 'Touring in Australia and New Zealand', WSRA Handbook, 1955, p35

31   Morgan, p36

32   Morgan, p36

33   Barbara Slotemaker de Bruïne, interview with Judith Fitzgerald, 2017

34   Interview with Judith Fitzgerald, 2017

35   Sheila Macintosh email to author, 4th February, 2016

36   Macintosh, 2016

37   Trove, McKay, Heather Pamela, (AM, MBE) (1941–) https://trove.nla.
      gov.au/people/714091, 21st September, 2016, p1

38   Terry Orvad, 'Visitors Clinch Squash Titles', *Illawarra Daily Mercury*,
      March, 1960

39   Squash Review: 'Australian Squash Pioneers', John Cheadle, p16

40   Sheila Macintosh, email, 2016

41   'Australian Squash Pioneers John Cheadle', *Squash review*, p16

42   'Australian Squash Pioneers John Cheadle', *Squash review*,p16

43   'Annual Report' Squash Australia, 2013, p45

44   *WSRA Handbook*, 1965

45   *WSRA Handbook*, 1965

46   Rex Bellamy, 'Heather McKay wins her sixth title,' *London Times*,
      February, 1967

47   'Slowing up says the Wizard', *Daily Mirro*r, February, 1967

48   Carol Murray, 'Team Manager's Report', 1975

49   Murray, 1975

50   Len Hill, 'Squash Corner', *Sunday Telegraph*, 5th September, 1976

51   Jan Honeycombe, 'Manager's Report', 1978

52   'World International Squash Players' Association', Wikipedia, https://
      en.wikipedia.org/wiki/Women%27s_International_Squash_Players_
      Association

53   'Vic Squash', January, 1981, p12

54   *The Belsham Years* 1976–1992, Australian Squash, p29

55   *Belsham*, p41

56   Margaret Zachariah, 'Manager's Report', 1985

57   'World Championships Squash Program', 1990, p24

58   Wikipedia, World Women's Team Squash Championships,1987 https://
      en.wikipedia.org/wiki/1987_Women%27s_World_Team_Squash_
      Championships

59   *Belsham*, p50

60   *Belsham*, p66

61   'Squash Australia News', Edition 5, October, 1992

62   Wikipedia World Women's Team Squash Championships,1992 https://en.wikipedia.org/wiki/WSF_World_Team_Squash_Championships

63   'Hall of Fame', Squash & Racquetball Victoria, http://www.squashvic.com.au/w/about-us/annual-awards

64   Meagher, letter, 1984

65   'News from Overseas', *WSRA Handbook*,1951, p34

66   Paul Vear, History of The Victorian Amateur/Open Squash Championships, unpublished document, p3

67   Janet Morgan, 'Touring in Australia and New Zealand', WSRA Handbook,1955, p35

68   Paul Vear, 'Vale Judith FitzGerald', https://thesquashsite.com/judith-fitzgerald-passes-away

69   Jan Tilly, email to author, 7th September, 2021

70   'Squash Player', August,1993, p13

71   Trove, 'McKay, Heather Pamela', (AM, MBE) (1941–), https://trove.nla.gov.au/people/714091, 21st September, 2016, p2

72   Vin Napier, *Squash the Australian Way*, Sydney, Paul Hamlyn, 1978, p12

73   Trove, 'McKay, Heather Pamela', (AM, MBE) (1941–), https://trove.nla.gov.au/people/714091, 21st September, 2016, p2

74   Life. Be in It.' 'Squash News', First Edition,1988

75   Napier, p13

76   Rex Bellamy, 'Heather McKay Wins Her Sixth Title' *London Times*, February, 1967

77   *Belsham*, p44

78   World Squash Program', 1990, p24

79   Annual Report', Squash Australia,1991

80   WA Squash 'Hall of Fame', https://wasquash.com.au/2017/11/13/2017-wa-squash-hall-of-fame-inductee-helen-muir/, 2017

81   Paul Vear, 'Robyn Howard honoured with Life Membership' http://www.squashvic.com.au/w/blog/robyn-howard-honoured-with%20life-membership, 4th September, 2020, p1

82   Vear, p.2

83   Vear, p2

84   Carol Murray, 'Manager's Report', 1975

85   Len Hill, 'Squash corner', *Sunday Telegraph*, 5th September, 1976

86   Queensland Squash 'Hall of Fame', 2006

87   'The Bancroft Women's Squash Open Programme', 1978

88   Smith, email to author, 2nd July, 2020

89   'World Championship Programme', 1976

90   Squash Australia, 'Hall of Fame', https://www.squash.org.au/w/about-us/hall-of-fame-members

91   Squash Australia, 'Hall of Fame', https://www.squash.org.au/w/about-us/hall-of-fame-members

92   'The Squash Player International', April, 1979, p41

93   Barbara Wall, email to author, 3rd July, 2019

94   'Life Be in It Squash News'

95   'The Squash Player International', October, 1978, p27

96   'Squash', Women in Squash, May, 1980, p26

97   'Squash', April, 1980, p31

98   Len Steward, 'Talking Points with Vicki' (source unknown),1988, p27

99   Vicki Cardwell, The Development of the Women's Game, 'Squash Magazine', 1996, p42

100   Aub Amos, 'Squash, Rhonda: As Aub sees her' (source unknown), p10

101   Amos, p11

102   WA Squash 'Hall of Fame', https://wasquash.com.au/hall-of-fame/, 2014

103   WA Squash 'Hall of Fame', 2014

104   WA Squash 'Hall of Fame', 2014

105   Di Davis, email to author, 12th August, 2020

106   'WA Squash News', 1985, p3

107   *Belsham*, p41

108   Margaret Zachariah, 'Manager's Report', 1985

109   WA Squash 'Hall of Fame', 2017

110   *Belsham*, p86

111   'Women in the News', newspaper article, source unknown, 1984

112   'Success Mystery even to Miller', *SA Newspaper*, 23rd June,1985

113   Wikipedia, https://en.wikipedia.org/wiki/Carin_Clonda

114   Wikipedia, https://en.wikipedia.org/wiki/Carin_Clonda

115   'Lambourne correspondence', 19th September, 2020

116   WA Squash 'Hall of Fame', 2012

117   'Lambourne correspondence', 19th September, 2019

118   WA Squash 'Hall of Fame', 2012

119   Belsham p23

120   Western Australia 'Hall of Fame', 2014

121   Wayne Smith, 'Squash advice not far away for Liz', *Courier Mail*, February, 1978

122   Paul Vear, 'Squash & Fitness News', 1993, p18

123   'Squash Player', June, 1993, p14

124   'Squash Player' June,1993, p14

125   'Squash Player', p14

126   'Squash Player', p12

127   'Sports Mad', Squash legends unite as Cassie Thomas interviews Michelle Martin, https://squashmad.com/breaking-news/interview-11-points-with-michelle-martin/ 2014, p2

128   'Squash Mad', p2

129   Squash Australia, 'Hall of Fame'

130   Wikipedia, https://en.wikipedia.org/wiki/Danielle_Drady-Harte

131   'World Championships Program', AIS Help Centre for Girls, 1990, p24

132   'World Championships Program' 1990, p19

133   Wikipedia, https://en.wikipedia.org/wiki/Danielle_Drady-Harte

134   Barbara Slotemaker de Bruïne, Interview with Sarah Fitz-Gerald, 2018

135   *Belsham*, p42

136   Margaret Zachariah, 'Manager's Report', 1985

137   *Belsham*, p50

138   Wikipedia, https://en.wikipedia.org/wiki/Sarah_Fitz-Gerald

139   'The Squash Player', 1997, p30

140   Andrew Shelley, World Squash Library, email to author, 2021

141   Squash Australia 'Hall of Fame', 2021

142   Wikipedia, https://en.wikipedia.org/wiki/Carol_Owens_(squash_player)

143   Martin Bronstein's Tribute, 'Squash Player', International edition 1, http://www.squashplayer.co.uk/magazine_test2.htm 12th January, 2004

144   Carol Owens, email to author, 21st December, 2020

145   Sam Porter, '*Racquets Sports Magazine*', Interview with one of Australia's Most Promising Squash Players – Rachael Grinham, 1998, p12

146   Wikipedia, https://en.wikipedia.org/wiki/Rachael_Grinham

147   Wikipedia, https://en.wikipedia.org/wiki/Rachael_Grinham

148   Wikipedia, https://en.wikipedia.org/wiki/Natalie_Grinham

149   Wikipedia, https://en.wikipedia.org/wiki/Natalie_Grinham

150   'Squash Review', 1980, p42 (exact date unknown)

151   Chris Sinclair, 'Vale', 18th January, 2019

152   Squash Australia, 'Hall of Fame', 2017, p2

153   Squash NSW, http://www.nswsquash.com.au/ Winner of the Sport of NSW Official of the Year Award 27th November, 2019, p2

154   Rita Paulos, emails to author, 2019–20

155   *Belsham*, p26

156   Robyn Prentice, 'Curriculum Vitae and various emails to author' 2020/21.

157   'Squash and Fitness News', May, 1992, p19

158   *Belsham*, p23

159   International Test Series, 'Team Programme', 1978

160   *Belsham*, p21

161   Jean Walker, 'Manager's Report', 1971

162   Barbara Slotemaker de Bruïne, interview with Carol Murray, 2000

163   *Belsham*, p10

164   Bob Finch, 'Vale', 26th January, 2016

165   Carol Murray, email to author, 12th May,2020

166   Carol Murray, 'Manager's Report', 1975

167   'Australian Women's Weekly', magazine article, (actual date unknown), 1961

168   'Australian Women's Weekly', magazine article, (actual date unknown),1961

169   Bev Garfield, email to author, 20th July, 2016

170   Bev Garfield, email to author, 20th July, 2017

171   Dot Debnam, 'In Mother's Footsteps', Melbourne Newspaper, (actual source and date unknown), 1959

172   Barbara Slotemaker de Bruïne, interview with Sarah Fitz-Gerald, 2018

173   Tricia Hunt, email to author, 2019

174   Ian Trengrove, *Geoff Hunt on Squash*, Cassell, London, 1974, p15

175   Tricia Hunt, email to author, 2020

176   Sam Porter, '*Racquets Sports Magazine*', Interview with one of Australia's Most Promising Squash Players–Rachael Grinham, 1998, p12

177   Andrew Shelley, email to author, 2021

178   Michael Morrisey, 'Squash Stats: Advancing Squash through Statistics', http://squashstats.com, April, 2020, p8

179   Morrissey, p9

180   Morrissey, p11

181   Morrissey, p10

182   Morrissey, p12

183   Message from CEO: 2023 A 'Ground-Breaking Year' for Professional Squash, 31st December, 2023 http://psaworldtour.com/news/message from-the-ceo ...p2

184   Squash Confirmed for LA28 Olympic Games, 16th October, 2023 http://www.worldsquash.org p1

185   WSF, Ted Wallbutton, 'A Sport with History: One Hundred and Thirty years of Squash', https://squashplayer.co.uk/history_of_squash.htm 19th May, 2017

186   WSF, 'Squash and the Olympics', https://www.worldsquash.org/squash-and-the-olympics/, p6

187   WSF 'Squash and the Olympics', p7

188   WSF, 'The Bid for 2016', https://www.worldsquash.org/wp-content/uploads/2011/04/110420_The-Bid-for-2016-Document-for-website.pdf p1

189   WSF 'The Bid for 2016', p1

190   World Squash Library, 'Squash Olympic bid failures, 2005 onwards', http://www.worldsquashlibrary.info, 27th November, 2020, p1

191   World Squash Library, 27th November, 2020, p2

192   World Squash 2020, 'World Squash at its Best', p1

193   Gough p2

194   Rod Gilmour, Squash one of five new sports in the running for the LA Olympics Green Light ,SquashMad,http://squashmad.com/breakingnews/squash-atill-in-running-forlos-angeles-2028-olympics-greenlight 23rd January,2024

195   Gough, p1

196   Bob Finch, 'Vale Jean Walker', 26th January, 2016

197   Chris Yeend, 'Interview with Sarah Fitz-Gerald, Australians Ruled the World Squash Court', https://www.abc.net.au/news/2020-07-18/what-happened-to-squash/12444178

198   WSF, James Zug, 'The History of Squash in Ten and a Half Chapters–a Sport with a History', http://worldsquashfederation.com/a-history-of-squash/, p23

199   Squash Australia, www.squash.org.au

200   Squash Australia, www.squash.org.au

201   Chris Yeend, Interview with Sarah Fitz-Gerald, 'Interview with Sarah Fitz-Gerald, Australians Ruled the World Squash Court', https://www.abc.net.au/news/2020-07-18/what-happened-to-squash/12444178

202   Squash Australia, www.squash.org.au

Quiz Answers

1. Heather McKay (Blundell); 2. Bev Johnson; 3. 9–0, 9–0, 9–0; 4. 1960; 5. Great Britain 3–0; 6. Sea; 7. 1964; 8. 1965; 9. Betty Meagher; 10. 16; 11. 'Blunders'; 12. A 4 leafed-clover necklace; 13. Barbara Wall; 14. 1977; 15. Jenny Irving; 16. Judith Tissot; 17. Janet Morgan; 18. Yvonne West and Fran Marshall; 19. 1960 and 1962; 20. Rhonda Thorne; 21. Sue King (Newman); 22. The position of the feet for the purposes of photography; 23. Fran Marshall; 24. Marion Jackman (Jackman); 25. 'Fairy Feet'; 26. Jean Walker; 27. Rita Paulos; 28. Speedie; 29. A thermos flask; 30. Rachael Grinham; 31. Natalie Grinham; 32. Michelle Martin, Danielle Drady and Sarah Fitz-Gerald; 33. Marlene Tierney; 34. Barbara Baxter

The names of girls at the end of the book (p328)–Michelle Martin, Sarah Fitz-Gerald, Danielle Drady, Robyn Friday, Liz Irving

www.ingramcontent.com/pod-product-compliance
Lightning Source LLC
Chambersburg PA
CBHW040408110426
42812CB00011B/2489